THE VERNEYS
OF CLAYDON

A Seventeenth-century English Family

Edited with Preface and Postscript by

SIR HARRY VERNEY, Bт.

ROBERT MAXWELL: PUBLISHER

Copyright © 1968 Pergamon Press Ltd.
First published by Robert Maxwell: Publisher
4 Fitzroy Square, London W.1
Library of Congress Catalog Card No. 68–29706
Printed in Great Britain by
Anchor Press and bound by
Wm. Brendon, both of Tiptree, Essex
08 00 7079 5

THE VERNEYS
OF CLAYDON

Sir Ralph Verney

TO
EDMUND

Contents

	PAGE
LIST OF ILLUSTRATIONS	ix
PREFACE	xi
GENEALOGICAL TABLE	xii

CHAPTER

1. The Early History of the Verneys 1456–1599 — 1
2. The Heir—and the Vagabond 1625–1642 — 13
3. The Scotch War and the Rising in Munster 1639–1642 — 22
4. The Raising of the Standard 1642–1648 — 31
5. Family Tragedies 1646–1652 — 49
6. Sir Ralph Back Home 1653 — 81
7. Sir Ralph Crosses Cromwell's Path 1654–1655 — 110
8. John Verney, the Industrious Apprentice 1653–1662 — 127
9. After Cromwell 1658–1660 — 143
10. London Life: the Plague and the Fire 1662–1666 — 152
11. The Squire of East Claydon — 169
12. Under Charles II 1675–1683 — 185
13. The Highwayman and the Undergraduate 1655–1688 — 198
14. Prologue to the Revolution 1686–1689 — 230
15. Exeunt Severally 1689–1696 — 242
16. Postscript—to 1900 — 250

APPENDIX: The Verneys in Parliament — 261
INDEX — 263

List of Illustrations

Sir Ralph Verney	*Frontispiece*	
Henry VIII as a child	*Facing page*	4
Claydon House	,, ,,	5
Sir Francis Verney	,, ,,	36
Tom Verney	,, ,,	37
Sir Edmund Verney	,, ,,	68
Mary, Lady Verney	,, ,,	69
Dr. William Denton	,, ,,	100
Sir Harry Verney	,, ,,	101
Staircase in Claydon House	,, ,,	132
Inscription by Florence Nightingale	,, ,,	133
Detail of door in Claydon House	,, ,,	164
The Chinese Room in Claydon House	,, ,,	165

Preface

THERE are about 30,000 letters in Claydon House from the seventeenth century. My Mother, Margaret Lady Verney, brilliantly created from these letters the story of the Verneys and in 1894 she published the result in four volumes. In 1905 these were reduced to two. This book is an effort further to curtail the memoirs and letters into one volume.

In the postscript the story of Claydon House and the Verneys is recorded up to 1900.

Thanks are due to the many people who have helped, but nothing could have been done without the skill and enthusiasm of Mr. Gordon Grimley.

H.C.W.V.

Middle Claydon,
Bletchley,
Bucks.

GENEALOGICAL TABLE

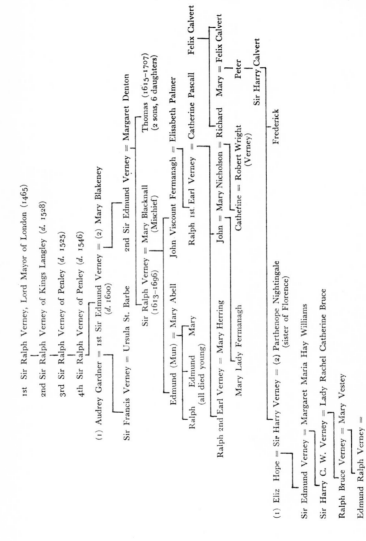

1st Sir Ralph Verney, Lord Mayor of London (1465)

2nd Sir Ralph Verney of Kings Langley (*d.* 1528)

3rd Sir Ralph Verney of Penley (*d.* 1525)

4th Sir Ralph Verney of Penley (*d.* 1546)

(1) Audrey Gardner = 1st Sir Edmund Verney = (2) Mary Blakeney
(*d.* 1600)

Sir Francis Verney = Ursula St. Barbe   2nd Sir Edmund Verney = Margaret Denton

Sir Ralph Verney = Mary Blacknall   John Viscount Fermanagh = Elisabeth Palmer   Thomas (1615–1707)
(1613–1696)   (Mischief)   (2 sons, 6 daughters)

Edmund (Mun) = Mary Abell   Ralph 1st Earl Verney = Catherine Pascall   Felix Calvert

Ralph   Edmund   Mary   John = Mary Nicholson = Richard   Mary = Felix Calvert
(all died young)

Ralph 2nd Earl Verney = Mary Herring   Catherine = Robert Wright   Peter
              (Verney)   Sir Harry Calvert

Mary Lady Fermanagh

(1) Eliz Hope = Sir Harry Verney = (2) Parthenope Nightingale   Frederick
                  (sister of Florence)

Sir Edmund Verney = Margaret Maria Hay Williams

Sir Harry C. W. Verney = Lady Rachel Catherine Bruce

Ralph Bruce Verney = Mary Vestey

Edmund Ralph Verney =

CHAPTER ONE

The Early History of the Verneys
1456–1599

THERE are different mentions of Verneys from the time of
King John: a slab to the memory of Isabella Verney, wife of
John Perrot, d. 1413, is in Tenby Church. She was the daughter
of Robert Verney by Eleanor, daughter of Wm. le Velans or
Valence. But Sir Ralph Verney, Lord Mayor of London, is
the first of the family of whom we gain a distinct impression.
He was a successful merchant living near the Great Market,
or Cheap, where was the hall of his Company of Mercers, close
to "Paul's Walk, the general resort for business and gossip."
He was chosen Sheriff in 1456.

After the battle of Tewkesbury, Edward IV celebrated the
triumph of the White Rose by knighting twelve London
citizens, of whom Sir Ralph stands first, on the very day that
the dead body of Henry VI was exposed to public view in St.
Paul's. The following year, Sir Ralph was elected one of the
members for London in the Parliament which settled the
succession.

Edward, "considering the good and gratuitous service rendered by Sir Ralph," granted him several forfeited lands in
Buckinghamshire; he bought back the old family property at
Fleet Marston, and purchased the manor and advowson of
Middle Claydon, on which he had advanced money. He did
not, however, live there, but leased it for a hundred years to
the Giffards, and died in 1478, when he was buried in the
church of "St. Martin's Pomary."

He ordered his tomb to be placed "between the quire and our Lady's Chapel"; but both church and tomb were destroyed by the great fire of 1666. His will is in English. He bequeaths his "soule vnto Allmyghty God in trinite, fardir, and sone, and holy gost, to the moost glorious virgyn, our lady saint Marie, modir to the ij^{de} person in trinite, our blissed Lord Crist Jesu my redemer and saviour." After providing for his widow Emme, his daughters Dame Margaret Raleghe and Beatrice Danvers, and his two sons, he gives legacies for the "reperacione" of the church of St. Martin: "100 marks to fynde an honest and convenable preest to syng for my soule, and the soules of my fadir and modir, my brothrene, my sustren, my children, and the soules of my speciall frendes Thomas Fauconere," &c. To the "oolde werks of the Cathedrall Chirche of saint Paule" he gives "xxs." He does not forget "poure and nedy prisinors" in Newgate and Ludgate, the Marshalsea, King's Bench, and other prisons.

His eldest son, Sir John, married the great-granddaughter of Sir Robert Whittingham, Sheriff of London in 1419, often confounded with Whittington of good cat memory. Sir Robert Whittingham was accused of treason after the defeat of his party; all his possessions and lordships, his rights of fairs and markets, his houses and advowsons in London, &c., were forfeited, and Margaret was left penniless.

But again the tide turned. Sir Robert took the field for the Queen, while Sir Ralph was as strenuous as ever for Edward VI in the City. The Yorkists soon regained their ascendency, however, and at the battle of Tewkesbury Sir Robert died an honourable death. Sir Ralph was returned to Parliament, and, in consideration of his own faithful service, the lands of her father were restored to his son's wife Margaret. The King had, however, given them for life to Sir Thomas Montgomery, and to his brother the Duke of Gloucester (Richard III), and for years the struggle with them went on unsuccessfully.

The battle of Bosworth changed everything, and Sir John Verney changed his tack also; he sank all mention of his father's services to the house of York, and brought prominently forward the sufferings and losses of his wife's father in the service "of the blessed Prince Henry VI." He took possession of the different estates of his wife, and they lived a quiet secluded life at Penley Hall, which he rebuilt.

The younger brother of Sir John, a second Sir Ralph, passed his life at Court. At the coronation of Elizabeth of York, in 1487, he rode as one of "two esquiers of honor, well-horsed, in gowns of crimson velvet, having mantles of ermine . . . on their heads hats of red cloth of gold, ermines, the beaks forward." They came with the lord mayor, next before the Queen. Soon after Sir Ralph Verney married Eleanor Pole, a lady-in-waiting to the Queen, and second cousin of Henry VII. Eleanor's brother, Sir Richard Pole, had married a cousin of the Queen's, so in right of her connection both with the Red Rose and the White, she seems to have had a considerable position in the royal household with her salary of 20*l.* a year. An account exists of a year's expenses of the privy purse of Elizabeth of York, and during that time Lady Verney lends the Queen "fifteen shillings suddenly," and is repaid; again she supplies "3*s.* 4*d.* as her Majesty's alms to a poor person," the same to the ferryman at Datchet when the Queen crossed the Thames, twice as much as to "an old servant of her Majesty's father," and 17*s.* on St. Peter's Eve, when there was always much jollification in the streets of London, bonfires, pageants, &c.; 3*s.* 4*d.* to Robert Fyll, "the king's painter," and 10*s.* "to John Reynolds," another artist, for "making of divers beasts and other pleasures for the Queen at Windsor." Then comes 20*d.* to a man who brought a present of cherries to her Majesty, to "Carvenelle for his costs, riding to the Princess [Catherine of Aragon], 5*s.*," "for making and lining a kirtle and other gear 2*s.*," "an offering at the altar of St. Frideswyde at Oxford on the Queen's progress into Wales in the summer of 1502, 20*d.*" The keep of the horse of Margaret Yone, a servant of the Queen's household apparently in attendance on Lady Verney, 4*d.* a day for 125 days, shows how all the ladies with their attendants went on horseback, as did the Queen herself on the "summer progress," which reads like a page out of the idyl "Guinevere."

Sir John was succeeded by his son the third Sir Ralph, who

was Sheriff for Bucks and Beds in 1511 and 1524. A MS. in the Lambeth Library [No. 285] gives the names of Sir Rauffe Verney as one of twenty-three knights who went in the Queen's train to the Field of the Cloth of Gold; of Sir Rauf Verney the younger as one of thirty-four knights in attendance upon her; and of John Verney as "Cupberer" in the Queen's chamber.

In the churchwardens' accounts of Wing, Bucks, is an inventory of church goods for June 1528, in which we trace the pious use to which Sir Ralph evidently put some of his gorgeous trappings after his return:

"A borther off clothe off goolde for the hey alter off the gyvyth off Syr Radulphe Werney."

Sir Ralph was three times married; his first wife, Margaret Iwardby, brought him the manor of Quainton, where she lies buried; her brass is in Quainton Church, with the effigies of one son and three daughters. His second wife was Anne Weston; she and her brother Richard were in the household of Elizabeth of York at the same time as Eleanor Lady Verney. After the death of the Queen she became maid-of-honour to Catherine of Aragon, and later Queen Catherine gave her a marriage portion of 200 marks and the custody of the lands and person of John Danvers, a minor, always a lucrative charge. Sir Francis Weston, Lady Verney's nephew, was afterwards beheaded with Anne Boleyn in 1536.

Sir Ralph was for the second time serving as Sheriff for Bucks and Beds in 1525, when his death occurred very suddenly; he made his will and died the same day. His estates comprised seven manors in the county of Bucks, and many elsewhere. His courtier uncle, who had been rewarded for his services to the late King and Queen with a valuable manor given by Henry VIII, died soon after. He was buried at King's Langley in 1528, in a splendid altar-tomb with coats of arms of the Verneys and Poles.

The fourth Sir Ralph was only fifteen when he inherited his father's large property; he married when he was nineteen, and took up his abode at Penley. Soon after we hear of a dispute concerning the estate at Claydon, with his tenant, Sir George Giffard. The house and church had been suffered to fall into

Henry VIII as a child, a painting in possession of Sir Harry Verney

Claydon House

ruinous decay, and Giffard at last agreed to pay 200 marks and to repair both, if Sir Ralph would renew his lease for 100 years instead of eighty, "to which Verney said he would not doe it for nothing." So Giffard said he would give him a hunting-horse which he valued at 30*l.* "so Verney consented to it." The church was repaired and the house rebuilt, "but the Verneys paid dear for the hunter," Lord Fermanagh adds significantly. The new lease is dated 1535.

Sir Ralph's marriage was supposed to be an excellent one, to Elizabeth, one of the six heiress daughters of Lord Braye, inheritor of the estates of Sir Reginald Braye; he was said to have found the crown in a bush after the battle of Bosworth, and to have set it on "Richmond's" head. For some time there was no male heir to the great Braye estates, but at last a boy was born to Lady Braye—"a youth of great promise, a paragon in court, and of sweet entertainment."

Sir Ralph seems to have been in bad health, and to have lived, like his grandfather, a secluded life at Penley. In 1537, however, we find him specially noted as one of the gentlemen present at the christening of Edward VI; and in 1539 he was appointed to help in receiving Anne of Cleves. In 1543 he was sent by Henry VIII with the army which inflicted terrible ravages upon Scotland. It was considered a hazardous expedition, and he made his will before starting; shortly after his return, ill and perhaps wounded, he died, aged only thirty-seven years, and was buried with his ancestors at Ashridge.

Sir Ralph left nine young children, and makes an earnest appeal to the "overseers" of his will to "maintain them in erudition and learning, and advance their welfare by good marriages and other promotion"; liberal legacies are left to his servants, and fourpence to each of his godchildren "if they require it." His death was a great loss to his family, for his wife married again and again—four times in all—and had other matters in hand than the care of her first husband's children.

The seven sons and two daughters were thus left to their own guidance, the eldest, Edmund, being only eighteen years old; he soon after married Dorothy Peckham, daughter of a

Bucks squire, cofferer to Henry VIII and subsequently one of the Council appointed to assist his "executours." He was afterwards executor to Anne of Cleves, who left him "a jugge of gold with a cover, or a crystal glass garnyshed with gold and sett with stones." Sir Edmund was chosen knight of the shire a few years after he came of age, and sat with his brother Francis, who represented the borough of Buckingham. The times were difficult; the sudden changes in religion and politics, as the different monarchs succeeded each other, must have been perplexing in the extreme. When a plot was brewing for transferring the crown to the Princess Elizabeth, it was among the younger members of Parliament that the Government looked for men likely to have joined in "Dudley's Conspiracy." Edmund Verney was arrested with his brother Francis and his brother-in-law Henry Peckham. Sir Anthony Kingston, "head of the late contemptuous behaviour of the Commons," Throgmorton, a Bucks squire, and some others were also taken. Several were put to the torture, others threatened with it, and all confessed excepting Throgmorton. The Verneys were not charged with treason, but for having "given in their adhesion." Edmund received his pardon—now in the muniment room at Claydon, dated July 1556—under the great seal of Philip and Mary. Francis Verney was tried and found guilty, but his punishment was afterwards remitted; it was given in evidence that he and Peckham had plighted their troth in a way still practised in the north. Peckham took a "demi-sovereign and broke it in two parts, one part thereof he traitorously delivered to Francis for an undoubted sign of their common consent to perform the said treason, and so the death and final destruction of their supreme lady the Queen and subversion of the Kingdom of England imagined and compassed"; the inversion of the sentences, the verb coming at the end, is curiously like the German construction.

Edmund Verney died in 1558, having witnessed the accession of Elizabeth (for which he had risked so much), and the triumph of Protestantism; he left no will, but had settled his land on his brothers, and was succeeded by one of them, another Edmund, a name which, with that of Ralph, is found henceforward in every generation of Verneys. Edmund, aged twenty-three, took up his abode at Penley, served as Sheriff twice for Herts and once for Bucks, and was very active in the public business of both counties during the reign of Elizabeth. At the time of the Spanish Armada he was appointed one of five captains who were to command the musters of the county; he was bound to bring in 300 men for the defence of the kingdom, and his contribution in money was large—50*l*. He married three widows in succession: (1) Frances Hastings, widow of Thomas Redmayne of North Marston; (2) Awdreye, daughter of William Gardner, widow of Sir Peter Carew, by whom he had one son, Francis; (3) Mary, daughter of John Blakeney of Sparham, co. Norfolk, who was also marrying for the third time.

Sir Francis Verney, eldest son of Sir Edmund, was only sixteen when his father died; he had lost his mother when he was but five years old, and seems never to have been under any control either from affection or education. His name appears in the Bursar's accounts of Trinity College, Oxford: he matriculated on 19 September 1600, aged fifteen. In 1604, when not above twenty, he was living in St. Dunstan's-in-the-West, in the neighbourhood of Alsatia, when one of his servants, Richard Gygges, was slain, apparently in a drunken brawl. He quarrelled with his stepmother at the earliest possible moment after he came of age; his brother was too young to have aggrieved him, but he petitioned Parliament to set aside the settlement made by his father of part of his estates on Edmund and of Lady Verney's jointure, which the Act of Elizabeth's reign had confirmed. A Bill for this object was brought in, and Randal Crewe (the celebrated patriot Chief Justice) pleaded before the House on behalf of Sir Edmund's widow. Several members who had sat on the Committee to which the former Bill had been referred gave evidence that "Sir Edmund Verney the elder did follow the Bill himself, and laboured divers friends in it, and the repeal would overthrow many purchasers, sixty at least." After "much dispute and argument" the Bill was rejected. Sir Francis had claimed as eldest son under a former settlement by his uncle Edmund, which had been annulled in the Elizabethan Act, and his claim had a certain appearance of equity. This was probably urged on his stepmother, for she resigned her dower house at Quainton to him in 1606. The young man was, however, stung to desperation; the dissensions and heart-burnings with his family, the keen sense of what he thought injustice, and the debts with which he was overwhelmed, at last determined him to sell everything and "forsake the friends who had injured him, and the country which had refused him redress."

Quainton was sold first; it consisted of about 800 acres with the advowson, and brought only 500*l.* Fleet Marston, where his ancestors had lived, went next; Penley, where his father died, followed, and the furniture was sold with it, as if to show that the break-up was final.

He then made a journey to the Holy Land; a letter exists from George Carew, English ambassador at Paris, "to my very good Lorde the Earle of Salisbury, principal Secretary of Estate at Court," telling how "the bearer hereof, Sir Francis Verney, since his retourne hither from Jherusalem, hath frequented the exercises of our religion at my house, which hath the rather moved me to give him this commendation to your Lordshippe, &c., &c." Lord Fermanagh notes that "this Francis was a great traveller and fought severall Duellos."

During the war with Spain, English cruisers were employed as privateers with commissions from the Queen herself. Sir Walter Ralegh's exploits were often little better than piracy, and the adventures of Elizabeth's famous Devonshire captains hovered perilously near to buccaneering. It is clear that Sir Francis was in command of one of these ships and was the terror of even English merchant vessels, for in 1609 Cottington, attached to the embassy in Spain, writes word that "Verney had taken three or four Poole shipps and one of Plymouth."

His reckless career went on for three or four more years of which we have no notice, till in "the most delectable and true discours of an admirid and painful peregrination by William Lithgow", published in 1623, we come on him once again. "Here in Missina (in 1615) I found the sometime great English gallant, Sir Francis Verney, lying sick in a Hospital, whom six weeks before I had met at Palermo, who after many misfortunes, exhausting his large patrimony, abandoning his country and turning Turk in Tunisis, was taken at sea by the Sicialian galleys, in one of which he was two years a slave, whence he was redeemed by an English Jesuit upon a promise of conversion to the Christian faith. When set at liberty he turned common soldier, and here in the extremest calamity of extream miseries entreated death. Whose dead corps I charitably interred in the best manner time would afford me strength."

The career of Sir Edmund Verney, who was now the head of the family, was in every respect, save that of courage, the greatest possible contrast to that of Francis—a high-minded, conscientious, chivalrous man, a most affectionate father and husband, devoted to his duties, "both public and private, both of peace and war." After his father's death he lived in Drury Lane with his mother, who had no home in the country for some time after she had given up her house at Quainton to Francis. At the age of twenty-two he married the daughter of a neighbouring proprietor "of birth and estate," Sir Thomas Denton, whose ancient house at Hillesden, with a large and beautiful old church close by, and an elm avenue leading to it along the crest of the hill, could be seen from the higher part of the Claydon estate. In later years "two black trumpeters in red used to sound a reveille, answered by two trumpeters from the other hill," says an unwritten tradition.

Margaret Denton was one of a very numerous family, but she had what must have been considered a good fortune— 2,300*l*.—equal to four or five times the sum at present.

Margaret was only eighteen, Claydon was still let to the Giffards, and it must have been a material and pleasant help to the young couple when the Dentons agreed to give their daughter and her husband "four yeares boarde." Sir Edmund seems to have oscillated between the house in Drury Lane, his chamber at Prince Charles's Court, and Hillesden, where his wife chiefly lived and where eight of their twelve children were born, the four eldest being boys, Ralph, Thomas, Edmund and Henry.

The estate at Claydon had all this time been a source of

great annoyance to Sir Edmund. It had been sublet to Mr.
Martin Lister, who cut the timber, ploughed up the pastures
(a great crime in Buckinghamshire, where they are exception-
ally good), and made himself otherwise disagreeable. The
lease, which had been renewed to the Giffards for 100 years
in 1535, had still fifteen years to run. Sir Edmund in 1620, to
put an end to the continual disputes, agreed to pay 4,000*l.* for
the surrender of the remainder of the lease. If he had had the
money it would have been an excellent investment, but as he
had to borrow it he was only involving himself in more serious
trouble. He had been at great charge in the service of "the late
most renowned Prince Henry and my ever most honoured and
famous Prince Charles, my loving master, and it pleased his
highness to promise to pay unto mee 4,000*l.*, by a thousand
pounds yearely for fower yeares. According to his princely
woord and promis he hath paid unto me one thousand pounds
of the same, and the said most worthy prince hath ever been
so just of his word and promise that he will no doubt give
order for payment thereof." "The princely woord and promis"
never led to the money being paid, and Sir Edmund continued
in more or less pecuniary difficulties to the end of his life.

The accession of the new King brought with it an improvement in Sir Edmund's position. He was made Knight-Marshal
of the Palace, a very ancient office which had been held by such
men as Baron Hunsdon and Sir Ralph Hopton. It was a troublesome post, and the duty of preserving order was no easy task.
During the reign of James the Court had been beset by a
"crowd of idle rascals and poor miserable bodies" from Scotland, against whom the King issued many vain proclamations.
"A multitude of idle and masterless persons" kept the place
in an uproar with their quarrels, and the danger of infection
was not slight in such gatherings at that very insanitary period.
A kind of market was held at the Court gates, where the "beefs,
muttons, veales, chickins," &c., were bought, which had of
old been supplied to the sovereign at certain low prices with
or without the consent of the owner. The precincts of the
palace must have been a scene of confusion, noise, dirt and
squalor, such as we can hardly conceive as surrounding a Court.

The state officers and the Royal tradespeople lived in the palace, with a number of workmen and hangers on; while innumerable petitioners, and beggars of all classes and descriptions stood about trying to obtain notice.

Many papers concerning the redress of these grievances are to be found at Claydon—one wherein the King gave orders that "the Knight Marshall shall continually ride both in the daytime and in the night about our Court," arresting and punishing the offenders: fortunately he was allowed a deputy and from four to six officers or vergers, which relieved him of many of these very distasteful duties.

For the two Parliaments of 1625 and 1626 Sir Edmund did not stand, but in that summoned in 1627–8 he was returned for Aylesbury. It lasted barely a year, but Charles seems to have felt that the presence in Parliament of one so respected and so independent, who yet had a strong personal feeling for his sovereign, was a help to his cause.

In his business affairs Sir Edmund had very little success of any kind. He began with a share in a patent for the sifting and selection of tobacco "within the realmes of England and Ireland, the dominion of Wales, and the towne of Barwicke" (which had still a separate existence), "with an allowence of fower pence in the pound." The tobacco patent came to an end in 1638, when the High Lord Treasurer, Juxon, demanded the surrender of the monopoly. Next came negotiations for buying some of the confiscated lands in Ireland, which, fortunately for him, came to nothing, or his money would have been absolutely lost.

Another patent in which Sir Edmund had an interest was for hackney coaches. These, it is said, first appeared in the streets of London in 1625, when a stand of them was established at the Maypole in the Strand. Under pretence, however, that "the King and his dearest consort the Queen, the nobility, and others of place and degree were disturbed in their passage, that the pavement was destroyed, and the streets pestered by the number of coaches for hire, the King began by limiting the power of hiring hackney coaches to persons who wanted to go three miles out of town." He then allowed licences to fifty persons, each holding twelve horses, the Master of the Horse, Lord Hamilton, being at the head. Sir Edmund's share often got him into great trouble with the coachmen, who were rebellious subjects in more ways than one. He was also partner in a "patent for sealing woollen yard before it was sold or wrought into cloth."

In 1640 the King borrowed 1,000*l.* from him, as from others of his household, and considering the uncertainty of affairs, Sir Edmund arranged that, in lieu of repayment of the principal, his heirs after his death should receive an annuity of 400*l.* for twenty years. The money was secured upon the "Aulnage," a tax paid for the measuring of cloth, and as he had only a life interest in his landed property, he left this annuity as a chief part of the provision for his younger children. It turned out a very bad investment, and after Sir Edmund's death the family were involved in endless legal proceedings, and petitions to Parliament, and in such a mass of correspondence, that the very name of the Aulnage has a terrible sound to any reader of the Verney MSS.

CHAPTER TWO

The Heir—and the Vagabond
1625–1642

THE strange variety of character in members of the same family is seldom seen in a more striking degree than among Sir Edmund's four sons. Ralph the heir was a prudent, cautious man, affectionate and conscientious, who spared no pains for those who loved him, and for many who behaved very ill to him, in the difficult times, which tried the spirit and temper of all men to the quick. Somewhat precise and formal in these early days, Ralph's long, elaborate compliments, painfully worked out in foul copies which he carefully preserved, fill his letters to the exclusion of what would be really interesting; one such is headed: "This was never writ to any one," and was evidently reserved for some transcendently important occasion which never came.

After all, his style is only an exaggeration of that usual in the letters of the period, which are full of provoking excuses, at the most important moments, that "there is here no news" or that the receiver "will have it from better hands." In 1631 the family were all living at Claydon—the four sons coming and going; the girls still children; and Dorothy Leeke, fair and lively, daughter of Sir Edmund's half-sister, a great favourite with the household, and not less so with Ralph's college friends.

The duty of a good father in those days required that an eligible marriage should be arranged for his sons at the earliest possible opportunity. A little heiress, Mary Blacknall, had been left an orphan at about nine years old; her father, John

13

Blacknall, Mayor of Abingdon, and his wife both died in 1625, "at one instant time," of the "great plaage," and their monument is yet to be seen in the church of St. Nicholas at Abingdon.

Mary, as an unprotected orphan, came under the jurisdiction of the Court of Wards. Four of her relations procured from the Court a lease of her lands and the custody of her person, with the privilege, when she should be fourteen, of bestowing her in marriage, for which they paid down 1,000*l.* to the Crown, and gave bond for the payment of another 1,000*l.* Sir Edmund agreed to take the child, and pay the 1000*l.* still due to the Crown, her uncle stipulating that she should not be forced in marriage, but should be well-bred, "and be allowed to make her choice at years competent." Still there were difficulties, but Sir Edmund procured a decree from the Court of Wards in his own favour, and in May 1629, aged thirteen, she was married to Ralph, who was not yet sixteen. The married couple did not live together for two years. Mary returned to her relations for some time, and an effort seems to have been made even then to induce her to repudiate the marriage.

Ralph, aged seventeen, was now studying at Magdalen Hall, where his father's friend, Edward Hyde, afterwards Lord Clarendon, and his young uncle, William Denton, had been before him. As Crowther, his Oxford tutor, writes to him during the summer vacation in 1631, exhorting him not to give up his studies for Hymen's delights, and tells him that the sweetness of a kiss will relish better after the harshness of a syllogism, with much in the same strain, it is evident that all is right between him and his wife.

In 1631, Mary Verney came to Claydon, where she and her young husband, in his eighteenth year, lived with the rest of the family, Ralph still going on with his studies at Oxford, and riding over twenty miles to his home, sometimes in such a storm of rain that his tutor Crowther laughs at him for his zeal. The marriage turned out a singularly happy one, except in the matter of health. With one of the sweetest tempers and most cheerful dispositions that ever woman was blessed with, Mary Verney had a backbone of sense and spirit and of high principle, which made her indeed, as Crowther wrote of her to Ralph, "your sweetest comfort." She kept the peace with the brothers —the selfish Henry and the scapegrace Tom; Edmund, who was warmly attached to her, always calls her "my sweetest sister."

Sir Edmund went very thoroughly into the management of the estate and garden, the letting of farms, &c., and sent frequent and minute directions to be carried out by Ralph and the steward; farm rents were much higher than at present: "The Gardner shall pleach noe Hedge this year," Sir Edmund writes . . . "if you fiend him fidle about his woarke, agree with him by the great for trewly I will noe longer indure his daye woarke; it is intollerable to beare with his knavery." "Bid Roades have a care for the timber of the ould barn att the Inn and lett him laye the ould thatch where itt may make muck or els uppon great Napson meadow, if hee thinck itt fitt." His horses were many, as was required in days when riding was the only means of going from place to place; but the farm horses were eked out by "plowing oxen." "I am not sorry the gray nagge is sould, though I should have been glad to have had more for him, but I will not part with the white geldenge, unless I may have £35 for him," a large sum for a horse in those days. "I am sorry to heare your horses thrive as ill as myne. I would send as many cart horses as I could to the fenns, there they would gather flesh at an easy charge."

It was by no means always on matters of business that the father and son wrote to each other. Scraps of "noos," absurd incidents, come in between the letting of the homestall and the close, the selling of the sheep, and the account of his dogs and horses. "To requite yor noos of yor fish, I will tell you as good a tale from hence, and as trewe. A merchant of lundon wrote to a factor of his beyoand sea, desired him by the next shipp to send him 2 or 3 Apes; he forgot the r, and then it was 203 Apes. His factor has sent him fower scoare, and sayes hee shall have the rest by the next shipp, conceiving the merchant had sent for tow hundred and three apes; if yor self or frends will buy any to breede on, you could never have had such a chance as now. In earnest this is very true."

Sir Edmund was consulted about marriages, then settled by

parents with more regard for the suitableness of the portions than for the inclination of the parties. He needs information about "Mr. Tho. Turvill's estate, because his sonne is tendered to a friend of myne for a marrage."

When Sir Edmund was with the King in the Scotch war, Ralph wrote to him: "I am infinitly sory to heare the Scotts continue in there stubbourness, for I feare if they come to blowes the business will not be easily ended, but we must referre all to God, and pray him to prepaire us for troubles here, and peace hereafter. I have hitherto been a little too negligent of getting my armes," says the unwarlike Ralph, "but now I will hasten them." He asks his father to inquire of Captain Sydenham "where and when I shall have my Pistolls . . . I pray send mee your opinion whither I had not best bespeake a Waggon presently and what other provisions I had best make. I would bee loath to bee utterly unprovided. You that are soe near and know more, may judg better of it than I can, therefore I humbly crave your advice. I confess I say not this that I am at all fond of the jorney, or that I can say I shall leave your affairs heere in soe good order as that I may conveniently come. I hope if need bee you can furnish mee with an horse, that will be readier than any that can be brought by mee."

This very uncheerful letter is a contrast to Sir Edmund's gay postscript to his reply, "I pray goe to Nedd Herbert [one of the Pembroke family] from mee, and tell him I will not wright to him till I can send him an inventory of the Skotts I have kild"; he still retained his buoyant spirit, little as he approved of the war in which he had to take part. "I will inquire for a nagg for you," he says another time, "but charity beginns at home, and I will first provide for myself if I can."

Fortunately for Ralph the campaign came to an end before he was able to join his father, and he went on diligently with the work for which he was so much more fitted, managing the large estates, some of them much scattered, of his wife and his father, helping his mother, looking after the affairs of his nine brothers and sisters, his uncles, aunts, and cousins innumerable, writing politics to Lady Barrymore, Lady Sussex,

Dillon, Burgoyne, &c., doing commissions in London for his most exacting friends, and finally, at the end of 1639, preparing to stand for Aylesbury in the Parliament which it was evident that Charles would soon be obliged to summon.

Of all sons "doomed their father's soul to cross" (for worse reasons, however, than that of rhyming), Tom Verney was certainly the most trying, and the most plausible. Sir Edmund had a fall from his horse, on his way to Scotland, and a report of his death reached his boys at school at Gloucester. Tom sat down at once and wrote his mother a string of pious platitudes, with a long list of clothes to be sent him "as soon as possibly you can, and I shall forever pray that you may live to see your children's children and comfort them all."

At eighteen he proposed to take to wife the "good daughter" of a Mr. Futsin, to whom he wrote, but without the smallest pretence of asking his own father's leave. "The thing was commonly spread about the house and I verily thought it came to my father's ears," he says jauntily, when reproached for his conduct. Sir Edmund, much displeased, resolved to send him out as a settler. The Puritan emigration to America had now been going on for several years; thousands of the best men in England—merchants, lawyers, farmers, scholars— were flying across the Atlantic; great landowners, like Lord Say and Lord Broke, were preparing to follow, believing that England would no longer be a free home for them; it was therefore quite natural that Sir Edmund should consider the opening a good one for his young son. Lady Verney undertook the arrangements with an emigration agent, who writes to her at great length setting forth the necessary outfit. He recommends that he do take three servants at least with him, which will cost 12*l.* for "passage and apparel." He had better "bringe up with him fether bed, blanquetts, and three payre of sheets, it is but a spare [pack] horse to bring them. Although many howshowlds in Virginia are so well provided as to enter-tayne a stranger with all things necessary for the belly, yeat few or non are better provided for the back then will serve their on turne." He must take some corn, "least ther should happen a scarsity in the cuntry, which some tymes doth fall out, through the covetousness of the planters, that strive to plant much tobacco and littell corne. I have already bought the flower, the fowling peeces, the strong waters and the grosery wares . . . if he settell a plantation for himself he shold have som seasoned men of his own."

In nine months, however, Master Tom was back again, and his outfit wasted, which in the state of his father's finances was a serious loss. Ralph, in the emergency, was most kind to him, and helped to make peace with Sir Edmund, who was naturally much annoyed.

Tom was next sent as a volunteer on board a king's ship, the "St. Andrew", in the ship-money fleet now cruising in the Channel, and he writes to his "loving and kind brother that we are bound to the French coast to see what they will say to us"; "there is a fleet of Spaniards lyes off Falmouth is the newes"; "there is warre proclaimed with France, the King of Spaine is soe much the more joyfuller, by reason that our kinge's fleet doth assist him in it." After which come the usual postscripts, "that you will speak for mee to my mother, for travellers ever want money."

A few months afterwards he is back in London, lodging with the keeper of the Marshalsea, a servant of his father's, to whom Sir Edmund "hath given express command" that no one is to buy anything for him without his leave, "which much discontents me, for now I must desire to have those things that are fitting for mee to weare."

He is next heard of in France: "my imployment will cost me 40l." He then begs for 20l., but desires Ralph to keep it from his father's ears, "lest it hinder me of that money."

At Paris.—"My Lieutenant-Collonel hath not restored to mee my clothes," he writes, "which doth very much discontent me. I wanted money to buy me a hors and other necessaries fitting me." He requests the money may be sent quickly as he has got some one to lend it who knows his family, "and I know you are of too good and loving a nature to see mee disgraced for so small a sum. Within two months after our fight, I will repay you with an innumerable of thanks . . . and I shall have more caus than ever I had to pray for the hous of Verney.

I have orders to march to La Chapelle, which was taken within this fortnight by the Spaniard. There we shall remaine most part of the summer. If it pleases God to send me life, after the fight is over, I shall by his grace send you a true relation of it."

During the rest of the year 1638 he is in London getting into debt and quarrels, or down at Claydon where his father sends him to keep him out of mischief. Before he starts he has a duel on hand, and he writes to his brother Edmund, "at the Pehatzo Coven Garden," for his countenance. "I would entreat you to be with mee by 7 of the clock in the morning, or els not at all, becaus I am to meet a gentleman att eight of the clock about some words which past between him and myself on Friday, and would entreat to make noebody acquaint with it, becaus I would not have it known. If you are not willing, I pray send me by the porter my russett shooes, and my greyest pair of worsted stockings with garters and ribbins to them, and laced band and cuffs if they bee don; if not, a plaine band, to put on tomorrow. I have a great company of young gentlemen with mee, which goes forth in the King's fleet, or else I had come over myself to-night."

Next he tries to make Ralph buy some horses of his: "as for the mare, you never had a better in your life"; but in another letter he acknowledges they are worth nothing, and sends him a "fox coat" in payment of ten pounds he had borrowed of him. The servants at Claydon and his grandmother at Hillesden were warned not to lend him money, or even a horse, lest he should sell it. His debts up and down appear to be many, and he is afraid that some of his creditors may go to his father; he declares they have good pledges, all but six and forty pounds, which he cannot account for.

The next spring "he is gone to the Barbathos," sent off in a good ship, with an ample supply of necessaries by his father. There seemed fair hopes at length that he was disposed of satisfactorily, for some time at least. In a few months came a long letter to Sir Edmund containing a clever and amusing account of the country. "I have obtained 100 acres of land, but not knowing how to dispose of it unless I can have such a supply as the invoise makes mention of, which, if I can have a supply according to my expectation, I make noe question but by the grace of God to rais my fortunes in a few yeares, nay, I shall be able in one yeares time to returne back the principall, which is a great incouragement both to you that doe disburs the money, and a greater to have mee continue here, which could never yett stay anywhere . . ."

After this comes a postscript, saying that his "new requests may perhaps daunt you, but 200*l.* will pay all"! and then follows an invoice of several pages in length, of every conceiv-- able kind of commodity to be sent out to him, from "twenty able men, whereof two to be carpenters, and a weaver who can weave diaper" to "swords, 30,000 nayles of divers sorts, pickaxes, butter, good sweet oyle, six cases of strong waters for the men to drink a dram every morning, to keepe them in health (for my part I drink non)"!!!

At the same time he writes to his mother, to try a little supplementary begging. "There is no newes worth your acceptance or worthy my labour, but that I am resolved by the grace of God to leade a new life, which I hope you will rejoyce when you heare of it from others as well as myself," he adds prudently. "For my owne part, I take no glory in boasting of mine owne actions, bee they good or bad, and soe I turn upon some better thing, which doth more befitt the time and my occasions, and that is concerning housekeeping. I am now a building a sorry cottage to harbour men when I have them." He wants "household stuff, plate, spoones, and the like, then pewter and brass of all sorts, and linnen of all sorts, both for mee and my servants." He will not trouble his father, "becaus this does not belong to him. I will leave them wholly to your own discretion, which knoweth better what to send, then I can in reason aske."

In May 1639 he repeated his demands on his father, sending a fresh and enlarged invoice of his requisitions, and forwarding a testimonial from a Captain Futter, who had authority in the island, and who certifies that Tom "is an extraordinary good husband and careful"!

In 1641 the vagabond, after getting into trouble and debt in Barbados, returned to England apparently penniless. He was given a fresh start by his long-suffering father, and sent back to his plantation in January 1642. With characteristic importunity he continued his requests for more supplies up to the eve of his departure from Gravesend, but whether the "doz. payer of tan lether gloves and two payer of summer bootes and six bands and six payer of cuffs" were supplied to him is not recorded.

Nothing more was heard of him until April, when he wrote to his father and asked him if, "with the great help of bridewell and the prisons," he could procure him 100 men in August: those that he took out had fallen sick, and he had been ill himself and unable to look after them, so he had sold them to a "chapman." On his return to England in the summer he finds it convenient to conceal this fact from the people at Claydon, where he wanted to find more recruits for his plantation.

Of the cargo he brought home, the cotton turned out to be worth little and there was a loss on the tobacco, so he could not make out a very good case for himself.

The breaking out of the civil war came opportunely for Tom, who was glad to defer his return to Barbados, and offer his services in the King's army.

B

CHAPTER THREE

The Scotch War and the Rising in Munster
1639–1642

LORD PEMBROKE's summons "to my very loveinge freind Sir Edmund Verney, Knight, one of the gentlemen of His Majesty's most honourable privy chamber," arrived on February 7, 1639. It announced that the King having resolved "upon a royal journey to York . . . His Majesty's royal pleasure is that all occasions sett apart you be in readines in your owne person by the 1st of April next at the city of Yorke, as a curassier in russett armes, with guilded studds or nayles and befittingly horsed, and your servants which shall wayt upon you horst in white armes, after the manner of a hargobusier, in good equipage." If his necessary occasions in his Majesty's service will not permit, some gentleman of quality is to be sent in his stead. The summons found Sir Edmund troubled in mind and infirm in body. He had been consulting a quack; Sir John Leeke hopes that "the Cobler may cure yᵣ sciatica which Mustris wroght me worde is your new name for an owld ach." Lady Sussex had thought him "very sade this crismas" at Gorhambury: "i fearede he hade been discontentede some way, but he tolde me it was not so, but that he was oftime in a grete dele of pane. i pray God he may get helpe or else it will shorten his time i doubt. . . ."

Little as he sympathised with the objects of the expedition, Sir Edmund made his will and prepared to follow his master.

His trust in Ralph is entire: "I constitute my son Ralph my sole executor, having had experience of his fidelitie unto me and of his love for his brothers and sisters." 20*l.* he leaves as a stock for the poor people of the parish. Annuities of 40*l.* a year to his sons Thomas and Henry; to Edmund and each of his daughters he leaves 5*l.*, they being provided for by the profits of the Aulnage. "To Doll Leake, my niece, 20*l.* To John Rhodes my faithful servant and bailiff at Claydon an annuity of 5*l.* . . ." To his daughter-in-law Mary, for whom his love was great, 40*l.* for a ring, "which I desire her to wear for my sake." To his mother 20*l.* "To my dear and beloved wife all such moneys as are in her custody at the date of this my will"; half his linen, with the use of half his plate and household stuff, which was to be shared with Ralph, all his "fuell of wood, furze and cole at Claydon, the coach and four of the coach horses with their harness and furniture"; "stuff for a mourning gown to the women & cloth for a mourning sute & cloak for the men legatees," etc. etc.

He left London with the King about the 21st of March. The expedition was more like a progress than the opening of a campaign. The "gay cavalcade" that accompanied them was not likely to overawe men who had taken up arms for a great cause, whatever Charles' councillors may have led him to expect.

Sir Edmund, writing to his son in the tenderest terms on his arrival at York, says: "Good Raphe since Prince Henry's death I never knew soe much griefe as to part from you, and trewly because I saw you equally afflicted with it my sorrow was greater; but Raph wee cannott live always togeather. It cannott bee longe ere by cource of nature we must be severd; and if that time be prevented by accident yett wee must resolve to beare it with that patience and courage as becomes men and cristians; and soe the gread god of Heaven send uss well to meete againe eyther in this woarld or in the next. The King has beene basly betrayd; all the party that hee hoped uppon all this while has basly left him; as we are this day informed: the two cassels of Edenbrough and Dunbarton are yeelded upp without one blowe; and yett they were boath provided soe well as they were impregnable soe long as they had vittle, which they wanted not. Dekeeth, a place of greate strength, wher the Crowne and Septer laye is yeelded to; and the Covenanters has taken them awaye and a greate deale of Armes and munition to; yett my lor Tresurer of Scottland undertooke to the King to keepe all that safe; and all these are given upp without one blowe. Aberdine wee heare is yeelded upp to and noe blowe given; and the King sent 4,000 of the choysest Armes hee had theather; soe that now I am confident the show of making a party ther for the Kinge has beene only to gett Armes from uss, and to feede us with hopes till they were fully provided.

"My Lord Clifford sent woarde this morning to the King, that the inhabitants of Carlile had left the towne uppon a fright they tooke of the Highlanders coming suddenly uppon them, but hee has putt 300 men into the towne and they saye they are resolved to fight it out. The Hilanders are in number 2,500 and 6 cannon as they heare; we cannot heare wheather my lord of Essex bee in Barwick or not, by tomorrow wee shall know; heere is this day gone from this country 2,000 men to second him. My Lord Trequare, the Treasurer of Scotland came last night to towne; & is this day confined to his chamber, wee expect some others may heare of it to, that I will not name for the King has been basly betrayed . . . and we shall all smart for it; saye little of this to the woemen least it fright them. . . . I heare noething of my Armes. Commend me to honest Natt Hubbard & the god of heaven bless you; remember to see Gorhambury as soon as you can; if Nedd Sidenham bee not on his waye . . . acquaint him with what I have writt; tell him and Charles Gawdy that I could wish they were boath heere, for the King has few about him, and that is a shame to uss all at this time when beleeve mee the danger is more than is apprehended, ther wher you are. I hope you have sent awaye my waggon. My man Peeter and I are parted; if hee comes to lundun bee not deceaved by any false message; write privately as much to Roades. The King goes to see the fortifycations at Hull on Thursday next."

He is afraid that many of his letters are "gotten into ill hands . . . trewly I have never failed sending twice a week at least. . . . I shall not wright often now for we shall goe into the feeld presently, nay the King himself & all his Army after we go out of this towne [Newcastle] will lodg in the feelds every night & noe man must looke into a village." He has received all his arms, "but praye hast awaye my pott & take care itt bee wide inoughe for this is soe much to little that noe boddy but a madd man could have beene soe madd as to mistake soe grosly, therefore take care it bee wide inoughe now; . . . this afternoone there is newes come for certaine that 2,000 Scotts are come within ten mile of Barwicke, they saye 8,000 more is coming after them & 2,000 more are gone to lye neare Carlile; we shall soone have blowes now, but I beleeve it will be skirmishes with the Hors & noe Battle till towards the end of sumer, it is folly to thinck any longer of a peace, we shall bee suddenly ingaged now." In the next letter: "I have tryed my Arms & the Hedd peece is verry much to little for mee; if the Pott I expect dayly from Hill [the Armourer] bee soe too I am undone; I praye send to him about it asssoone as you receive this lēr; this will come upon noe part of my hedd it is so very little; the rest of my Armes are fitt. . . ."

Dr. Denton seems anxious to keep his friends at home well frightened about Sir Edmund, in which he entirely succeeds. In his next letter he says that he will not thank Ralph for his book until he sends him "a paire of barbinge sissers; . . . y^r father is yett well in body & att a good distance from the borders. the King goeth towards Barwicke on Thursday next & intends to intrench himselfe wthin 5 or 6 miles of it, but on this side Tweede & soe long as he keepes there I presume we shall be in safety." He hopes that the King will not fight this summer, but will tempt the Scotch to bring out their forces, and by that means exhaust them, "but I feare he will be cozened for I beeleeve that they be as cunninge as they be wicked. The newes of theire beinge 12,000 in a body wthin fore miles of Barwick is false; this is the best cordiall that I can send you at this distance. Be confident that I will leave noe stone unmoved that I conceave may knock y^r ffathers fightinge designes on the head & preserve him; if I can but keepe him from goinge out in parties, I hope he will returne wth safety. I shall be very sensible of any the least hazard that I shall thinke he may be in & if all the witt & power that I have, or can make, may prevent it, it shall be noe fault of y^r assured lovinge uncle."

There are constant letters from Sir Edmund during this anxious time. "Every hower now produces eyther something that is new or some alteration of our former resolutions; the King makes all the hast with this little Army into the feeld that possibly he can; . . . he has sent for 8,000 men more with all speede; Lasly threatens to fight uss, but if hee comes not quickly, he slipps a faire occation, for when we are intrencht and thes men come to uss wee shall not much feare him which now wee do, for if he bee able to bring 10,000 men to uss any time thes twelve dayes beleeve mee we are in verry ill case."

Sir Edmund's next letter is labelled "Leslys pride." They were now encamped within two miles of Berwick, and had seen no enemy as yet; "we heare lasly is within 12 miles . . . wee fiend all the meaner sort of men uppon the scotch Border well inclyned to the King and I beleeve when time serves they will express it well; but the Gentlemen are all covenanters, and I beleeve most men are weary of the government ther now, for they lay Heavy Burdens uppon the people. . . . in earnest the King is most willing to suffer much rather then have a warr, soe that I hope it will prove a peace. Lasly has now the title of Soverain amongst them, and the best lord amongst them sitt att a great distance below him, and under a lord noe man putts on a Hatt in his presence; all the Government of the warr is comitted to him and of the state to, which is to mee verry strange; we heare the man is soe transported with this greatness that he gives offence to all the Nobility, and I beeleve they will desire a peace to free themselves of him againe. I have beene heere this three dayes in the camp ordering of things ther for the King's coming tomorrow to lodg ther."

On 18 June 1639, peace was declared and the Treaty of Berwick signed. The extraordinary uncertainties of Charles's mind appear by the perpetual changes in his intentions; a fortnight after Sir Edmund's return (so that the smallest consideration from the King might have saved him two long and painful journeys), he left Berwick for London, accompanied by Sir Edmund, riding the whole way in four days. There were great rejoicings in England for "the blesedness we heare of Pease," as Lady Sussex writes; the Cavalier poets broke out into the most extravagant congratulations; Cowley wrote a pompous ode on his Majesty's return out of Scotland.

But the armour was scarce hung up before it was taken down again; and in a few months the war with Scotland was renewed —"the second Bishops' War," as it was called. Edmund was sent to Flanders, and his father writes letters to Captain Apsly and Captain Homwood for the young soldier to take with him; "they will gett him assistance and directions what to do. He had best land at Flushing and soe goe directly to the Army."

Sir Edmund found much troublesome business of his own and other people's awaiting him in the south. He spent part of the Autumn at Bath, accompanied by Ralph; he was suffering and anxious, and behind all private troubles lay the thought of the probability of a renewal of the Scotch war, which must have been as painful to Sir Edmund as to his namesake son, who wrote in the winter from Utrecht: "I heare that the King hath vast summes of money given him by his subjects, and that these forces are lyke to goe against Scotland; the former part I wish to be true, but shall ever pray against the latter."

So ended the year 1639. In Ireland, Strafford had ruled for eight years sternly but successfully; when the strong man was removed the seething discontent gathered force. There were rumours that the Catholic population was to be uprooted; the rebellion broke out in Ulster and spread to the South. The tidings reached London in November 1641, and every post brought news of fresh cruelties practised by the rebels. Sir John Leeke writes to Sir Edmund at the end of the year, in the greatest distress.

"The frights and terrors wee heere live in, cannot welbe expressed but by such as suffer and feele the distraction, whereof many are com for England that cann relate itt as eie witnesses, which you will hear of befor this letter cann come to yoʳ hands, as the noble Incyquin and Mr. Jepson. . . . I protest I am most miserable, for though I have friends, yet noe frinde to lend me tenn pounds. No man will part with a peny of money, and by all that is good in heaven and earth, I nor my wife have in purse 40s.—We have 20 good cowes, wee may have none tomorrow, such is the case of many men. I have barreled beefe and porke and some littell wheat and mault for a moneth, God healp us and send the English forces to us, oʳ hearts wowld be light and our corrages stronge, for thes English wee have here have gott good things abowght them, and themselves and ther goods gott into stronge townes. The country is abandoned and in my Lords country is nothing left but ther cattell and a servant or tow in ther house. . . . P.S.— Barrymore taks the field tomorrow with 60 dragowns and 70 lancers. Browghall goeth to the rendezvous as stronge if not stronger." He asks that a case of pistols may be sent him "for I will not stay in Yoghall, but will into the field with Barrymore, and see something that may inable my knowledge. I lack a sword wᵗʰ a garded hilte, I want other armes, but have no way to have them—bee we as patient as we can."

In March Sir John writes again: "Sir Charles Vavesor, a noble gentillman who doth assure me he left you well, and took his leave of you the day before he sett one his jorney for Irelande hath brought over 1,000 as brave carcases of men as ever I beheld wᵗʰ my eies and would fayne be in the feild and fightinge. they had well hooped that they should have fallen to pillaging the Irish of the towne of Yoghall, and meetinge wᵗʰ some Irish wemen that hadd mantells and crucefixes abowght ther neckes, wᶜʰ the soldiers teore from them, but by ther commander were quieted, the preests are all stole out of the towne and noe masse sayd yesterday, beinge Sunday . . . wee expect this day or tomorrow to see my Lord of Incyquine, if the wind hould fayre as itt is. The very noyse of the landinge the troops have blowne away rebells, that laye neere Yoghall, but abowght Lismore, where Browhall hath killed and hanged many, some loss he hath receved as a brave gentillmann his Cornell. The Rebells did use much cruelty before ther departure by dragginge a gentillman out of his howse, and bindinge his hands, layinge him on a banke, and shott him to death; 4 poore English that wer ther, they hanged, drawinge them up to a hovell post, and held them until they were dead, and this was done within

Lismore precincts; the rebells were 71 colours in one place and 8 or 9 in another, but they vanished in a moment to the mountaynes. Ther Gennerall the Lord Mount-Garratt is fallen from the Lord Roch and gone into his one contry, with 6,000 men. . . . They marched to Mallo, wher were tow castels, Mr. Jepson's house is very stronge and well appoynted, the other not bigger than an ordinnary steeple, but 25 good men at Least and a stowt commander; the Rebells summoned the castell but they were answered wth muskett Bulletts, in short they killed neere 200 Rebells, and hurt many, att last powder faylinge, they accepted quarter and went to Mr. Jepson's castell; the English lost very few. The next day the Rebells parted ther army. Kilnalmechy keeps his towne of Bandon Bridge . . . this last week he fell most bravely on the enimy: 400 of the Rebells came neer Bandon with some p^{r}vision and necessaries of usqubach, wine, bread, some munition and ther apparrell, 3 cartloads. Killnalmechy drew out 200 musket-teeres and himselfe and 70 horse, putt them to route, and running killed 104, tooke prisoners and hanged them, many prime gentillmen were slayne. . . . Our lands are all wasted, and we shall have no profitt this many yeares." He entreats Sir Edmund to get him a company or to lend him some money. "I have gott four soldiers to keepe the house. . . . Here no man hath anythinge, nor shall not this many yeares; the stocke of English sheep and cattel are almost destroyed, the Rebells stole English sheepe from a frende of mine, but some dayes after the English troops tooke some of the sheepe and other cows from the Rebells; the troopers sell the sheepe for 12*d*., 8*d*., and 6*d*. when ther skinne were well worth 16*d*. and so sould thus all turnes as mischeefe to the poore English; little or noe restitution unless the proprietor be in pursuit and recover, God healp us. . . . Tom Badnedg [his son in law] is . . . now Capt. of the gard of our Yoghall, it is creditt but not a pownde proffittable. his diligence and care is a great security to the towne. Wee have many Irish and few trew harted as wee feare but o^{r} English are a bridell in ther nose; yett the townsmen pfesse and pteste much loyalty. . . . While I am writing a messenger is come in from the army that assures us my

Lord President hath regayned Dungarvan wth the slaughter of many, the castell howlds out, but cannot Longe; in itt are men of qualitie, as Sr Nycholas Welsh and some of the Bullers . . . ther are 5 or 600 cooped in betwixt the sea and the blackwater wch must falle. My Lord Barrymore is in the field wth the President and hath most bravly and loyally behaved himselfe, to the great terror of his countrymen; itt wilbe a most bloody warre, for none can be spared; the Irish women are most cruell in execution; I pray God bless you in England and knitt your harts in unitie. trust no Papist for here they betray ther dearest frendes. . . . I Intreat you^r cowncell and comfort to yor poore brother John Leeke."

He writes again a few days later:

"My Lord President with his one and the regiment of Sir Charles Vavisor have rescued Dungarvan with the castel from the rebels, killed 300 att least, and gave quarter to 80 that were in the castel, the reason of that favour being the suddayne risinge of the Lord of Muscary, who contrary to all menns expectations and his own vowes and protestations is now with 7,000 men within 5 myles of Corke, the President is not withstanding got into Corke, but hath not power sufficient to keep the field, but doth strengthen all our townes until new supplies come and then he will not be pent up. . . . I am most miserable, money I have none, rent none to be paid, the rebels within a mile of the towne, the river only between, our towne supposed not to be sownd at heart, I mayntayned a gard of 4 men and a boy and a mayd to dress theire meate until 3 weeks since, from 9ber, wch was hard for me to keep tow houses, . . . my long service to his father and himself are forgotten. . . . If I may not get a company I cannot here live, no man can see to the end of this rebellion, nether will (if we had peace) 7 yeares reduce us into order and that time is more than I can expect to live."

A few months later Lord Barrymore was killed. After this date there is little more correspondence between the Verneys and their unfortunate Irish friends. Sir John Leeke, ruined and hopeless, took refuge in England, and was followed by Lady Barrymore and her family.

CHAPTER FOUR

The Raising of the Standard
1642–1648

THOUGH Sir Edmund did not join the King at York until July 1642, he had made preparations for the war which seemed inevitable. He wrote to his steward to get his horses into condition in view of a campaign: "I praye take upp my mare . . . and lett her be kept att house. I shall shortly send for my coach mairs. When my mare Lea hath foaled, let the foale bee knockt on the head, and the mare taken to Howse, for I cannot spare her this summer. . . . There will be a press shortly in the country. I praye let there bee care taken to thinck of some able boddyed young man to goe in King's roome for I am loth he should goe." "When I sent for my Arms I forgott to send for one peece as I thinck, and that was for my Gorgett, it is that which goes about the neck, I pray lett Will Browne looke for it, and faill not to send it to mee to bee heere on Tuesday. . . . Send mee woard wheather Tom Isham has bought mee another gelding or noe, you shall receave a saddle from Mr. Busby, lett it bee well layed upp, bidd the groome bee carefull of my Horses." Ralph had also written for "a paire of my father's Pistolls of the Best sort; my father tells mee there is a paire that have White Stocks, and part of the Locks are Blew, and they are very light. Let Moses bring them upp, and bee carefull to keepe them from wett, and let the Moulds, and other implements belonging to them come upp with them."

On 11 July it was declared by both Houses that the King had begun the war. He had granted commissions for raising

31

cavalry, and had placed himself at the head of a small force at Beverley. It was resolved in the Commons that an army of 10,000 men should at once be raised, and Lord Essex was appointed general.

Sir Edmund now writes to his steward from York, with sad anticipation of the bad times to come: "I praye have the carbines att home in reddyness for the defence of the Howse if need bee; and gett powder and Bullets reddy; for I feare a time maye come when Roags maye looke for booty in such houses; therefore bee not unprovided; but saye noething of it, for that maye invite more to mischeefe that thinck not of it yett." Again: "I praye have a care of my howse, that roages break not into it, have stoare of bullett and powder, and gett some boddy to lodg in the howse that maye defend it if need bee."

War preparations were vigorously carried forward on both sides. The 22nd of August 1642 was a memorable day in Sir Edmund Verney's career. The king set up the royal standard at Nottingham and confided it to his keeping. There were several "Knights, Baronets, and three Troops of Horse to wait upon the Standard and to bear the same backwards and forwards with about 600 Foot Souldiers. It was conducted to the Field in great State, before His Majesty, the Prince [of Wales], Prince Rupert, and divers other Lords and Gentlemen . . . besides a great company of Horse and Foot in all to the number of 2,000." At the last moment, when the trumpets were to sound and the herald at arms was to make a proclamation of the causes of setting up the standard, the King, with character-istic vacillation, called for the paper, made some hasty erasures, and gave it back to the herald, "who proclaimed the same to the People though with some Difficulty after his Majesty's Corrections . . . and the whole Multitude threw up their Hats and cried God Save the King." The standard was carried back into the castle at night, and the same ceremony was gone through in the King's presence on the two following days, "with sound of drums and Trumpets."

In reply to the King's proposal the Parliament had refused to treat until the royal standard should be taken down, and the charge of treason against their members withdrawn. Ralph had taken the oath of adherence to the Parliamentary cause, and was now therefore in avowed opposition to the King and to Sir Edmund.

In September Lady Sussex writes to Ralph: "I am truly sory to hear the Kainge is returnede from Nottingham i fear he will make this a tedious bissynes, and much blode will bee spilte before ther be ane end of it. . . . Sir tomis chike i belive is not att all pleesed with his sone rogers being strenth [aide-de-camp] to my lorde Harfort. As i am thus far of my litter i hear the Kainge hath sente an other mesege to your parlyment, i pray God it bee a good one: your father will suffer many wayes i fear if the Kainge gos on in this way he begines; sende not my letter to him, i pray, till you mete with a safe messenger."

On the morning of the battle, 23 October 1642, the King was at Edgehill and on the "edge" itself is a solitary old inn, "The Sun Rising." Here the King breakfasted attended by Sir Edmund Verney.

In the battle the struggle round a smaller standard was "furious in the extream." Sir Edmund "adventured with it among the enemy in order that the souldiers might be engaged to follow him." He was offered his life by a throng of his enemies upon condition he would deliver the standard; he answered that his life was his own but the standard was the King's and he would not deliver it while he lived and he hoped it would be rescued when he was dead, selling it and his life at the rate of sixteen gentlemen which fell that day by his sword.

Later in the day Sir Edmund's hand holding a piece of the standard was recaptured and buried in the crypt of Middle Claydon Church. On one of his fingers was the ring given to Sir Edmund by the King and containing his miniature. The ring is preserved in Claydon House.

Sir Edward Sydenham's account of the death of Sir Edmund at the battle of Edgehill, written from "Ano on the hill," close by, was sent by hand to Ralph. "For all our great vycktorie I have had the greatest loss by the death of your nobell father that ever anie freind did . . . he himselfe killed two with his owne hands, whereof one of them had killed poore Jason, and brocke the poynt of his standard at push of pike before he fell, which was the last account I could receave of anie of our owne syde of him. The next day the kinge sent a harald to offer mercie to all that would laye downe armes, and to enquire for my Lord of Lynsee, my Lo Wyllowby and him; he brought word that my Lo Lynsee was hurt, your father dead, and my Lo Willowby only prysoner; he would nither put on armes or buff cote the day of battell, the reason I know not; the battell was bloody on your syde, for your hoorss rann awaye at the first charge, and our men had the execution of them for three miles; it began at 3 a clock and ended at syx. The kinge is a man of the least feare and the greatest mercie and resolution that ever I saw, and had he not bin in the fylde, we might have suffered. My Lord of Essex is retired in great disorder to Warwick, for the next morninge he suffired his cannon to be taken away within muskett shott of his armie, and never offired to hinder them; it is sayd ther was killed and run away since, eaygtt thowsand of his armie."

The news that Sir Edmund was slain filled his family and household with horror and consternation, Ralph writes to Lady Sussex:

"Maddam, Last night I had a servant from my Lord of Essex Army, that tells mee there is noe possibillity of finding my Deare father's Body, for my Lord Generall, my Lord Brooke, my Lord Grey, Sr Jam Luke and twenty others of my acquaintance assured him hee was never taken prisiner, neither were any of them ever possessed of his Body; but that hee was slaine by an ordinary Trooper. Upon this my man went to all the ministers of severall parishes, that buried the dead that were slaine in the battle, and none of them can give him any information of the body. One of them told him my Lord Aubigney was like to have been buried in the feilds, but that on came by chance that knew him and tooke him into a church, and there laid him in the ground without soe much as a sheete about him, and soe divers others of good quality were buried: the ministers kept Tallies of all that were buried, and they amount to neare 4,000. Maddam you see I am every way unhappy."

Lady Sussex replies the same day: "My soro is beyonde all

that can bee sade; it is not possible to bee greter then it is."

Sir Edmund had left home in his usual health; the children and servants had since seen his grooms and his horses starting off to join him—there had been no illness and no funeral—Claydon had no tangible proof that the beloved master was actually dead.

He had told Mr. Hyde: "I will willingly join with you the best I can, but I shall act it very scurvily. My condition is much worse than yours, and different, I believe, from any other man's and will very well justify the melancholick that I confess to you possesses me. You have satisfaction in your conscience that you are in the right; that the King ought not to grant what is required of him; and so you do your duty and your business together. But for my part I do not like the quarrel, and do heartily wish that the King would yield and consent to what they desire; so that my conscience is only concerned in honour and gratitude to follow my master. I have eaten his bread and served him near 30 years, and will not do so base a thing as to forsake him; and choose rather to loose my Life (which I am sure I shall do) to preserve and defend those things which are against my conscience to preserve and defend. For I will deal freely with you, I have no reverence for the Bishops for whom this Quarrel subsists."

Sir Ralph Verney's case was equally complicated. Only one member of the House of Commons, says Mr. Gardiner, amongst those who had remained at their posts at Westminster after the first months of the Civil War—Sir Ralph Verney—refused the Covenant at the end of 1643, preferring the miseries of exile to the soiling of his conscience.

A Parliamentarian in the King's prosperous days, a Puritan under Laud, a Churchman under the Presbyterians, dubbed a Royalist under Cromwell, Sir Ralph's conscience always drove him into a minority, especially when his interests lay on the other side. He is the type of idealist who raises the level of political life, but is disliked by practical men.

During these difficult days Parliament carried on with Sir Ralph generally in his place. The rule still held good that "noe man was allowed to take noates" of what went on in the

House of Commons. But Sir Ralph in his careful and methodical way prepared to chronicle their proceedings; his notes are written in pencil on folded sheets of small foolscap paper, evidently held upon his knees and carried in his pocket. Sir Ralph's notes deal with many abuses, from which this patient country is not yet delivered. But the most thrilling moment of his Parliamentary career was that in which he saw Charles enter the House to arrest the five members.

As an eye-witness account written on his knee, he completes our knowledge of that memorable day. The scene over, the Commons at once adjourned with the sense that they had just escaped a massacre.

The precious papers are in Claydon House.

Tom meanwhile had "proffered his service to his Majesty," which had been accepted. In January 1643 he writes from the Fleet to tell Sir Ralph how the troops he was with had been besieged in Chichester and forced to surrender upon quarter, "But were all taken prisoners, and plundered of all except the cloths wee had then on our backs, which hath caused mee to be destitute of everything. For what I have hitherto done, I will maintaine with my life that it is warrantable . . ." He then begs for 10*l.* Tom is unapproachable when he poses as a philosopher and a divine; but it is to be feared that his letters were much less diverting to Sir Ralph than they are to us. He has found another cause for complaint: "I was informed by a friend how scornefully I was spoken of, att the horne taverne in fleet street, by three or foure gentlemen that were in mourneing. The words were thees; that I was a great malignant and had deserved hanghing. . . . More over they were pleased to applaud you, in saying that you were both wise and discreet and in much favour in the parliament hous; now one of thees being by made this answer; why you (being in soe great favour) did not seek my releasment from my close imprisonement. Another of his associates did reply, that you took much distaste at a letter which I lately sent to you, therefore you would neither meddle nor make with mee." He goes on to reproach Ralph furiously for making a brother "a laughing stock and talk to every unworthy rascall."

Sir Francis Verney

departures; but many "bundles" are coming up from Claydon by degrees. He was evidently preparing for a long absence. The "bundles" go through sad adventures. A certain Dixon was to convey some of them to Rotterdam. Dr. Peter Chamberlain writes from thence to say that Dixon has arrived, but without Sir Ralph's goods or his own, "like a spider he hath turned the sweetness of your favours into poison . . . we have fallen into the hands of Turkes, the seamen we had to deale withall are most exquisite knaves. . . . Noble Sir, wee are here in a strange country all nacked, till your freindshipp & wisdome helpe us out of these troubles."

Other things are despatched to Amsterdam and Rotterdam, and later on Will Roades sends up "an inventory of 17 bundles of linen, pikturs and stores, whereof 10 of them are sent to London, and the last seaven are to com up this present 17ᵗʰ Novemb. 1643."

The luggage sent on amounted to fifty-one "percells," including some trunks of valuables which relations had confided to his good nature. Other property was hidden away in London; but troublesome as these arrangements must have been, they were as nothing to the complicated business to be settled at Claydon.

A protection from the King and one from the Parliament had been obtained for Claydon House to defend it, if possible, from either army. Sequestration was imminent, and to ward it off all sorts of legal fictions were resorted to. The estate was vested in trustees, and fictitious leases to friends were drawn up to protect Sir Ralph's London house, and his interest in the Aulnage.

There were the five sisters to be provided for, whose names read like the chorus of an old song. There were Sue and Pen and Peg and Molly, and unruly little Betty, who was only ten years old. Except Susan, who was boarded with the Leekes, they were all to remain at Claydon under the care of Mrs. Alcock, with occasional visits from their brothers, and from their uncles and aunts at Hillesden, which was sheltering a large party of Dentons and Ishams. They were dependent on their eldest brother not only for protection, but for bare subsistence.

Meanwhile matters in Parliament were growing more and more serious. Sir Roger wrote of "three members that refused to take the covenant yeisterday, for which they are only suspended from the Howse during the pleasure of the howse, and untill such time as a punishment be agreed uppon by the howse for to be inflicted uppon the refusers of it." Again: "We heare nothing concerning the three gentlemen . . . the punishment is not yet brought forth, but the Com^{tee} is now in travaile; I wish it prove not a monster." Mr. Pierpoint was refused an interval to consider the question.

Nothing remained for Sir Ralph but to be gone with all speed if he was to retain his personal freedom.

Having apparently wound up his business, private and political, he sits down in utter grief and weariness, and draws up, *more suo*, two melancholy papers, docketed in his usual tidy fashion, as expressing his wishes—"If I miscarry," to be left with Sir Roger, about the disposal of his goods, the payment of his debts, and a provision for little Jack at Claydon.

This done, he made a rough draft of a letter to Lady Sussex, in which he took a ceremonious leave of her, "for I am now hastinge to the shipp, wch perhapps may bee my grave." Alas! there was no need to hurry. There were still many tedious weeks to be got over, spent chiefly, it appears, under Lady Sussex's hospitable roof at Gorhambury, to which loving farewell letters are addressed by different members of the family. "Nattycock and Nannycock" (the playful names of happy Claydon days for Sir Nathaniel and Anne Lady Hobart) send 10,000 loves. His aunt, Mrs. Isham—a King's woman to the core—who quarrelled with his going from the opposite point of view to Sir Roger Burgoyne's, writes that she cannot hear of some clothes sent to Claydon for the children:

"Now the armies is aboute, and Mr. J. [Isham] and I could wishe you thire too, thinkeing it the rites cause, and in time I hope youre mind will change, if it be in the ronge, or else not, and in the mene while my pray shall be as god would gide us to take his side which ever it be, and so a due wisshing you as well as mine one soule."

There is a little brown scrap of paper at Claydon labelled

"a Pass for Sir Ralph Verney with his lady, etc., when they retired into France under the names of Smith"—a time-honoured *alias*, which did good service with all refugees, and in later days sheltered Louis Philippe on his flight to England. The pass is addressed "To all Captaines and others whom it concernes." "London. These are to require you to permitt and suffer Mr. Ralph Smith and his wyfe and his man and mayde to passe by water to Lee in Essex and to returne. So they carry nothinge of Danger. By warrant of ye Ld Maier, Jo: Beadnege."

The tempestuous wintry weather added indefinitely to the sufferings and hazards of the journey. Two or three weeks seem to have been spent in vain attempts to get across to France. "My very cloathes were on Board," writes Sir Ralph, "and I myself lay privatly in a close corner ready to bee gonn." The weather is so bad that their late kind hostess listens anxiously to the wind howling among the trees at Gorhambury, and thinks of them tossing about in the Channel. The terrible voyage over at last, Sir Ralph wrote to her on the last day of the year, 1643, from Rotterdam: "This letter hath noe other errand then to acquaint your Ladyshipp that from the first of this month till Friday last, wee lay winde bound, in wch time I spent all my little stock of patience, and then seeing noe hopes of better weather, a shipp or two being ready for Holland, I resolved to come heather. Wee had a most tempestuous and violent winde for 12 hours, but through God's greate mercy on Sunday night wee all arrived heere in saifty. I humbly thank your Ladyshipp for your Furre, certainly you did fore see or phrophicie my coming into this cold country. My stay heere is very uncertaine."

After a fortnight's rest at Rotterdam, Sir Ralph is arranging to move on to Rouen; he sends "26 percells of goods for my use there, marked R.V. No. i to 26," "in the shipp caled the Fortune"; he writes to an agent, "I hope to bee at Roan before they come, but if I should be stayed longer by any misfortune, I must then intreate you to take care to get them sett upp in some saife dry place...." "The goods containe wering apparrell, Linen, Pickturs, and other Household stuffe, all of it hath been used; there is noe Marchandice amongst it. I pray use some meanes that the Searcher may not open anything till I come with the Keyes, a little money perhapps will Blinde his Eyes, or at least make him deferre the opening of them till the Keyes come"; custom-house officers remaining unchanged, with all that has come and gone, since Sir Ralph's travelling days.

Settled at Rouen early in 1644, but not at all reconciled to his lot, Sir Ralph writes: "The difficulties of my last journeys, and the doubts and feares I have for my little family, together with the miseries of my native country, have made me soe conversant with afflictions, that this World is growne tedious and life it selfe a Burden to mee. . . . This place is full of variety of newes concerning England; every one reports as hee would have it—out of w^ch, I (that desire, and pray for peace) can gather nothing but ye expectation of a generall ruine."

The news from England, so ardently desired, was sad and startling enough when it came. Hillesden, which had been a second home to all Dame Margaret Verney's children, had been besieged, taken, and totally destroyed by fire.

Hillesden lay in an important position—between Oxford, where the King was in garrison, and Newport Pagnell, which was held by the Parliament troops under Sir Samuel Luke, with a communication by Aylesbury, securing the north road from London. Early in 1644 Colonel Smith took command of the place for the King, built barns and stabling for cavalry, and dug a trench half a mile in circumference, enclosing the house and church; far too large an extent for his troops to occupy.

The country in all directions was swept by forage parties from both sides; Colonel Smith, with a body of troopers, carried off a drove of cattle, with money and other valuables, belonging to a tenant of Mr. Hampden. When they reached Hillesden a violent dispute arose as to the partition of the spoil; Major Amnion, "an uncommon frenzy man," claimed all the horses and a large share of the booty for his troop. A general mutiny took place, and the major, who had imprisoned several soldiers, was obliged to release them, and give up his claim. This was not the only ill-consequence of the expedition. The owner of the cattle arrived at Hillesden to ransom them, probably annoyed much at having been attacked from a house belonging to a relation of his landlord. He was made to pay 80*l.* for his stock; upon which, indignant at his loss, he claimed compensation of 160*l.* from the Parliamentary commanders at Aylesbury, which first showed them the danger of permitting so strong a Royalist garrison to hold Hillesden. A surprise was attempted by a force of 300 horse and foot, but unsuccessfully; upon which Sir Samuel Luke prepared for a regular attack. One half of the men marched, under the command of Colonel Oliver Cromwell, to Steeple Claydon, where they encamped for the night around a barn, still known as the Camp Barn. The Royalist garrison had meantime been hard at work. They had summoned all the country people, manufactured a wooden cannon from an elm tree stoutly hooped with iron, and had obtained five small pieces of ordnance from Oxford, with ammunition, which they stored in the church. Nearly 1,000 labourers were employed to complete the trenches and throw up a mound on which to mount the artillery. But it was too late, and seeing themselves unexpectedly surrounded on all sides, they sent out a flag of truce. Finding, however, that they could obtain no terms short of unconditional surrender, Colonel Smith proposed to defend the works; but the ditch was only knee deep in places, and the assailants overwhelming in numbers: the defenders were obliged to retire, some into the house, others to the church. A second assault was made, and the church carried—marks of the struggle being still seen in bullet-holes in the old oak door; Colonel Smith, seeing the hopelessness of any further defence, surrendered on promise of quarter. The prisoners, and amongst them the master of Hillesden Sir Alexander Denton, M.P. for Buckingham, and his brother, were marched off to Padbury, a village some three miles away, "where they passed the night in great discomfort." The next day they were taken to Newport Pagnell. It is difficult to ascertain the exact truth about the treatment of the garrison of 263 men; the *Kings News* accuses Sir Samuel Luke of great barbarity; the Parliamentary reporter admits the death of thirty-one men.

The morning after the surrender, a trooper, striking his musket against the wainscoting of one of the rooms, discovered a large sum of money; further search was made, and more treasure found concealed, particularly under the lead roof. Later in the day came news of the advance of a body of troops from Oxford, and it was determined to evacuate the place. Luke withdrew to Newport, Cromwell to Buckingham; the house was set on fire and burnt almost to the ground.

A letter from Sir Alexander to his steward has been preserved, written from Newport: "Blagrove, I woulde have you send mee by Tyler that bag of silver w^h Berney left wth you long since and Seale it upp. . . . Bid him also take a viewe of ye house y^t was burnt upon Tuesday, y^t I may have some certayne information of w^t destruction is fallen upon mee, and whether it bee possible to rebuild those walls that are standing if ye distractions of ye times should settle. I thancke God I am yet in health notw^tstanding these many misfortunes are fallen upon mee, and my comfort is I knowe myself not guilty of any fault."

He was afterwards removed to London, and committed to the Tower on 15 March 1644, whence he wrote a few days later to Sir Ralph:

"S^r,—I was gladd to see your servant, allthough in a place I have not till nowe beene used unto, the tower of London, whither I was comitted uppon Saturday last, beeinge taken at my owne howse by Liuetenant Generall Cromwell with some 4,000 horse and foote with him, I only cominge accidentally thither some 2 dayes before to remove my familye, the kinge havinge placed a garrison there." "Those officers that commanded that place were taken and some 150 men, and some 19 killed on both sydes, the howse pilladged, all my cattell and wine taken away, my house the next day burnt downe to the grounde, and but one house left standinge in that end of the toune. Captayne Tho. Verney taken prisoner that came only to see his sisters, and all my own servants are as yett detayned. It endamaged me at the least 16,000*l*. . . . My children and neeces not fayrly used yett noe imodest action, and the resydue of my family are yett at Sir Ralph Verney's howse." Penelope, who with Ralph's other sisters was in the house, writes: "When it pleased God to lay that great affliction on my uncle, I was more consarned for him, but I did stand so great a los in my own particular that it has been a half undoing to me. We were not shamefully used in any way by the souldiers, but they took everything and I was not left scarce the clothes of my back." Mrs. Isham described how "Hillesden parke pales be every one up and burned or else carried away, and the Denton children like to beg."

Tom Verney remained a prisoner for many weeks, part of the time in St. John's College, Cambridge, whence he writes furiously to Roades for more money: "ffor shame; rous up your drowsye and decaying spiritts that the world may not say we have a foole to our governour. Sir Ralphe is liable to the censure of the world, that he being a wise man should chuse a foole to govern his brothers and sisters." "I shall find a freind that will furnish mee with as much as will bring me to Claydon: then I hope to have my peniworths. It shall not be your great language or your fleareing looks that shall any wayes daunt mee." Ralph does send him a few pounds, so with the help of Mrs. Tom Verney's friends his ransom was made up, and he was set free.

Sir Alexander never regained his liberty; he was removed on his own petition to Lord Petre's house, used for prisoners when the Tower was very full. Mrs. Isham sends a pitiful account of him a few months before his death, she being with her husband in the same prison. Some of the prisoners hoped to get leave to go out for a time, but he is not likely to be of the number, "and then I knoe he will not lett me goe, for he doth say as he should be half dead if myselfe was not with him. I must confes he had hath anofe to a broke any mans hart, but that God hath given him a great dell of pachance, for on the seven of Augst last his sunn John was slaine within a worke att Abtone [Abingdon], as Sr. Will Wallers forces had made . . . To tell you how it was done I shall want the wordes of wore, but nevor did I heare of a more bravor pice of sarvis done, and if his life had bine spared, the hole Towne had bine his one. They came on so Galiently as there tooke ye Pickes out of the

Enemies handes, and then a drak [a brass field-gun] wente of and kiled him in the Plase and 7 Bollets was found in his Brest, and beside himselfe they was but 7 or 8 kiled, none of note but him, for they all retreted when thay see him fall for he commanded in chefe. This you must thinke is a grete troble to his father as did love him so well."

In September 1645 the blow fell that poor Ralph had so much dreaded, and which he had hoped to the last might have been averted. He was deprived of his seat in the House of Commons. Sir Roger, deeply grieved, writes of it under a thin disguise. ". . . My friend is voted out etc. the 22nd of this instant; and it was his servants fortune to be at it, who had not been ther long before: his endeavor and care were not wanting in anything he could do. Writs are to be issued for new elections for that place; he is likewise to be sequestred, I would to god I might know his pleasure in all things speedily . . . it was for no crime in the world," he adds later, "but only his long absence; others were laid to his charge of having been in the King's quarters, but a servant of his who was ther present did fully satisfy them to the contrary (who, I may say for him thus much that he did leave no means unattempted, nor friend unsolicited to prevent that sad misfortune). . . .

Ralph, with his heart wholly centred on England, seems to have given but little thought to the country of his banishment; writing was his absorbing occupation, letters from home his greatest solace; he kept a calendar in which he entered an abstract and sometimes a full copy of letters written and received. Sir Thomas Hewytt only echoed Ralph's own thoughts when he wrote to him: "The separation of friends I find to be worse than the sequestration of estates, from the continuance of which I daly implore our good God with a piece of our old Letany."

As mistress of the family Mary has at least the comfort of being very busy; they can keep but two maids, and one little boy, "soe we are but 7 in family, and I know not how to do with lesse, because of the children"; the housekeeping does not always go smoothly; Mr. Ogilvy writes from Orleans to apologise not only for the bad service of "that graceless boy that I was so unhappy to prefer to your Ladyshipp, but also for his impertinent speaches which shall be the cause that he shall hardly find another maister."

That some of the refugees treated their French servants in the overbearing spirit traditionally attributed to the Englishman abroad, and that the quick-witted Frenchman cheated them in return, is evident from the letters.

Amongst his wandering fellow-countrymen who passed through the town, none was more welcome at Sir Ralph's board than the light-hearted and eccentric Sir Henry Newton, who found much in common with Mary's ready witt and merry humour. The friendship was of long standing, as Sir Henry's father, Adam Newton, had been a colleague of Sir Edmund Verney's in the households of Prince Henry and Prince Charles. Sir Henry, who had set up house at Rouen, writes to Sir Ralph: "I forgott in my last to acquaint you with the parting of my Boy Estienne, Who having of a long time play'd some prankes, made mee at last resolve to pay him his arrearages, Chiefly 3 or 4 dayes before having been very rude to Mrs Cochram and in his words defi'd both her and mee, And telling her if I beate him once I should never doe it twice, wch I understood him was by runing away. And though hee knew he was complain'd of, hee was so sencelesse as for a whole afternoon when my wife and I were abroad with a coach to neglect us and bee debauch'd with another lacquay should have been also following the coach. The next day I bestow'd a little beating of him, and did it heartily, though without passion: Upon wch hee ran to the doore and call'd for his things, and swore hee never would enter again, though a thousand devills drove him, But I over hearing him, sent one that was too strong for him and brought him back, and tooke a little more paines upon him, to shew him hee was mistaken. For I would beate him twice; And to bee beforehand with him, made him unbutton, that so hee might goe his way, as naked as hee came, if hee thought good. This startled him, but heardly wrought peccavi from his high stomach. But I perceiving hee would not stay long and might take some worse opportunity if I permitted it, dispatch'd him going, but with his cloaths, out of the sole respect I have to some at Blois that are his kindred."

So much for the foreign lacqueys. English servants were more trustworthy, but if they did not consume whole turkeys for supper, they quarrelled with the foreign food, and were as hard to please abroad as their successors of to-day. "I know noe English maids will ever bee content (or stay a weeke)," wrote Sir Ralph, "to fare as thes servants faire. . . . Noe English maide will bee content with our diet and way of liveing: for my part, since this time twelvemoneth, I have not had one bit of Rost meate to dinner, and now of late, I rost but one night in a weeke for Suppers, which were strainge in an English maide's oppinion." But though Luce and Besse quarrelled with a diet of "potages" and "légumes," and doubtless thought Sir Ralph's political scruples sadly misplaced, they followed the fallen fortunes of their master with exemplary fidelity, and when Ralph writes to Mary in England as to the comparative merits of bringing out an English maid or of getting a French one on the spot, his description of the latter makes one's hair stand on end; "it is hard to find one here especially of our Religion"; he has heard of one whom he recommends his wife to take "with all her faults," "her 2 sisters are but Ramping girles," "but truly she is a civill wench and plays well of the Lute, she is well cladd and well bredd, but raw to serve, and full of the Itch"!

Many English parents were sending boys abroad for education. Rouen "is very unfit" for the purpose, wrote Sir Ralph from thence in answer to an inquiry about a boys' school, "for heere most men speak worse French than the poore people doe English at Northumberland, and there are noe Protestant masters alowed to keepe a schol heere. All things exceeding Deare, but higher in the country. There are divers Universities at Sedan, Saumur, Geneva, and other fine places, and as I am told at noe unreasonable rate and not only protestant scholemasters, but whole colledges of protestants."

Among the smaller worries which Ralph had to endure in France was that of wearing a periwig, a fashion from which England was still free. The bills for the wigs themselves, the ribbons, the pomade, and the powder come again and again. Ralph sends minute directions about the length, style, and thickness, and encloses a pattern lock of hair; "let it be well curled in great rings and not frizzled, and see that he makes it handsomely and fashionably, and with two locks, and let them be tyed with black ribbon . . . let not the wig part behind, charge him to curl it on both sides towards the face." The cost of this wig was 12 livres. Good powder seems to have been hard to obtain. Sir John Cooke sends "a small phiole of white Cyprus powder, which I beseech you present to my Lady as an example of the best Montpelier affords, for I saw it made myself. It must be mixed with other powder, else it will bring the headache. There is a powder cheaper, but not so proper for the hair."

When Mary is describing the presents from Paris that her English friends most value, we learn that "wooden combs are in greate esteeme heare, butt truly I think they buy them very neare as cheape heare as there"; there is not "anything that will be soe wellcom as gorgetts, and eyther cutt or painted callicoes to wear under them or whatt is most in fashion; and black or collered cales [calash, a hood] for the head; or little collered peny or toe peny ribonings, and som black patches, or som prety bobbs, butt ye pearle ones are growne very old fashion now." Kings may be dethroned and Parliaments may totter, but Fashion still rules society with a rod of iron!

CHAPTER FIVE

Family Tragedies
1646–1652

THE EARL OF DEVONSHIRE had taken refuge in France not long
after Sir Ralph went there. In 1645 he was sent for to return to
England under pain of the confiscation of all his estates; he
writes to ask Sir Ralph to return with him. Ralph replies that
he wishes his affairs were in such a state that he might take
advantage of Lord Devonshire's friendly offer; "you are now
under the Lash and that of the most severest masters that ever
yet were read or heard of, and from first you knew full well
'tis bootless by delays or otherwise to vex them." The Earl,
after his arrival in England, was kept as a sort of hostage at
Latimer, his place in Bucks.

For a whole year the question of what course Sir Ralph
should take is debated between him and his friends in England.
In December 1645, Parliament resolved that privileges granted
to persons "coming in" "shall be understood of such persons
onely, as shall testifie their affections to the parliament by
taking the covenant," so that, as he says in a letter to Lord
Devonshire, his remaining abroad was "upon the same terms"
as heretofore. To Henry he writes: "You know I never was
within the king's quarters nor never contributed, or in any
way assisted against them: absence is my onely crime, and
you know I have highly suffered for that already and was
neaver soe much as somoned to returne soe noe contempt
can bee layed to my charge; neither have I refused to pay
taxes."

Sir Roger Burgoyne writes that he has procured an order "that the com^tee shall certifie the cause of their sequestration wth power to examine witnesses uppon oath . . . if you could procure us certificates of y^r living soe and soe longe in this and that place happily they may be useful to us."

The sequestration of Claydon appears to have been only absolutely carried out in September 1646, though the ordinance was dated 1644 in which Sir Ralph had been named a delinquent, and his tenants formally warned that all rents would have to be handed over to the Committee of Sequestration, sitting at Aylesbury. His friends had been able to show that his estate was in the hands of trustees for the payment of 900*l.* a year of debts and annuities, but Roades was compelled to account for all the residue of the rents to the committee.

Sir Roger had advised Mary to petition the Army about the sequestration, but public affairs continued in so unsettled a state that for many weeks it was useless to expect any private business to be attended to. Mary writes rather indignantly that Lady Warwick "never soe much as sent to enquier after me . . . though she knew I lay in in London and was then in all the troubles when she was glad to runn out of towne." Her conduct was probably to be explained by her husband's critical position, for in a former letter Mary wrote: "Lady Warwick's husband is one of them that the armye demande; I hear they are much in disorder in that house."

Ralph writes carefully and minutely about the clothes that he and the children require, which Mary, ill and distracted with domestic anxieties, has scant leisure to attend to. "Now let me tell you, ye silke stockinges are good, though much to bigg, but that's noe matter, but the Thred ones have made amends, for they are soe little that they will not come over my Toes; my Foote is bigger than yours, but for your comfort these will neither serve me nor you. As for Mun's gray stockings they are about a handful too short and almost an inch too Little, soe I have layed them upp for your sonn John, and you must buy Mun more. . . . Besse is as well fitted, for Luce sent her 2 paire of Shooes that will come as soon uppon her head as upon her Heeles; soe we laugh at you both." Mary, in return, sends them directions about the house-keeping: "You must needs buy some suger both fine and course, and some spice, and a few reasons and currants"; she does not think the children require any more clothes, "but I think it will be necessary to give faireings to those that you gave unto last yeare." There is a great annual fair at Blois, and Ralph, as she suggests, buys presents for various neighbours, but when he has done so, he finds he has no money left for the sugars fine and coarse, the raisins and the currants!

Mary's summer visit to Claydon had been a very sad one; to so careful a mistress the state in which she found the place after four years' absence was indeed heart-breaking; she writes to Ralph that "the house is most lamentably furnished, all the linnen is quite worne out," . . . "the feather bedds that were waled up are much eaten with Ratts" . . . the fire irons, "spitts and other odd things are so extreamly eaten with Rust thatt they canot be evor of any use againe," and she will have them sold by weight: "the cloak of the Musk-coloured stools is spoyled, and the dining-room chairs in Ragges." Ralph is anxious lest the "Moathes" should destroy "the Turkie Worke cushions," and "I pray see that the Armes [Sir Edmund's] doe not want cleaning and Oylinge, least they bee spoyled with Rust."

Mary returned to London from Misterton in October 1647, leaving Jack and Ralph at Claydon. "I am soe weary," she writes to her husband on the 21st, "that tis a payne to me to hold ye penn, but yet I cannot conclude, untell I have chidd thee that thou dost nevor give me an account how thyselfe and boy and gerle have your helthes, and yett I have intreated itt of you before now: tis a duty I weekly performe to thee, and I assure you I expect ye same from you, for my deare hart ther is noething in this world soe nearly concernes me. . . . I can not express to thee how sadd a hart I have to think how long tis since I saw thee and how long twill be before I come to thee," and again she complains that he tells her everything except what she wants most to know, "how thy Deare selfe and my children have been."

Her instinct did not deceive her; both children were very

ailing and little Peg, who was never to learn how to hold up her head in this world, was down with dysentery and fever. Ralph, knowing how she loved her little daughter, had not the courage to tell her of it; he wrote of her sufferings borne with sweet patience to Dr. Denton, but never mentioned them in his letters to Mary; and while she was writing her tender inquiries the child was dying.

"I am soe full of affliction that I can say no more but pray for us," he wrote to Dr. Denton, and his next letter of 10 October is but a sorrowful fragment: "Oh Dr. Dr. my poore Peg is happy but I am your most afflicted and unfortunate servant. Tell mee how and when this shall bee made knowne to her mother." He wrote this all unconscious of another loss; Mary's baby had died suddenly at Claydon, and Dr. Denton had a doubly heavy task in breaking the news to his beloved niece. He writes to Ralph of this second sorrow: "Your own wofull experiences have prepared you for any disasters that any of Job's comforters can present to you, god hath taken away what he gave, I meane your youngest son by convulsion fitts. My wife mett me by the way to let me know soe much and that she had broken it to her. . . . I found her in her bed lamenting and very inquisitive of me alsoe how her children did, express-inge that you had sent her noe worde of them for a month or longer."

Dr. Denton writes in November 1647: "Your wife I thanke God is very well . . . she hath not been abroad since I told her of her daughter, but I expect her this hour to come and eat a goose: for all you condemned me to plum pudding and puddle ale, yet I believe landlady will tell you that she hath found good nappy ale to be very comfortable and to fatten her. As for your petition I putt it yesterday into a good hand (Sir G. Lenthall), and I have promised him 40*l.* and he will give me an account of it very shortly." A petition is to be presented to the House in the name of "the Lady Verney, wife to Sir Ralph Verney, that the whole business of the sequestration be referred to a committee of Lords and Commons," and a few weeks later Dr. Denton writes an account of how it was carried.

"Deare Ralphe, I told you in my last that I would drive on

the naile furiously, and I have beene as good as my word for the very next day I drave it beyond all the Pikes of the house against the advice of most. . . . . The truth is there was digitus Dei, eminently in it, for beyond all our projects, designs and contrivances, God cast us into a gentlemans hands in the turninge of a hand that very morninge, nay that very moment, as he was goinge into the House, that very nobly and handsomely carried it through a very harde chapter, in soe much that some laughed and jeered att mee to thinke how I would be cozened, because that very moment there was high and mighty expectations of Scotch and Army papers ready for readinge, and by the opinion of all it was not in the power of the most eminent leadinge man there, to have promoted it singly and nakedly. But thus it was. Mr. J. Ash, who was by order to bringe in reports from Goldsmiths Hall (our petition beinge in Frank Drakes hands), was moved by him and two more of us in his passage through the Hall that he would sit quiett whilst F.D. moved it which he absolutely denied, but beinge made sensible of the business, and of the equity and quick dispatch it would receave uppon very easy intreaty, very much like a gentleman undertooke the delivery of it, soe before he sate down in the midst of his business he gott it read, and soe it passed with some, but not much regrett, and yet the House was fuller (about 300) then in a longe time before. . . . We have had some of our good frends with us att dinner, our bellies are full and I have noe more to say. . . ."

Mary writes the same day: "Our petition is granted and I trust as God hath wonderfully pleased us in itt, soe he will continue his marcye still, and bless our endeavours thatt wee may suddenly dispatch thy busenes which hath cost me many a sadd and tedious hower. Our frends caried in the house to every creatures greate amazement, for twas a mighty full House and att the very same time they had buseness came in of very high concernment."

At length the case came before the committee, and the sequestration was taken off. Mary writes the good news to Ralph on "January ye 6th and twelveday," "thy buseness was yesterday donn according to thy hartes desire, and I have

c

this day onely time to tell thee soe . . . Lady Warwick hath at last in some measure playd her parte, butt I putt her soundly to itt for I have bin 4 or 5 times with her this week; her husband was there and brought others with him whoos pressence did much good; I went Imediattly from the Comittee to give her thanks last night, where her hus: was gott home before me soe I gave them both thanks together."

Ralph could not as yet return to England, but the removal of the sequestration put him in a fair way of paying his debts by degrees, and Mary prepared to rejoin him in France. Ralph had been planning her journey ever since the previous September. "I expect your summons, the winter is come and ye weather soe cold that unlesse you wrapp yourselfe extraordinary warme, I shall welcome you with a good Cudgell," he writes in September 1647. "I know you will have a care to keepe Jack from cold, and when you land you must not throw off much, for that Towne [Calais] standing uppon ye seaside is subject to bitter weather." Mary had been urging him not to leave Blois too soon, as neither the date nor the port of her arrival were settled: "I know thou wilt have a tedious time of itt to wayt long at Diepe. Itt may be I may wayte att Rie a week for seasonable weather at thatt tim of the yeare which you know is something Blusterous." Sir Ralph tries to persuade Dr. Denton to accompany her by praising "the rare effect of a sea vomit."

Before Mary can leave London, there are 200*l.* of small debts to be paid, besides her husband's larger creditors, and she has also to take a journey into Suffolk to settle money affairs with the Sydenhams. She sends minute directions to Roades for bringing up little Jack, to join her in London. As he will lie but one night on the way, his maid need not come with him; "I would have John Andrewes or some lustie fellow, come up a foote by your horse to helpe the child if any occasion should be, and lett him be sett upon a pillow and wrapped extreamly warme with one of the little cradle rugs and a mantele aboute him." She also orders him "a pare of russett shoose pressently, lined with Bais, the sole within the shooe to keepe him warm."

Ralph had advised her not to bring clothes for the children, "unless you can have a very great peneworth, for they are ordinarily cheaper heere than with you, and we must take the thriftiest way. Truly Muns masters and books cost me above 20 pistolls a yeare now, and he must have cloathes too"; but Mary is resolved that her husband at least shall be made smart: "Prethy send me word whether men weare black cloth still there, and how much will mak you a sute and cloke, for I have a great mind to bring you some over because I know you will rather weare any old rusty thing then bestow a new one upon yourselfe." Also "I think you had best take a glove of my boy Mun's and cutt the bigness of itt in paper . . . and I will buy some gloves for him hear." In a former letter Ralph had playfully teased her for not having worn her new garments: "Sure you meane to sell them and bring mee a minte of money, or else the vanitie of others hath abated your pride, and theire prodigallity made you miserable. Certainly wee are much of a humour at this time about our cloathes, for did you but see how I am patched upp with old Frippery, you could not but admire it; but I deferre all my bravery till you come (with a minte of money) and then ile make it fly, doe not doubt it." He desires her to get little presents for all their friends at Blois, "men, women and children," and he proposes to purchase some pewter plates, "they are very much better and cheaper than they are with you: if you send me a pattern I will match them and buy toe dossen more, for I remember mine were handsome and of a good size."

In contrast to the Verney's simple way of living, Mary describes how "Mr. Pierpoint is now gon out of toune: he hath bin hear about a fortnight or 3 weeks and hath spent a thousand pound: he keepes a coach and fower footemen and toe gentlemen, beside grooms and porter at his doore and cook and very fine coach and liveries, but the very same man he was at Blois. . . . Mr. Smith is with him still . . . but I beleeve will not travayle with him as he is hard a wooing." Ralph sends a message to Mr. Pierpoint in February to tell him, "heare hath beene balls in 14 nights together: if hee please to visit this neglected place . . . the joy of his presence will make the toune forget Lent and give at least as many more." When Sir Roger writes, "I breathe not in a French ayre so cannot complement, . . . civility begins to be look't upon as a monster now," Sir Ralph replies: "S^r complements are a very cheape commodity, & abound too much in this flourishing climate, but . . . should I live ten thousand yeares among these pratlinge people, I thanke God I have not soe much courtshipp, nor soe little honesty, as to learne this flattering quallity."

At length, on 10 April 1648, husband and wife were reunited. Dr. Denton writes lamentably to Ralph of the loss of her company; he had intended to go with her to the coast, but his child's sudden illness and his wife's "whinnelling" (Mary says her jealousy) stopped him; "she will as soone give him leave to goe to Jerusalem, but you know what tis to be bound to a wife, and though you doe not," she adds merrily, "yett he must obey."

Meanwhile Tom had got into one of his worst scrapes, signing a bill of exchange belonging to Sir Thomas Elmes, who had lately married his sister Margaret, to whom he behaved very ill; Doctor Denton wrote that Tom was "in danger of hanging in Paris and of the pillory in London." He would not, however, stir from France without being bought off by Ralph, who employed a friendly Doctor Kirton to treat with him, while Edmund had to use all his eloquence to persuade the scapegrace to go home. "I am hugely affrayd he will linger and bee caught by justice." Doctor Denton, who had no scruples in alarming his friends, observes, "I heere Tom Elmes is in Paris, wch I am much troubled at, for I doubt Mun will have him by the eares (and truly if he would crop them and slit his nose I should not be overmuch troubled), and I doubt be the death of him if he give him noe better satisfaction concerning Pegge, and I should be very loathe that he should have his hands in blood, and so I have sent him word."

The merciless conduct of Parliament to Sir Ralph had made no difference in his opinions; neither he nor his wife "font leur cour" to Henrietta Maria on any of their visits to Paris, so that "Mistress Mary" may have had real difficulty in bringing the Queen's "coch" to the Verney's door; while the Gardiners had behaved so unkindly to Cary when she was left a widow, that Ralph had no very great desire for the company of the maid of honour, who was inclined to dabble in the intrigues of the little court at the Louvre. She afterwards married Sir Henry Wood.

The negotiations in favour of the King lingered long. Edmund, still at "S^{nt} Jermynes," writes to Lady Verney at Blois: "I have wysely, though not pollitickely, placed all my happinesse in attending you—wisely in reguarde it would give me the truest and most vallued content, but impollitickly in reguarde it iss soe dissonant to may fortunes and my wandring profession that I am not allowed soe much ass hopes of enjoying it. My joyes are momentary and come ass it were to swell my afflictions, for Suckling tells uss truely, pryvation iss a missery ass much above bare wretchednesse ass that is short of happinesse. I have experimentally founde it ever since you left Paris, and yet I find a strange pleasure in thiss discontentednesse, because it iss so evident an argument of the vallue I have for you. . . . I shall never esteeme any person in the worlde above you. . . . My service to little Wagge" [his nephew].

Mun had better intelligence of public events than Ralph, and in his letters he often passes on the latest news from England. He joins Lord Ormonde at Havre, hoping to find "my lady Marquese, but as she resolves to stay in thiss kingdome [France] till it be knowne what will become of our Irish affayres," he goes to kiss her hand at Caen, which takes him a week there and back, some fifty miles. "My Lord Lieutenant undertooke the lyke journey . . . & most narrowly escaped drowning. He had some 8 or 10 leagues to come by water, & an ignorant seaman coming before the tyde served him, splitt his boate against the ground; my Lord was a greate part of him under water, but with much a doe got into a small cocke-boate, in which he rowed about all night, expecting to be cast away every minute, the waves beating into the boate, but by God's mercy is brought safe to land this morning; I have been with him above this houre."

When the sequestration was removed, the first money which Ralph received—little enough for his own necessities—was employed in assisting his brother. "I am very sensible," replies Edmund, "of the charge I put you to, and your noble and free way of parting with the money. I confesse I receive not any thing from you but with a trouble, and that I would rather be out of the world than continue chargeable to you. I hope the way I am now going will eyther mend my condition or end me." "Havre.—The Prince of Wales and all hiss fleete are gone for Holland to victual themselves, and my Ld Warwicke with about 17 shipps came into the Downs last night. Though victualling iss reported to be the cause of the Prince hiss drawing into Holland, yet I doubt he wass perswaded not to stand Warwicke, ass being thought too weake, for he hath not above 4 tall shipps, the rest are frigots and small vessels. . . . Wee cannot passe into Ireland now without great danger by reason of my L^d of Warwicke, and woe be to us if we are taken, but I hope better fortunes are decreede for uss. Wee have a gallant vessell with 36 gunnes and shall be well manned, and if wee are not very much over matched shall fight hard before wee give ourselves up. I believe this totall defeate of the Scotts has put the queene, Prince, and all theire Councell soe much to theire witts' end that they know not which way to turne themselves now. I spake with Sir Baldwyne Wake, who came lately from the Prince, and reports it wass really beleev'd that the Prince should have been marryed to Duke Hambleton's daughter." "There iss noe jealousy of duke hamilton's betraying the army, but lieuet.: generall Bayly who gave up the foote iss much talked of, and duke hamilton's courage somewhat questioned. The Scotts are in trueth but in a sadd condition. . . . God send them better fortune, even to the downefall of our present Tyrants, for whyle they reigne England can never be happy. . . . I am of opinion if wee can by any meanes settle Ireland I shall be in England with men next spring."

Colchester had been captured by Fairfax, and Edmund was horrified to hear that "they had been so inhumanely bloody as to put Lucas and Lysle to the sworde"; "Fayrefaxe's own party doe soe exclayme against the butchery . . . that it's thought there iss an end of proceedings in that kind. The Parliament are selling the Scotts common prisoners to the

Barbados and other plantations, which I conceive to be about 12,000 or 14,000 men, and artickle the merchants for theire not returning. I thinke they meane to transplant the whole nation." Again and again Edmund returns to the tragedy of Colchester: "I shall adde something now which must render Fayrefaxe's murthering those gallant gentlemen the more odious, and their own diurnalls confirme my argument, for upon the question what mercy wass, it wass resolv'd by Fayrefaxe hiss own commissioners in hiss name 'that it wass to kill or save whome the generall pleas'd, but he had given that frequent testimonye of hiss civillity to such ass fell into hiss power that none neede suspect severity, nevertheless he would not be obliged to mercy.' Now let any person judge whither thiss answer and exposition of mercy did not implicitely promise lyfe to all, but it wass a high tyranny to bring thiss extreame into his power, for ass every gentleman and souldyer is obliged to a punctuall observance or the trust committed to him by defending to hiss utmost all persons, townes, and forts under hiss command, soe there iss a civill and honourable custome, and soe authenticke that it may not impropperly be called a lawe, amongst souldyers to give noble and honourable conditions to theire enemy though in the greatest strength and necessity. I shall only give two examples, and those from noe meane souldyers, and yet when the besieged could not hold out an houre; the one iss from the last prince of Orange to those in the Basse [? Boise-le-Duc] after he had sprung hiss mine and hiss men upon the rampiers, upon a parley beaten of by drumme, he caus'd hiss men to retreate and gave the besieged theire own conditions, and thiss after sixe or eight monthes siege. The other iss from the Earle of Callender to Sr Edmund Cary, governour of Hartlepoole neare Durham. Caryes souldyers conspired to deliver him up, and sent thiss offer of theires to my lord Callander then before the towne, but my lord abhorring thiss treachery, sent in theire base engagement to the governour by a trumpet of his own, and withall hiss name to a blanke sheete of paper, and desired him to write hiss own conditions. These gentlemen of Colchester tooke up armes by the prince of Wales hiss commission, and entered into parley for surrender of the towne assoone ass the Scotts (which were theire expected reliefe) were destroyed, and a council of warr would have condemn'd them had they surrendred sooner, but ass the rebellion of England iss the most notorious of any that ever wass since the beginning of the world, soe certainely it iss prosecuted and justifyed with the most mercilesse inhumanity and barbarisme. . . . The sufferers have dyed with honour and glory and the actors live in horror and infamy."

In April Sir Henry Newton writes: "My lady Marquesse is sent for to Ireland. I thinke it will turn the sanctuary for us all." Things were indeed looking so serious in Ireland for the Parliament, that Cromwell himself prepared to take command of the army, but before he could land there, Colonel Michael Jones, who had been attacked by Ormonde in Dublin, came out in force and utterly routed the Royalists. The slaughter was tremendous, and a false report reached England which Dr. Denton forwards to France. "On Mun his regiment of foot and on Vaughan his regiment of horse, fell all the slaughter. Mun his regiment were killed all on a heape, not one of them as I can heare but fought it out to the last even against horse and foote,—Mun is for certaine slaine, not wth out much regrett, even to his adverse party. Jones himself strooke his hands on his breast, and said he had rather have had him alive than all the prisoners he had, and he should have been as well used as ever was prisoner. . . . It was 1000 to one but Ormond had beene taken, on whom there lights infinite blame, though not fit for any of Mun his friends to say so, he being at tick tak and continued playing after the alarum. . . . My hart hath beene so sad since the newes of Mun as I thinke hath not beene since Edgehill, but we must not repine, it is God not the Sabeans, that takes all away, let him do what seems best in his eyes." The letter goes on to say that Jones had had Mun honourably buried. This circumstantial story proved to be entirely false. To have been killed in battle would have been a better fate for the brave soldier than that which awaited him. Cromwell hastened his departure, and was followed by Ireton and the remainder of the army. Lord Ormonde threw all his best troops into Drogheda under Sir Arthur Aston, a first-rate officer, and entrusted his own regiment to the command of Sir Edmund Verney. "The defences of the place were contemptible," and Ormonde was unable to attack the besieging force. On 9 September both Aston and Verney sent despatches to him.

On the morrow Cromwell began the bombardment and Aston penned his last written words. Drogheda was taken. Inchiquin on 15 September 1649 reported to Ormonde: "All conclude that no man [had] quarter with Cromwell's leave, that yet many were privately saved by officers and soldiers . . . Verney, Finglas, Warner, and some other officers were alive in the hands of some of Cromwell's officers 24 hours after the business, but whether . . . they are yet living they cannot tell." Sir Ralph on 4 November was still "between hope and feare concerninge deare deare Mun," and it was not till 30 November that he received Mr. Buck's letter from Caen announcing the death of "your Brother and my deare Freind, Sir Edmund Varny, who behaved himselfe wth the greatest gallentry that could be—he was slaine at Drahoda three dayes after quarter was given him, as he was walkinge wth Crumwell by way of protection, One Ropier who is brother to the Lord Ropier, caled him aside in a pretence to speake wth him, beinge formerly of acquaintance, and insteade of some frendly office wch Sir Ed: might expect from him, he barberously rann him throw wth a tuck, but I am confident to see this act once highly revenged; the next day after, one Lt. Coll. Boyle, who had quarter likewise given him, as he was at dinner wth my Lady More, sister to the Earle of Sunderland, in the same Towne, one of Crumwell's souldiers came and whispered him in the eare to tell him he must presently be put to deth, who rising from the table, the lady asked him whither he was goeinge, he answered, Madam to dye, who noe sooner steped out of the roome but hee was shott to deth. These are cruelties of those traitors, who noe doubte will finde the like mercie when they stand in neede of it."

Here is the relation from the opposite point of view: Cromwell, writing to Bradshaw, from Dublin, says, "It hath pleased God to bless our endeavours at Tredah. After battery we stormed it. The enemy were about 3000 in the town: they made a stout resistance, and near 1000 of our men being entered, the enemy forced them out again. But God gave a new courage to our men, they attempted again, and entered. . . . Being entered, we refused them quarter: having the day before summoned the town. I believe we put to the sword the whole number of the defendants. I do not think thirty of the whole number escaped with their lives. Those that did are in safe custody for the Barbados. . . . This hath been a marvellous great mercy . . . the enemy had put into this garrison almost all their prime soldiers under the command of their best officers. . . . There were some 7 or 8 regiments, Ormond's being one, under the command of Sir Edmund Varney. I do not believe . . . that any officer escaped with his life, save only one lieutenant . . . I wish that all honest hearts may give the glory of this to God alone." "I am persuaded that this is a righteous judgement of God," wrote Cromwell to Lenthall the Speaker, concerning the wholesale slaughter of men who had submitted, and the selling of hundreds more into slavery. "The defendants in Tredah consisted of the Lord of Ormond's regiment (Sir Edmund Varney Lieutenant Colonel), of 400"; &c., &c. Considering that Lenthall was a kinsman of the Verneys, this could hardly have been an agreeable communication from "your most obedient servant, Oliver Cromwell."

In 1648 Ralph and his wife stayed for several weeks at Paris on their way south, partly no doubt in order to meet Edmund, who was soon to embark on his last journey to Ireland, and perhaps because of a natural shrinking on Mary's part from coming back to Blois where both her young children had recently died. A few weeks after their return thither she writes of being weary of the place. Ralph went by himself to Tours to seek fresh quarters, but could find nothing suitable, and they had to resign themselves to remaining at Blois. The dullness and stagnation of a French country town where, as Ralph declares, "no newes is ever heard" and "nothing ever comes to pass in this woful place," must have told heavily on one fresh from the interesting society of London—seeing and hearing some of the best men and women of that most stirring time—society in which she herself was so well fitted to join and indeed to shine. When one reads how her uncle-doctor brought "parliament-men" and lawyers to her little lodging, it is clear how he reckoned on the power of her charm and capacity for business to influence and persuade them. Now she had nothing to do but to look after her little household and her two boys, who were most of the day with their tutor, the French *pasteur*, and to cheer the tedious life of her husband.

The progress of public events at home was most disquieting. Dr. Denton writes: "Here is at present a strange consternation of spiritts amongst all people, for the Army hath interposed about the treatie, and the generall expectation is for worse and more sad times then ever." "Drake is att this present in the hands of the Army with many other members, some say 50, others more, others lesse, which was seised uppon yesterday goinge to the house. What the issue will be God knowes. . . . It is an ill time now to treat about land; . . . noe man will touch uppon that stringe, for the Army is att the Parliament doores, and secure all the members they can light on that they suppose will vote contrary to their remonstrance, particularly they have seized of your acquaintance Drake, Wenman, Ruddier, Nat ffines, Prinne, Sir G. Gerard, and I know not how many besides." After some details about business the Doctor continues his account a little sarcastically: "The Army doe not to-day as yesterday catch and imprison the members . . . but now they only stand att the doore with 2 roules, and if their names be in such a roule then they may enter, if in the other then they may not. Soe that none enter now but our frends, and you shall see we will doe righteous things at last. Most of the secured members lay in Hell last night, and are now gone to the generall. There is scarce enough left free to make a house."

The party in power was bitterly hostile to the King. The Commons passed an ordinance instituting a High Court of Justice by whom he was to be tried. The Upper House, or what remained of it, made a futile attempt at resistance. Dr. Denton wrote, "I heare the L^{ds} on Tuesday last voted all null since ye army siezed ye members . . . It is not to be told ye confusion we are in, ye L^ds have adjourned for a weeke; the Commons now declare the legislative power to be in them only. I pray God send peace on earth & write all o^r names in ye booke of life. Deare Raph I am thine in peace or war." "A[lexander] D[enton]'s creditors . . . see there is nothinge but land to be had, & they will rather venture all then take it, soe troublesome & cumbersome a thinge is land growne now, it is soe liable to quarter & taxes, & makes one's estate soe visible & consequently the persons more liable to sequestration, for it is almost a crime to have an estate in these days. . . . I doubt before this come to you our Kinge will be defunct, and it is feared the sword will govern instead of the crowne. The complexion of our confusions growes every day more sad & black then other. Y^e scaffolds are buildinge for the tryall of the Kinge, & ye terme putt of for 20 daies for that very reason. It is almost every man's opinion that nothing will satisfie but his head, & I am clearly of ye same opinion except God miraculously divert or divide, or confound councells. Our divines preach generally against these proceedings & not without great vehemence, & some of them begin to writt against them alsoe. Our cavalier L^ds have offered to ingage life & fortune for ye King's performance of whatever he shall grant of their demands. The Scotch have mediated & declared absolutely against it, yett nothing will doe, they are resolved of their course for ought I can find."

Even Sir Roger Burgoyne, strong parliamentarian as he was, writes: "I could be content to be a monke or hermit, rather than a statesman at the present conjunction of affairs. . . . What will become of us in England God only knowes. The passages of late presage the saddest of times." Dr. Denton writes again: ". . . It is now the dismallest time here that ever our eyes beheld. Noe mediation by Ministry, Scottland, Cavaliers, L^ds, or of any body else for ought I can heare, can disswade from doinge execucon uppon ye kinge. I heare the Queene of Bohemia is cominge over if not landed, her son's mediation hath not yett prevailed any thing, & I doubt hers will prevaile as little. Y^e confusions & distractions are every where soe great that I know not where to wish my selfe but in Heaven. . . . It is thought there will be a risinge or combustion in every country of ye kingdome at once, soe generally are people's hearts agst these proceedings."

Ralph received tidings of the final tragedy from Mr. Cockram, an English merchant at Rouen in February 1649. "I doubt not but ere this you have heard the dolefull news of our King's death, whoe was beheaded laste teusday was seaven night, at tow of the clock, afternoone, before Whitehall, the moste barbarous Ackt, & lamentable sight that ever any Christians did beholde. The Numerous guarde of horse and foote of Armed Tygers did binde the hands and stopp the mouths of many Thousand beholders, but could not keepe their eyes from weeping, for none but harts of flinte could forbeare. His maies^{tie} appeared uppon the scaffold with admirable constancie noe way dismayed, did make a very worthy speach shewing his Innocency of what hee was accused & condemned for; & yett with greate charitie did freely forgive all his enemies in rehearsing the example of St John. And to satisfy the people concerninge his Religion hee theare declared that hee dyed a trew Christian according to the open profession of the Church of England, as it was lefte by the deceased king his father: And soe with sundry expressions of piety & godly exhortations hee submitted to that wofull ende, which makes all honest menn's harts to bleede; And is a beginning of England's greater Miserie than ever hath bin hitherto."

For nearly a month there are no letters from Sir Roger or Dr. Denton, when their silence is thus accounted for: "The newes . . . of most publique concernement I am confident is long since come to yor eares; as the kinge beinge executed by Whitehall yeisterday being 3 weekes since, I had not failed to have given you notice of it the same weeke, but that the D^r would not suffer me to send the letter I had written, there being a generall stoppage of all letters," and Dr. Denton adds "We are now in the maddest world that ever we mortalls sawe."—"If I am not disappointed you shall have the king's booke [Eikon Basilike]. It hath beene hitherto at 8*s.* and 10*s.* price. . . . It hath beene much suppressed, the first printer and impression plundered and presses broken." "The king's booke, with his deportment, indurance, att his tryall and on the scaffold, hath amazed the whole kingdome to see soe much courage, Xstianity, and meekness in one man. The women generally are in mourninge for him, ye men dare not, only some few." Sir Henry Newton writes from Paris: "I find a Court heere sadd & hugely discomposed, but as much for want of money as for anything else; their poverty must needes bee very much, when to this houre the Qu: & D. of Yorke's footmen & many others are not in mourning. I have kiss'd all their hands, & passed a whole day betweene dukes & civilitees."

The bad news of public affairs in England must have weighed all the more heavily on Ralph, as his wife's health caused him growing anxiety. Some months after her return to France she fell dangerously ill of what Ralph calls "a kind of apoplexiy or Lethargy," in which she lost her sight for a time. She recovered from this illness, but was in delicate health; the doctor advised her drinking the waters at Bourbonne les Bains; they spent some weeks there, and expected to have the company of the sprightly Sir Henry Newton, who wrote to Ralph that he was anxious to "returne time enough to tipple with my lady at Bourbon, against when I have resolved for so much water that I promise you to deale in none till then, not thinking it an element to bee us'd that way except phisically." "I am growne very weary of good veale and wine; my mind runnes much on water, therefore beleeve me, S^r, I sitt in thornes untill I can bee a man of my word both unto you and my lady." In spite of these fine phrases, he never came, and in his next letter it appears that he had flown over to England.

Dr. Denton expresses his satisfaction that Mary is better, and hopes that she need drink no more—"it's possible to have a surfeit of water as well as wine. Sir Richard Winn hath mett with it, not to the life but to the death." He "cannot gett a booke for landladie's pallett"; the works on controversial divinity that the doctor so zealously recommended may well have been heavy reading after the baths in the hot valley of Bourbonne in July. They went to Paris for a time, and then Sir Ralph was anxious to take his wife to the South. "Shee should order you better," wrote Dr. Denton, "then to lett you ramble like Tom a Bedlam ten leagues beyond the wide world's end."

Avignon, he heard, was visited by "les trois fléaux de Dieu" —famine, pestilence, and the sword—and the plague was also at Nismes, but he hoped to get to Montpellier. Sir Henry laughs at him for his roving spirit; he says he has received his last letter, "but where hee is that sent it the Lord knowes."

Mary has been shopping in Paris for Mrs. Sherard, and Ralph writes to her that "my wife . . . hath ventured to present you with a paire of French trimed gloves, a Fan, a paire of Tweezes & an enamiled Box with patches; I blush at her boldnesse but more at my own Folly, for suffering of her, but you know she weares the Breeches & will doe what she list."

Tom turns up at Paris again. "My dayly study now is to serve God, and to avoid the banquier apprehending mee": he is "forced to lye in bed, being destitute of bootes and stockings." When at length he returns to England "he follows his old tricks still." For a time he appeared "clinquant & in wonderful equipage both for cloathes and money," but it was only due to what he "threatened" out of his aunt Ursula (and probably from unworthy gains as a spy), and then came the usual *da capo*—prison and pious penitent epistles, of which Dr. Denton writes: "to see now his letters you would thinke him a St. or a preacher at least. He goes far that never turnes. God can doe much. Paul persecuted till he could noe longer kick against the pricks." But no miracle of reformation was to change Tom's wretched career.

Dr. Denton writes from Oxford in September 1649: "Two daies since the souldiers of this garrison discarded their officers & are all turned levellers, & it is thought most of the regiments of the army are of the same mould." Sir Roger also writes: "The Levellers have begun to play some more prankes about Oxford, but it is hoped that they will suddenly be quasht, although some much doubt it; it is pitty that souldiers formerly so unanimous in the cause of God, should now begin to clash one with another, but it is verily thought that there are some knaves amongst them which I hope God will one day discover. They talke much of the Kinge of Scotlande having the better upon the seas, & that Ormonde hath beaten Ld. gen. Crumwell since his coming over, the rather because he hath sent over for fresh supplies . . . but I presume you are too discreet to bestow your beliefe upon any fabulous report." However incredulous about political news, Sir Roger seems to have no doubt about another story. "Great store of crown crabs were taken in Cornwall among their pilchards"; four of them were sent from Plymouth to London; they were "as bigg as halfe crownes, have shells like crabbs, feet like ducks, faces like men, & crownes on their heads, theire faces & crownes seem as if they were carved upon their shells."

Mary was getting gradually worse, but many merry messages still pass between her and the good Doctor, sent and received by Ralph. "You must needs send landlady over in wonderfull post hast to me, for I hear her old prosecutors the Hydes are makinge enquiry after me & except she come to out scold them, I must goe to Billingsgate and I doubt I shall not match them nor her there. I thinke I mumpt her there!" The Doctor has at last succeeded in letting their London house for 65*l*. "for this next yeare to the Countesse of Downe." His absence about their affairs "hath so routed my business that I am like a crowe in a mist, or rather like an owle at noon." He attacks Mary again, who asks about some commissions he was to do for her: "She is a lyinge slut. . . . for I doe not or will not remember that ever she writt to me for nuttmeggs; how ever, tell her she shall neyther have nuttmegg nor stockins, nor meat neither by my good will, nor money which is worse, nor anythinge but druggs till she write her longe—longe—longe promised letter."

Then comes the death of Mary.

In Sir Ralph's calendar of letters addressed to Dr. Denton are the following entries:

"$\frac{15}{5}$ May 1650. I writ Dr. word I received his letter, but could write of no businesse, Wife beeing soe ill."

"$\frac{22}{12}$ May 1650. Oh my deare deare."

"$\frac{29}{19}$ May 1650. Friday the $\frac{20}{10}$ May (at 3 in ye morning) was

Sir Edmund Verney

Mary, Lady Verney

the Fatall day & Hower. The disease a consumption. . . . I shall not need to relate with what a Religeous and a cheerful joy & courage this now happy & most glorious saint, left this unhappy & most wicked world. . . ."

Ralph was quite determined that at all events nothing so precious to him as his wife's body should remain in France, and he immediately had it embalmed; but there were many difficulties in the way of getting it carried to England, and he dared not send it "uppon uncertaine termes; least it should bee tossed and tumbled from Place to Place, and being discovered . . . run ye hazard of some affront." For months it remained in Ralph's house at Blois, and he wrote: "though it bee locked upp in a Roome by itselfe where noebody comes, yet you must needes thinke it noe small affliction to me to have it soe neare mee. You know when Sarah died Abraham made hast to bury the dead out of his sight."

At length a safe-conduct for a coffin was found. Sir Ralph followed the ship in thought with loving anxiety, "every puffe of winde that tosses it at sea, shakes me at land"—the honest Doctor saw it reverently interred in Middle Claydon Church on 20 November 1650.

The state of Ralph's affairs did not admit of his returning home, and he wrote to Dr. Denton: "My mind runs more after Italy; not to delight myselfe with anything there, for since my deare Wife's death I have bid adieu to all that most men count theire Happinesse. The Arabian deserts are now farre more agreeable to my humour then the most pleasant Grotts and Gardens that Rome it selfe affords. Ah Dr., Dr., her company made every place a paradice unto me, but she being gonn, unless god bee most meraculously mercifull, what good can bee expected by your most afflicted and unfortunate servant."

"An absolute detestation of all manner of Businesse" and of society fell upon him. "Ah, Deare Doctor," he writes, "the sorrows that possess my soule are my companions in every place, and make the sollitary corners of the world the most agreeable to my humour; for there (when words are wanting) I have liberty to weepe my Fill, and when these Floodgates can noe

longer runn, my sighs and groanes bewaile the most unutterable
losse, that now afflicts, Your most disconsolate and unfortunate
servant."

Of the seven children born to Sir Ralph and Dame Mary,
two only survived her; Edmund, aged 13, had now been absent
from England more than six years, and John, aged 9, had been
at Blois since his mother brought him back with her from
Claydon in 1647. These little boys, with a French manservant
and an English maid or two, formed Sir Ralph's household,
managed with painful and scrupulous economy. In the autumn
the family party was increased by the arrival of the two little
Eure girls, with Luce Sheppard now their waiting-gentlewoman.
Better days were dawning, as the sequestration was taken off
Sir Ralph's estate; but creditors were clamouring to be paid,
and he was honourably anxious to cut down all expenses,
except those necessary for the boys' education, till he could
satisfy them in full.

Sir Ralph's genial friend, Sir Henry Newton, after his last
visit to Blois, had gone off to Holland to look after "a certain
Cosen of mine, Mrs. Jane Puckering, that was stolen away out
of Grenwich parke last Michelmas, by the Walshes of Wor-
cestshire, who forcing her upon landing to say something for
their advantage, sue her upon a marriage, and have made a
shift to gett her into a Monestery at Newport [Nieuport]
where shee is a perfect prisoner, and in great distresse".

Sir Henry's mother was Catherine, sister of Sir Thomas
Puckering (or Pickering), Bart., M.P. for Tamworth in the
parliaments of 1620 to 1627. The "stealing away" of Sir
Thomas Puckering's daughter and heiress in October 1649,
while walking with her maids close to her own home, was one
of the *causes célèbres* of the day.

To run off with an heiress and force her into a marriage had
been no uncommon feat for the wilder spirits amongst the young
Cavaliers; but the Commonwealth, with its anxious provisions
for public morality, afforded to women a protection they had
never known before. Prompt measures were taken by the
Council of State; the difficulties made in Holland about
surrendering Mistress Jane were met by a still more peremptory

demand. Soon after Sir Henry's visit an English man-of-war was sent over to bring her home, and an indictment of felony was found against Joseph Walsh and his companions. Sir Henry inherited her fortune at her death, and took the name of Puckering-Newton.

On his way to visit his cousin he writes to Sir Ralph in his airy way of a duel he had fought with Colonel Bamfield, who had behaved very badly to his wife's sister Anne Murray. "I mett at sea with a rencontre of a person who bored some few holes in mee at landing, which have done mee this only despight, that they kept me away so much longer then I intended from my Cosen, and you; of two pricks scarcely worth the naming, one of them hath been kind to mee about the belly, but the other now seven weekes in cure I doubt will domineere among the sinewes a moneth longer before I gett my arme at liberty." This letter was written in ignorance of Dame Mary Verney's death. Sir Henry, who with all his jests and oddities had a warm heart, was shocked to hear of his friend's bereavement.

On Christmas Day a party of thirty English exiles met at dinner, and Sir Henry Newton writes from Rouen that he would gladly have made their number thirty-one. He still retains an affectionate remembrance of the noble company at Blois, "who if they were to be purchased with gold, I would not grudge to give my bookes, or the wayte of them for Mr. Gee, for Mr. Cordell and Mr. du Val, but chiefly for Sir Ralph I would give myselfe." As he could not keep his Christmas among friends and Cavaliers, Sir Henry proposes to himself, as an action of charity suited to the day, to try to forgive the Presbyterians; but he feels this to be almost an impossible task, and cheers himself with the assurance "that God Almighty will not."

When Luce Sheppard and her little charges passed through Paris, Lady Browne was kind to them; and charged Luce to find at Blois, perhaps at the great annual fair, some fur which she could not buy in Paris. Luce failed to do so, but Sir Ralph, glad to show Lady Browne any mark of respect, came to the rescue. "Madame," he writes, "Finding by Luce, you had occation for some Fur, and that she could not fit you in this Towne, I haveing such a one, as I guessed might possibly serve your turne (though I could not then come at it) have adventured to send it now, togeather with some other odd Trifles wch I must beseech you to accept, though I confesse they are not worth receiving. Madame, had I not a very greate experience of your goodnesse, I should not have presumed to tender such inconsiderable Toyes as these, to a person of your Meritt."

Sir Ralph keeps a note that "with this letter I sent her:

A greate White Furr to cover a Bedd.

2 Paires of Frenchpain Gloves.

12 Paires of Eng: White Gloves.

12 yrds of Eng: Scarlet Ribbon, 6 penny Broad and 12 yrds of 2 penny Broad to it.

A paire of Scarlet silk stockings, with a paire of Turkey Garters to them.

An excellent Spanish pocket cover with Scarlet Taffaty, and a Box of Dried Grapes with 4 laires 3 p. besides the Box."

A gentleman might now hesitate to send to the wife of the English Ambassador at Paris "a paire of scarlet silk stockings, with a paire of Turkey Garters to them"; but in such evil days Lady Browne took these additions to her wardrobe in very good part, lamented the "small capacity" she and her husband now had to serve Sir Ralph, and signed herself "untill some happy opportunity of Requitall, in all gratefullnesse" his most obliged humble servant; her son and daughter are also Sir Ralph's humble servants. This daughter was the wife of John Evelyn; during his absence, to settle his affairs in England, she remained for a time at Paris, "yet very young, under the care of an excellent lady and prudent mother," Lady Browne did not long enjoy her "greate white furr": she went to England the next summer for her daughter's confinement, and soon after caught scarlet fever and died—"an excellent and virtuous lady," says her son-in-law, "having been so obliging on all occasions, to those who continually frequented her house in Paris, which was not only an hospital, but an asylum to all our persecuted and afflicted countrymen, during eleven years' residence there in that honourable situation."

Sir Ralph's letters from England were sad enough; public affairs were very unsettled, and each member of the family had his or her own troubles: "Elmes hath Tom in prison uppon 2 suites. . . . Betty wants cloathes and there is a small crosse caper about her going to Pegg; D^r made Pegg cry about it and will bee at her againe, Harry also told her her owne, as D^r heares." Penelope has lost a baby, Sir Ralph's godchild, who only lived long enough, as the poor mother put it, "to be maid a Christian sole." Mary needed an "adishon" to her allowance, "for the times grow harde," and Henry is so unpleasant that Sir Ralph will rather "dispise the Deedes of such a desperate Dick then suffer himselfe to be dared out of anything."

Sir Ralph was planning a journey to Italy: he would allow himself three months to wind up his affairs, then give his address to none but the Doctor and Sir Roger, with power to the Doctor to burn his letters. The tangle of debts between himself and young Edmund Denton is so complicated that he is in despair: "if all that I can write shall bee called a labarinth and scrupulous, and looked uppon as meerely dillatory, I can say noe lesse then that *None are soe blinde as those that will not see.*"

Hopeless of fulfilling his many obligations, Sir Ralph had considered, soon after he became a widower, whether he ought not to sell Claydon. He is not very hopeful that even this desperate step would clear him, for the market is so glutted with the sale of "Church lands, Crowne lands, and Malignants' Estates" that purchasers are shy, and Claydon would sell cheap. "But if there is no other remedy," he writes, "I had rather sell it all, then a part of it, and if it must goe, the sooner tis gonn the more money will bee left. And if I must bee soe unhappy, I wish I knew it now, for if I sell this land I shall forever bid adieu to England, and then I would not burry my deare wife there, for whensoever it pleaseth God to call me to him, I much desire, and (as shee did) shall make it my request, to have my Bones burried by hers (and if I tooke care for that, she bid mee lay her where I pleased), soe that when our soules and bodies shall be reunited, wee may goe hand in hand to Heaven togeather."

The three months Sir Ralph had given himself to wind up

his money matters extended to six, and yet the business seemed but little advanced; however, in March 1651, he is making his last preparations at Blois for a prolonged tour. He doubted whether to take his eldest boy, Mun, to Italy; he could not afford a tutor as well as a travelling servant, and "a French Preceptor is fitter than an English and more useful; 'tis better be without than take an ill one." He thinks "Mun is too young to profit by his travel, and his Body too thin to endure it"; but his piteous appeals seem to have turned the scale. A few years later, when there was any question of his spending an hour with Mary Eure, Sir Ralph could not hope for his son's society; but this heroine of a romantic chapter of Mun's youth was still in pinafores; he had all a schoolboy's contempt for girls, and vehemently objected to be left with Luce Sheppard and the little ones, when he had been used to the society of his father and his father's friends.

So it was decided that "the young gallant," as Sir Roger called him, should go on the grand tour. Sir Ralph gave up his house, settled Luce and her two little gentlewomen in "Chambres garnies" at Madame Juselier's, and sent "poore Jack" to Madame Testard, widow of the Protestant *pasteur*, where he was to board and attend classes under Luce's super-intendence.

No definite plans were made, but letters from England were to be addressed first: "For Mr. Raphe Smith, a Monsieur Monsieur Remy, chez Monsieur Le Sueur Sculpteur de Roy, aux Maraiz du Temple, Rue de Bretagne, au Soleil levant, à Paris"; and afterwards: "Chez Monsieur Le Sueur, Rue des graveliers vis à vis de la petite Hotte"; then to await his arrival "chez Monsr Monsr Cesar Gras, Marchand Bourgeois, prôche le plastre a Lyon." "Mr. Gape's men," Henry Foukes and Francis Lloyd, "are to send him the Diurnalls weekly."

Sir Roger Burgoyne writes to Sir Ralph in May 1651: "I shall desire thee to make all the hast thou canst back againe, as may stand with the gravity of the father and the youth of the sonne, I trust that betweene you both you will trace it very orderly." "Orderly," Sir Ralph was sure to be, and there is a careful list of the clothes that Luce Sheppard is to send after

them to Lyons, including —"6 Fine night capps Laced marked
V in black silke, and 2 Fine night capps plaine," to frame his
care-worn cheeks when the majestic wig was taken off at night;
and "4 new plaine capps, marked V in Blew silke," to surround
Mun's fresh, boyish face, such as we see it yet in a picture painted
the following year; many elaborate shirts with lace and "New
Cambrick double Ruffe Cuffes, marked V in blew thread,"
which must have been a great anxiety to pack; "5 paires of
little Holland Cuffes for Mun, 3 Paires of Cambrick double
Boot-hose"; a large number of "fine Holland Handkerchers
Buttoned" which would be puzzling to the modern nose; "2
Tufted Holland Wastcoates Lined"; "2 Dimothy Wastcoates,"
one "Greate Fustian Dressing Wastcoate"; "4 Face Napkins";
and in case of accidents, "2 old Handkerchers and 2 paires of
old Linnen Stockings." Later a "Black trunke with 3 lockes
and Wooden Barres, is packed at Lyons, to go on to Florence,"
and Sir Ralph keeps a careful list of its contents. There was
a great deal of the heavy mourning which the etiquette of grief
required: "Black cloath Doublets," new and old; "Black
Breeches and Cloake, Blacke Cloath Cape for a Cloake, and 2
other peeces of Blacke Cloath; Black Hats and Hat-bands;
old Black Tafaty garters, and new Black ribbon roses; and
severall peeces of extra crape."

Even the shades of night and the privacy of the bedchamber
did not allow of any relaxation of woe; Sir Ralph could hardly
take his black bed about with him, but he did take "2 Black
Taffaty night-cloathes, with the Black night capps, and Black
comb and brush and two Black sweetbaggs to it, and the
Slippers of Black Velvet," and "Blake Paper." There were
more coverings for the head than ever: "6 serge undercapps
and 6 Browne callico under-capps," to be worn by day when
the wig was taken off; and besides "3 plaine new night capps
coarse," and "30 Fine Peaked night capps," there are "2 Night
Periwiggs." The complexion is also cared for; his toilet equip-
ment includes "Muske for powder, ciprus Powder, and a
Puffe, 12 Tortus shell Agendas, 2 gold picktooths, Hair Powder,
2 Paires new Barbing Larmes, sizars, and 3 Head-rubbers."

Sir Ralph was virtuously anxious to provide for repairs,

as he took a "Black Leather needle-case with a greate gold Bodkin, Papers of Pinns, Blew Thread, Shirt Buttons and old White Round Buttons, Cap-strings, and Tape"; but none of the honourable company seemed capable of making use of them, and after some months' absence from Luce's needles and threads, there are lamentable entries of black silk stockings of which only one is whole, and of "2 Night Cloathes burned, and one old one with out Buttons" and such like.

In May Sir Ralph and his son are at Montpellier, famous for "pure ayre and faire women," having passed through Bordeaux, Toulouse, Carcassonne, "and divers of the best towns in Languedoc"; "the violence of the Plague and Famine" prevented their intended visit to the North of Spain, and they settled down for some weeks at Lyons, where Sir Ralph provided Mun with a Latin master and devoted himself to answering the great budget of business letters that he had found there. The Spanish army encamped near Turin, and the "multitude of peasants in Savoye which practise the trade of bandittis, more dangerous to travellers then the Spaniards," make it difficult to reach Milan. Sir Ralph found Toulon and the towns on the Rhone intolerably hot in July and August, but he had a horror of Switzerland; mountain scenery being too rude for the elegant taste of a seventeenth-century gentleman. Roger North wrote of the soft beauty of the Lake country: "We went through a plain but stony road, in the view of hideous mountains." If this was the effect of Westmorland, the Alps could only have been repulsive and terrible.

Evelyn, who also left England in the winter of 1643, and was tossed about by the same November storms that kept Sir Ralph and Mary so long waiting to cross the Channel, has left us a vivid picture of the discomforts of Swiss travelling. The age of flannel shirts and homespuns was not yet, and it seems an irreverence even to fancy Sir Ralph stumbling through "an ocean of snow" on a pass, in his Paris periwig, his "new Cambrick double ruffe cuffes," and his "tufted Holland Wastcoate"; or lying his "Fine peaked Nightcap" to rest on the coarse sacking of the Swiss "beds stuffed with leaves" thrown down on the mud floors, "or in cupboards so high from the ground that they climbed them by a ladder." Nor was the coach better fitted to encounter "the greate cataract of mealted snow and other waters" which poured down Alpine roads after a sudden storm, than he himself was to put up with such "infamous, wretched lodgings"; so he made his way to Italy.

This September the echoes of the Battle of Worcester brought dismay to the various knots of English exiles abroad; that stout Parliamentarian Sir Roger Burgoyne wrote exultingly of "a late and very remarkable providence of God in reference to our Parliament forces," and "the absolute overthrow of our enemies"; but to the unwarlike Sir Ralph it was a great sorrow to hear of more English blood being spilt by English hands.

Sir Ralph is delighted with "the Duke of Florence's garden of Simples, his gallerie of rareities of all sorts" and the "Miracles of art"; but Florence is "a deare Towne for strangers"; Siena he finds a "cheape place to live in"; Naples "a noble rich king-dome but a bad people," the Spaniards courteous, the Italians cloudy and jealous.

Coffee, the new "Turkish drink," is just coming into fashion: "2 spoonfulls in a pint of boiling water boiled by a soft fire half an hour," Sir Ralph prefers taking it cold. Seals and stones for rings are much in request at home, and "one Col. Atkins in Florence, at Mr. Amies the English House, hath more varietyes for stones with seales, then all Italy besides." Dorothy Osborne tells us how the fair Saccharissa wears "twenty strung upon a ribbon, like the nuts boys play withal," "the oldest and oddest are most prized"; "oreng Flowers dried for sweetbags, are also in request."

Sir Ralph spent Christmas of 1651 at Rome and returned thither for four months after a visit to Naples, where he found letters awaiting him "in clusters." He studied Italian, in which he found it difficult to converse, and both he and Mr. Cordell took much interest in Italian politics. Rome was very full; the old Pope Innocent X was occupied with building on a magnificent scale, entertaining Spanish and Austrian princes, beheading a treacherous secretary (Moscambruno) and his accomplices, and ornamenting Pont Sant' Angelo with their bodies.

At Venice Sir Ralph buys for Mrs. Isham the famous drug for her family medicine chest. "I see by your sending of me Venice trekle," she writes, "as you thinke I stell deale in Phisicke, but my traviles hath binne so a boute in Inglande, as I have allmost forgote all Phisicke." "Hee that is most famous for Treacle," Sir Ralph notes, "is called Sig^r Antonio Sgobis, and keepes Shopp at the Strazzo or Ostridge, sopra il ponte de' Baretteri, on the right hand going towards St. Mark's. His price is 19 livres (Venize money) a pound, and hee gives leaden potts with the Ostridge signe uppon them, and Papers both in Italian and Lattin to show its virtue." This celebrated and incredibly nasty compound, traditionally composed by Nero's physician, was made of vipers, white wine, and opium, "spices from both the Indies," liquorice, red roses, tops of germander, juice of rough sloes, seeds of treacle mustard, tops of St. John's wort, and some twenty other herbs, to be mixed with honey "triple the weight of all the dry species" into an electuary. The recipe is given as late as 1739 in Dr. Quincy's *English Dispensatory*, published by Thomas Longman at the Ship in Paternoster Row. Vipers are essential, and to get the full benefit of them "a dozen vipers should be put alive into white wine." The English doctor, anxious for the credit of native vipers, proves that Venice treacle may be made as well in England, "though their country is hotter, and so may the more rarify the viperine juices; . . . yet the Bites of our Vipers at the proper time of year, which is the hottest, are as efficacious and deadly as theirs." But he complains that the name of Venice goes so far, that English people "please themselves much with buying a Tin Pot, at a low Price of a dirty sailor . . . with directions in the Italian tongue, printed in London," and that some base druggists "make this wretched stuff of little else than the sweepings of their shops." Sir Ralph could pride himself that his leaden pots contained the genuine horror. It was used as "an opiate when some stimulus is required at the same time"; an overdose was confessedly dangerous, and even its advocates allowed that Venice treacle did not suit every one, because forsooth "honey disagrees with some particular constitutions." Sir Ralph is also much taken with some "old men's house boots," called Scarfaroni, made of felt, bound with leather, "si tengono in piedi per stare caldo a scrivere"; these cost 8 livres a pair. He keeps the addresses of glovers and glass shops that he may order goods after his return to England.

From Venice Sir Ralph turned his face homewards, passing through Frankfort and Cologne, Rotterdam and Amsterdam, and reaching Antwerp in September. There he met Dr. George Morley, a life-long friend of the Verneys, who had suffered much for the King, and was now ministering to the "distressed English loyalists" at Antwerp. His personal habits were such as to recommend him to Sir Ralph. He rose at five and went to bed at eleven, "not having a fire nor his Bed warmed in the severest season of the year, nor did he eat more than once in the 24 hours." If he had a weakness it was his dislike of the Scotch; he wrote of the "Originall and Eppidemicall sins of that Nation, I meane lying, flattering and boosing"; yet several loyal Scotsmen were amongst his friends.

Sir Ralph is anxious to revise his will, and cannot do it away from all his papers. Since the last was made in 1643, he has lost both wife and daughter, and its provisions are now obsolete. "I would doe some other things about my estate before I take any more long journeys, for I am old," he writes wearily, "and the times sickly." He had just completed his fortieth year.

There is an outburst of joy amongst his friends at home at the first mention of his return. He has his own doubts about the prudence of it, and is considering whether he should conceal his name or "lie publickly" in lodgings. He has many offers of hospitality. Mr. Wakefield has "a little Island at Edmonton where you may bee as private as you will desire and very well-come." Monsieur Duval is ready to share with him the modest rooms he is preparing for his wife near St. Martin's Church. Trusty Roger is beside himself with delight. "I am now come to Lodgings in the Strand over against Yorke House, where if I may have the happinesse to see my dearest friend it will make my old legges to Caper, and with excess of joy." He cannot, however, recommend the Strand. "It is so moist a Place" that he thinks of removing into the City.

Sir Ralph prefers to be in his old neighbourhood of Covent Garden; he dislikes a boarding-house, but will not object to going to a cookshop for his meals. "Oxford Kate dresses meate well, but I heare Oxford John as well and cheaper." Dr. Denton, as his wife complains, neglects all his own business to run after his nephew's. Sir Ralph writes from Brussels: "By the next I doubt not but to tell you the very day I intend to set forwards towards London. . . . I purpose to bring noe Boy with me, but I must have at lease one that knowes some service, and can doe a Message; . . . if you can meet with none little, take one of 16 or 17 yeares old; if I like him not 'tis but losing his livery and leaving him behinde mee; all servants are good at first, and therefore I doubt not but to bee well served for soe small a time. I purpose to come in a Coach from Dover, with our company. . . . Order matters soe as we may chatt a whole day, before any other know I am in towne." He returns several times to the important matter of the footboy: "One that knows service and can doe a Message hansomly is of more use to me at present than anything, which I doubt noe Raw Country Boy can doe. . . . If Sir Tho. Hewyt, Nattycock, or Aunt Sherard had such a Boy, I would take the liberty to borrow him for a moneth, which is the most I intend to stay in England, at this Bout; and then return him to them againe in his old Livery and take away mine. This is ordinarily done, both here and in France, therefore I presume it will not bee woondered at in England, but that you know best and must tell me." He has some thoughts of bringing over the boy who waits upon him at Brussels, "though hee know noe more English than I doe Hebrew; . . . hee is honest and drinkes only water." He writes again: "I love not to take a servant with a friend, for all servants tattle. . . . If my Lady Lisle's boy bee fit, and shee will part with him without thinking she doth me a favour, I shall take him, though, 'tis hazardous taking any from persons in authority, for when they are corrected, they may tell tales and accuse or betray a Master. . . . Court noe body to come to me, but if you take any, let them learne to order Wiggs."

CHAPTER SIX

Sir Ralph Back Home
1653

ON SIR RALPH's return to England at the end of January 1653, after nearly ten years' absence, all his friends and relations were clamorous to see him, and some months elapsed before he was able to settle down at Claydon after a round of visits. Many changes had taken place in the family: Susan and Edmund had both died; the other brothers and sisters wrote to welcome him home after their manner. Tom was detained by very particular business from waiting upon his brother, being in durance vile in the Fleet. Henry, who in middle life played the rôle of a young man as naturally as Sir Ralph played that of an old one, was prevented by an equally characteristic engagement from kissing his brother's hand; "beeinge att my Lord of Petterborough's [Henry's foible for paying court to great people was well known in the family], My noble Earle tells mee hee has this week a progress of pleasure to take, for 10 or 12 dayes, to visset his freindes; soe that untile that bee over, hee will not dissmiss mee on noe pretence whatsoever, though I pleaded with him on this occation moddestly for my liberty." Sir Ralph could wait without undue impatience.

Sir Ralph's preparations to set up house again at Claydon give us a very complete picture of his household and house-keeping. He had written to Dr. Denton from Brussels: "If I must keepe house which I am willing to doe if you advise it, I will keepe but one woeman kind, who must wash my small Linnen (bed & board linnen shall bee put out) and cleane all

81

both house & Vessell which she may doe for I supp not: if she could cooke also I should not bee sorry, and for men I intend to keepe only a Coachman & 2 footmen; or a Vallet de chambre & one footman; or which I like much better a Page & a Footman, but if persons of my condition keepe not pages in England I will not bee singuler, though they are used both heere and in France, & by reason they ride behind the coach, not in it, are better than any Vallet de chambre. If I keepe any other meniall servant, I thinke twill bee a young Cook, since Besse Heath & her husband have noe children, I shall not scruple at their being married: but imploy them at Claydon if they desire it; but I shall not sue to them, nor can hee bee usefull to me at London (for there wants neither Bakers nor Brewers) but at Claydon, hee may for both & also take care of my stuff, for he knowes it, & how to order it better than his wife, my mother bredd him to it, but I cañot keepe them all ye yeare, because I am like to bee 3 or 4 months in a yeare at Claydon, & that only by fits & spurts." His mother's housekeeper, Mrs. Alcock, who married "an ordinary grazier," had continued to live at Claydon, and farmed the grass-land round the house.

"Tell me what Family Mrs Alcock hath in my house, what Napkins, Table Cloathes, Sheetes & Pillowbeeres; what store of Beds she can make both for Masters & for Servants, with Blankets & coverlets, and how many of them will have curtains; also what silver spoones and salts she can lend me. I presume there are dishes, pyplates, candlesticks, Basons, Wooden Trenchers, Beere & Wine glasses, great & small candles, spitts & such like matters of my owne in the house already. . . . Tell me what scollop dishes there are at Claydon for Frute. . . . and the prices of Beefe, Mouton, Veale, Lambe, Rabbets, Pidgions & Poultry; Butter & green morning-milk cheeze."

Sir Ralph's larder is evidently well stocked; he has also a variety of game in the autumn: his pheasants and partridges are said to be a worthy "present for my Lord Maier, for hee hath noe such ware in his shoppes" in London. The garden is to "bee planted with ordinary usefull herbes, if there is noe Borrage nor Burnet, plant or set it quickly." Luce Shepherd is buying French shrubs and vegetables. "I pray forget not to bring the seeds. . . . some five or six souls [sous] worth of Cardon d'Espaigne ye best and ffairest comes from Tours, also some good Mellon & seeds of Roman Lettuce, Lettuce Frizé, Chou de Millan, Chou frizé, bestow about 30 or 40 sols on all these seeds and such others as you think fit beside what you pay for the seeds of the Philloray. . . . I also desire any sorts of eatable grapes out of the best & choycest gardens; . . . in my old garden there was woont to bee good Eateing grapes of severall sorts."

He continues his directions to Roades: "Tell me if the Locks & Glasse windowes are in order, if not glaze the Parlour & my Studdy by it, the Dining Roome & Best Chamber: tell me if the Water pipes are in order, & let the cisterne be clenged. Repaire the chickin house next the slaughter house quickly as you & I agreed, that I may not bee troubled with Workmen when I come. Tell me if the grate is upp in the Kitchin Chimney, & what Wood, Seacoales, & Charcoales, you have ready for me . . . Tell me if there bee not white sillibub pots in the house. If Mrs Alcock cannot brew Ale, a brewer must, 6 Barrells for my table and the Hall, strong, will not be stale enough in time, I doe it for any of my Tenants that may come to me, tis cheaper then Wine and will please them better . . . make them welcome, & being they have nothing but Bread, Cheeze & Drinke it must be good & in plenty too, or else, they may justly blame both you & mee."

For his own table he sends down "in a Browne Hamper 2 dozen of stone Bottles with White Wine. They are all sealed with Black Wax, & by one Seale, I pray observe if the Seales are whole, & set them into sand in the Wine cellar by themselves, & sometimes cast Water (that's well salted) upon the sand." Six stone bottles "of Vergus, Vinaigre, and Ink," follow later in "a greate hamper," to be put in the cellar but not in sand. "I hope you have few chickins, & other poultry to bee a little fleshed, before I come, or else they will not bee to bee eaten at present." Roades is also to get "some young Turkies, though they are noe bigger than a chicking of 6 pence, or 8 pence price."

Sir Ralph sends down a new cook, but is afraid that "Idle-nesse may spoyle him," so the steward is to exhort him to use his leisure in learning to read and write, and in baking French bread in the great "Brasse Baking Pans." The cook greatly prefers the making of hare pies to literary pursuits; "hee is wilde to get a gunn" to shoot the hares: but Sir Ralph will not have the hares shot, nor his game disturbed in May. He is anxious to know how the cook "carries himselfe," and whether Mrs. Alcock approves of him. "I shall suffer noe man that's either debauch or unruly in my house, nor doe I hier any servant that takes tobacco, for it not only stincks upp my house, but is an ill example to the rest of my Family."

Sir Ralph, alive to the importance of a good water supply, thanks Mr. Abell of East Claydon for his courtesy in letting him bring down water from a spring which has supplied Clay-don House ever since. "Perhaps Mr Sergeant at Brill can take the height of it with a Water Levell, & my owne [spring] too, & I hope they goe high enough to come into the Leaden Cesterne in the Water House, as it now stands, without any forceing of them upp. Tast & smell the Water of that Spring & of my owne too that's neare it, & try if either of them will beare soape; but doe it privately." Coals were selling in London at 27s. a chaldron, having just fallen from 33s. After this they had to be carted down to Claydon. Sir Ralph is assured that he may "buy Wood cheaper than coales at these rates, considering the carriages." The Claydon woods supplied many villages with fuel. In the autumn of 1650, when there had been no sale at Claydon for two years, the poor were up in arms: all the hedges were pulled down, and they would "not be kept out"; "The country wants wood, for all their old stock is gone." So Sir Ralph authorises a great clearing in Muxwell wood, "where there is at least three yeares sale." The firewood yields from 4l. to 10l. an acre, according to the season—generally 7l. to 8l.

A tenant farmer had pleaded for more time to pay his rent, but when he was heavily in arrears he disappeared one summer morning with his stock. "Collins cannot carry away 68 sheepe & 12 cowes soe as not to be found," wrote Sir Ralph to his steward; "for if he went away on Satterday he durst not drive them on Sunday; ask Mr. Busby if I may not send hue & cry after him & the cattle, for since he played the knave soe grossly, when hee was soe well used, make him an example; . . . never trust any tenant soe much hereafter; but let them all know, if they cleare not all arrears before the next halfe yeares day that shall follow, you will not trust them with theire cattle, but sell them at the best rates you can, for forbearing of Tenants, you see, tempts them to bee knaves."

Besides the small farmers and the labourers in regular work owning cows, there were a number of destitute people who had been much on Sir Ralph's mind in his long lonely evenings abroad. At Christmas time 1648 he wrote: "I am told that Claydon is poorer than ever, & that the poor want work"; and again, to Roades: "About 2 yeares agon you writ me word, there was non at Claydon that asked almes at any man's Dore, either within the Towne or without. Tell me if there is any that doe it now and who they are; . . . also name how many receive weekly or monthly assistance from the Towne, & what the Towne allowes them." He wrote a careful memorandum on "How to relieve Claydon Poore"; those "which receive noe Almes, are perhapps," he says, "fitter objects of charity than the Beggars." He desires Roades to confer with their richer neighbours about the apportionment of labour, "so that all men that can work, want work, and are without work, shall be given work according to theire abilities." He helps the young people to start in life by paying apprentice fees or by finding them places; he is willing to pay for the board of a poor little village child whom no one will own; "but then security must be taken to keepe it like a Christian." He will give immediate help to the most destitute; 6d. a week to "old Newman . . . & to Andrewes & his wife 3d. a weeke a peece, from mee towards their present subsistence," "200 faggots" are to be divided between "John Lea, Widow Croton, Nan Heath, and Judye May"; but he longs to see something done for the aged poor more permanent and more business-like than these uncertain doles. He desires Roades to think over a scheme which might start at "some considerable charge" if the village would keep it going by a common rate of which he would bear

D

his full share. His own plan would now be called a co-operative cow club; the cows are to be bought by subscription, and to remain the property of the club (the club at first being Sir Ralph), the men to pay for the cow-run and to have the produce of the cow, taking more cows as they can afford it. He would introduce a good breed of cows at Claydon, as those belonging to the poor were "old and naught, & dry many months in the yeare." But this scheme proved to be full of difficulties: there were local jealousies, and the cows themselves did not rise to the occasion: "a cow that was worth 5*l.* at May day was not worth 50*s.* at Michaelmas."

Two pious tasks filled Sir Ralph's mind on returning to his old home—to build alms houses for the poor, and to perpetuate the memory of his dead.

The monument, after all the time and thought bestowed on it, proved worthy of Sir Ralph's good taste and of the memories it was destined to enshrine. "My hopes of seeing you at the D^tors were dasht," Sir Roger complains. "Its your pleasure to live still amongst the tombes, and to keep company with ghosts. I pray be no longer intomb'd, least I prove interr'd before you come." "Cousen Smith, Lady Haile and cousen Hobart meet Henry at Claydon, to see the house and tombe." But Sir Ralph is absent and "noe dinner do they gett." Tom "cannot but begg the freedome to take a view of that well beseeming monument or tomb you were pleased to bestow for the memoreye of yours and my deceased freinds, ffor the which you have for ever eternized your name & deserved to be chronocled in the book of fame, soe sayeth Sir, Your most cordiall brother & very humble servant."

In August 1653 Sir Ralph is planning a gathering at Claydon; Sister Gardiner and Mr. Stewkeley are hospitably pressed. "Hee and all his house shall be most welcome heather, though not so finely fed as I was lately at Preshaw." He will send two horses to meet them. "I wish they could cary trebble, that your coach might bee lesse charged; however I hope you will order matters soe as not to leave a Hoofe behinde. The Honest Farmourer will guard the House sufficiently doe not doubt it. In earnest, the more you bring, the sooner you come, & the longer you stay, the greater will bee the obligation to, Deare Sister, your most affectionate Brother & Servant.''

Sir Thomas Elmes replies to Sir Ralph's invitation: ''Your sister & myself do live so unlovingly together, that I have no heart to come to her freindes; neither do I like to have my freindes come to mee, least they should take notice of her unkindnesse to mee.''

Edward Fust, of Hill in Gloucestershire, and his wife Bridget Denton, were also invited. They were a very attached couple, and their youngest daughter, Peg, was one of Sir Ralph's special friends.

It must have been sad for Sir Ralph to receive Mary's luggage, which kept arriving from Blois; there were trunks to be unpacked marked "M.V." in brass nails, containing odds and ends of women's goods: "fringes, cordes of stooles, cushions and such like," and the guitar that Sir Ralph had so loved to hear her play. The boxes had gone through many perilous adventures, owing to "the pyrates and other sea robbers" in the Channel, and "the porters and such starvling fellowes that steal at the Custom houses, where there are as many filchers as searchers." The delays were infinite in getting them from London to Claydon. Sir Ralph's agent in town had arranged with the carrier to take them, but though the goods were brought two hours before the time appointed, the waggon was full, and they had to be warehoused again.

The carrier might well have been alarmed at the bulk and number of the packages: besides the "long elme cases of linnan," the "square Box of Drawers," the "great iron bounde Trunkes," the "yalowe haire sumpter trunkes," the "presse for napkings," the "Cabanet in a case," there were "great Bundels" past telling of bedding, carpets and hangings, "hampers of glasses, potts, and trumpory," and a "Bundel" of the unfortunate picture frames that had already been so knocked about the world. The Vandykes themselves were still waiting, rolled up at Rouen, for a safe means of sending them home. Inside the "glasses and trumpery" Luce Sheppard packed "two pound of bisquet, a dozin of oringes, and summe liquerish." The luggage sent by carrier often came to grief by the way. Dr. Denton was reproached for despatching a box to Claydon without sufficient care. "The D^r," he replies, "is out of tune, maugre jeers & flouts, for he did not only tye the black box with its owne stronge leather, but alsoe coarded it with a packthread, as porters use to coard a trunke."

Sir Ralph is planting his park and orchard. "Cherry stocks will be two shillings by the hundred, gathered out of the woods: but any better and biger ones from the gardens will be from three pens to twelfe pens a pece. The holly setts price are eighten pens the hundred . . . the holly beris are not cald for as yet." John Hanbury, of Preston Court, sends him grafts of good apples for cider. "30 or 40 couple of Does [rabbits] are to be turned out to feed in the orchard, and the grass must be mown if it be too sour and long for them." Cousin Gee is inquiring about lime trees in Flanders, where "they doe abound almost everywhere, especially about Lisle, where they are to bee had of what size you please for a very small matter," and Mr. Wakefield offers to import for him 800 abeles, which he says will be much better than "the Lindeboomes." A few of the old abeles still flourish at Claydon.

A nursery of young trees is started "in the Kodling Knoll in the Garden," whose seeds are to be carefully saved "and writt upon severally." While Sir Ralph is in London these young trees are much on his mind. All the "Ewes" and ashes are to be staked. He will have some alders set in the wet places of the woods for a trial. In July the new trees are to be constantly watered, "especially the firre trees & Lime trees in the Garden, and those in the whitening yard, and lett a Loade of water be carryed to the Wallnutt trees in Barley yard." Michaud, who has no scope for his confectionery talents while Sir Ralph is absent, may help to carry water.

In a country without stone, brickmaking is one of the most important outdoor industries at Claydon. The brickyard is to be trenched and the brickmakers will come as soon as the weather permits; there is a list of the tools, wheelbarrow, and moulds "delivered to the Brickmen." Sir Ralph is getting "Brik pavements" from a neighbouring village; they are 9 inches square, and he inquires whether if he "take soe great a quantity as 12 or 15 hundred together . . . six oxen would not well draw 500 at a loade, for they are not near twice so heavy as brick, and any ordinary cart will bring 5 or six hundred of brick at a loade, now the wayes are good." The brickmaker is paid six shillings a thousand for making and burning bricks, one shilling a quarter for burning lime, and five shillings a hundred for making and burning "pavements." Stone-gatherers should be set to work on some of the fields. Sir Ralph "would expect to get some fields measured and plotted for a penny the acre, if the ditches were perfected."

Tom, the importunate debtor, now appears again.

"To imitate historians in putting prefaces to their books, I conceive I need not, for I am confident you are so very sencible of my want of clothing. Sir my last request to you is for a slight stuff & coat against Whitsontide, which may stand you in 50s., the which I will repay you by 3s. weekly till you be reimburst. In former times my own word, would have passed for such a summ, but now they require securitie of mee, becaus I live in soe cloudy a condition. God put it into your hart once to releive my nakedness & you shall find a most oblidgeing brother of Sir, your humble servant Thomas Verney."

So runs one of the frequent begging letters addressed by Tom to his long-suffering brother. "Faithful Abraham," and "righteous Job," St. James and St. John, are all pressed into the service to teach Sir Ralph the duty of almsgiving; when this well-spring of charity threatens to run dry, other members of the family are put under contribution. "I have sent to my hard-harted Aunt, only for two bottles of her table-beare . . . it is my greatest refreshment, soe it be fresh & brisk"; Uncle Doctor is encouraged to send Tom those expensive luxuries "a few oranges or lemons" if he is indisposed, or at the least "some cooleing barley broth." This is a list of his modest requests when meditating a West Indian journey; "First for a provision for my soul—Doctor Taylour his holy liveing & holy dyeing both in one volume. 2^{ly} the Practise of Piety to refresh my memery. The Turkish Historye, the reading whereof, I take some delight in. Now for my body." A list follows of provisions of all kinds, Westphalian hams, Cheshire cheeses, Zante oil, beef suet, everything to be "of the very best quality." He will not ask for "burnt clarett or brandy," though he requires it, "for I must not, Sir, overcharge you, for you have been highly civill to me"!

Liar and braggart as he was, Tom's personal courage had never been doubted, and if his ill success in Virginia and "the Barbadoes" had shown his lack of aptitude as a colonist, he might still have earned his bread honourably as a soldier; but "having flown over many knavish professions, he settled only in rougue."

His younger brother Henry, with his cynical lack of high aims and worthy occupation, at least behaved like a gentleman in the ordinary affairs of life, prided himself upon the good society he kept, and continued to be Penelope's favourite brother till death. But in that large family of brothers and sisters Tom had not one chum. He alienated the love of his first wife and disgracefully neglected the second. From being idle and extravagant, he had become, at the time we have now reached, actually dishonourable and dishonest, and the doors of the old home were at length shut against him. If he visited Claydon at all, it was by private appointment with the steward, for Roades as long as he lived could only behave kindly to the son of his old master. The informer and forger might not claim the familiar intercourse of a brother, though Ralph still continued to supply his material needs.

Plausible and quick-witted, with an evergreen hopefulness that would have been admirable had it led to better things; born of a Puritan family in an anxious and conscientious age, Tom stands out as a man absolutely without either care or scruple. While the ship of the state is labouring in stormy waters, and men are struggling in agony to bring her into port, Tom follows her course with the keen and hungry eye of a sea-gull, indifferent to her fate, but ready to swoop down upon any scraps thrown overboard.

His share of the family correspondence lays us, however, under a deep debt of gratitude; he depicts social conditions to which the admirable Sir Ralph must ever have been a stranger. We learn something of the shifts and tricks to which a debtor in the seventeenth century was driven, and are forced to admire the cultivated and ingenious letters the wretch can write in most unsavoury surroundings, hunted down by creditors and racked with fever and ague. To give the scapegrace his due, he was not generally addicted to coarse self-indulgence.

The habits of fashionable society after the Restoration made Tom's nephews and cousins old men at fifty; and it speaks much for his sobriety of life that he continued hale and hearty to his ninety-third year, surviving all his generation. Rogue as he is, his very audacity compels us to attend to him, and (as has been said of the cuckoo) "the world has always a fondness for interesting scamps."

In the fateful year 1649 Tom Verney crosses the path of John Lilburne, and the fierce blaze of the Leveller's invective sheds light upon passages in Tom's life but dimly known to us through the Verney letters. Lilburne was at this time in prison, and, according to his own account, Haslerigg and Bradshaw were employing "one Thomas Verney, a quondam Cavalier . . . to plot and contrive the taking away of his life" by getting him to commit himself in writing

Tom wrote to Lilburne in the Tower expressing his sympathy and assuring him that he could bring 3,000 or 4,000 men into the field to back him, and that it would not be difficult to gain over the City of Oxford to his cause.

Such magnificent offers from a stranger excited Lilburne's suspicions. He was asked, if ink and paper were kept from him, and his speech were free, to instruct some friend to treat with Tom by word of mouth on his behalf; or to give him a list of his adherents in Bucks. Tom pretended to have heard from a friend of Lilburne's, who was to meet him at the George Inn, Aylesbury, "one Mister William Parkins," a creation of Tom's fertile brain. Lilburne consented to see Tom at last, taking with him two of his fellow-prisoners as witnesses, who feared lest Tom might try "to stab or poyson him in a cup of wine, or the like." They did not know their man. Tom bragged a good deal of his own services to the King's party "five years ago," and "that his Father was slain at Edgehill, being the King's Standard-Bearer," and protested that he abhorred the very idea of being a "Derby House agent." Lilburne called him "a juggling knave" and "a Judasly villain," and repeated some of the choice stories he had heard about him "from a citizen of London, a Colonel, & a Gentleman Cavalier." "At which," Lilburne says, "the gentleman (with the impudentest face and undaunted countenance that I have seen) denied all". . . . "O pure Rogue!"

Lilburne did his very best to pay Tom out; he desired that the matter should be brought to "the Committee of State," and sent copies of the letters to "Master Hunt of Whitehall," which if they had expressed Tom's genuine sentiments were certainly sufficient to hang him.

There were obscure reports on the other hand that Tom had tried to sell himself to Charles II, and had been obliged very hastily to leave the Hague. The gossip-loving newspaper *Mercurius Eleuticus* has a wild story that, having stolen a horse in France, Tom took refuge in a monastery, "when for some small time, he dissembled himself a zealous Catholique, &, as the sonne to so honourable a gentleman as Sir Edmond Varney, had great respect & favour shown him untill hee found an opportunitie to steale away sundry priests' vestments, pictures, & other things consecrated to a holy use, & of great value, wherewith he fled to Calais, & there sacrilegiously sold them."

He was so cordially disliked that the marriages and births carefully registered in each branch of the family have not been recorded in his case, except for a scornful entry that he had many wives and left no children. It is therefore difficult to disentangle his domestic history. In 1644 we heard of him with an affectionate wife, Joyce (family unknown), a woman of good fortune and position; perhaps her parents, who were Royalists, had left England in the troubles, for Tom airily alludes to a "wife that I have at Mallaga." Sir Ralph was afraid of meeting her abroad: "Tell me how Tom is, and in what Towne in Italy his Wife is, for I neither desire to visit her nor to bee visited by her. I doe not beeleive shee is dead, tell me if he spake of it, before hee went a wooing to another"; but Tom declared that he had had too much trouble with one wife to undertake a second.

He wrote without any embarrassment to Will Roades that he had counterfeited his signature for a sum of "20*l*. or 30*l*." to get rid of a creditor, and there were rumours of a more serious forgery. Tom was released from the Fleet under the Act for the Relief of Poor Prisoners, having to swear that he was not possessed of more than 5*l*.; but he found his way back again in a few months' time.

On Sir Ralph's return he received from Tom a ceremonious letter of welcome: "The nois of your landing affoarded mee more joy and comfort than a wife can receive att the report of her deare husband his arriveall from the Indies, after seven yeares voyage, etc. etc. . . . My greatest stock is now come to one poore groat . . . and how I am able to subsist 5 months with one groat . . . I appeal to you and to all rationeall and judicious persons."

Tom was deeply in debt to the landlady of his lodgings, and when she took to calling on Sir Ralph, he was sensible that she "was an eyesore to him." The woman "had resented his conduct very ill," he writes piteously to Dr. Denton. "Feareing that I should play the knave with her, shee (not withstanding my then weakness) betrayed me into the prison of the fleet, and I was brought thither by 8 of the clock the last night; which I feare will be a meanes to putt mee into a second relapse; for I was forced to walk in the yard all night, haveing neither fire, money, but one poore groat, nor roome to shelter mee in from the coldness and rawness of the night." "The grave of the Living" the Fleet was called, "where they are shut up from the World, the Worms that gnaw upon them, their own Thoughts, the Jaylor and their Creditors." Tom, little fastidious as he was, could not face the horrors of the common wards nor pay those "great rates the Gaoler exacts" for better quarters.

Sir Ralph lost no time in getting him a private room (the lowest price being about 8*s*. a week, besides extra fees), wretched as it was at the best, but his "enlargement" was more difficult to compass. Tom writes again: "My confinement is soe very chargeable, my chamber soe extreame cold, my habitt soe thinn, that I did by letter make my desires knowne. . . . Good brother, here is now some cold snowie weather approaching, which incites mee to putt on warmer cloths. I must confess I am moved for a coat of shagg'd bayes, but you are suspitious my cloak would be then pawned. Hunger will break through strong walls, and I shall be soe plaine with you, as to let you know that rather then I should starve, cloak, coat, and all that I had should goe to relieve nature: But thanks be to God your charities and brotherly affection hath soe amply appeared to mee that I have not knowne what hath belonged to want since teusday last."

"You are that founetaine," he wrote again two days later, "from whence all my joy, delight, and comfort comes, and long may you live to see, what you principally aime att, my amendment. He goeth farr that never turns. Wors livers then my self have seen their errors and have returned home like the prodigall: why may not I? God hath endued mee with a reasoneable understanding; and I question not a reall conversion, since I have soe courteous, soe kind, and so tender a harted brother to help mee up before I am quite downe. . . . I begg the continueance of a weekly supply dureing my restraint. Eighteene pence a day, which amounts in the week to 10s. 6d., is as low as any one that is borne a gentleman can possibly live att, let my wants be supplied by noon, that I may have a dinner as well as others."

Tom was released before dinner time, but then immediately rearrested. "I have been now ever since Sunday at night in prison, and have not come within a payer of sheets or a bed, or have had a fire or any meat to eat, but what I bought with my groat; and if this be not hard measure for one that hath been lately desperately sick, let the world judge . . . and if I perish I perish."

Sir Ralph is exerting himself, and Tom writes again: "Deare Brother,—Your pious (though unmerited) charitye ought to be registered in the chronicle of fame as a memoriall to future ages. Be confident, I shall not be spareing in exerciseing the office of a herauld to proclaime your worth. You may conceive mee a flatterer, but in truth I am not; for I am an enimye to all such sort of persons. . . . One thing more, I beseech you, take notice of: which is, that I must this night and soe for the future, lodge without sheets, if I pay them not two shillings; for I have layen in my foul ones a fortnight, and would, if I could possibly prevayle with the turnekey, who receives money for his sheets, keep them longer, but that civilitye I am denyed, as I am all others where now I am: therefore I must pay 2s. for a cleane payre; which I begg of you to send mee, and yet I cannot but blush for my mentioneing a thing soe inconsidereable, and of soe small a moment."

The fees for beds were exorbitant: even those who provided their own "paid fees for the privilege of lying upon them, without some one or more of their fellow-prisoners being told off to share the bed with them."

"Deare Brother," he writes on his release, "I conceive it, both in point of honour and gratitude, to be huge gentleman-like to returne you a letter of thanks for what civill favours I received from you dureing my restraint, which, in truth, were many. I shall celebrate them particularly in my soul, whereby to be able to acknowledge them in the least presenting serviceable occasion, and live allwayes with this will, never to dye beholding to you, but yet my most truely esteemed Brother your most acknowledged thankfull servant, Tho: Verney."

The old Fleet Prison, with which he was so familiar, perished in the Fire of London. Sir Ralph mentions the new Fleet Prison in 1688, when Lord Monson the regicide was confined there. As Lord Monson owned a deer park, and was in a position to ask high prices for his deer, it is difficult to understand what he was doing among the debtors; but a man who was in prison both under Cromwell and under Charles II must have had a perfect genius for getting into trouble. Sir Ralph found him "somewhat shy, and carelesse of parting with his Deere, though he confessed clearly they cost him money, and yeelded him neither profit, nor pleasure," and finally Lord Monson asked him to do his best for a poor prisoner. But to return to Tom, he begs again in his "huge gentlemanlike" manner, five days after his release, for means to leave the country. "If I may be furnished with tenn shillings I will goe downe to Wapping and there take a lodging in a place where I am not knowne, and soe I can, by accompanieing my self with seamen, have dayly and hourely intelligence what shipps are bound either westward or southward, and learne both their burden and strength, and what convoy, and allso when they will be ready and soe communicate unto your knowledge the truth of all things."

He promised if he reached Malaga to send Sir Ralph "the knowledge of my wife's and my greeting, together with the scitueation of the place, there manner of government, and with what else that I shall esteeme worthy your reading." But he has no special preferences, and next desires "to be transported in a shipp that is bound for the Barbados. . . . Courteous Brother, That Island, and all the Indies over, doth wholly subsist by merchandizeing: and that person that aimes to live in creditt and repute in those parts must be under the notion of a merchant or factor, planter, or overseer of a plantation, and he that lives otherwise, is of little or noe esteeme. . . . I could (soe it might not occasion an offence) prescribe you a safe way how to send mee thither, like a gentleman, like your brother, and allso to equall my former height of liveing there: but you may perhapps find out a way (unknowne to mee) how I may subsist and have a being like a gentleman till you can heare I am safely arrived there or noe."

How Tom was to have "a being like a gentleman" was a problem which all the family had tried in vain to solve; but Sir Ralph sent Robert Lloyd to make arrangements for his departure, and if he would only betake himself "anywhere, anywhere out of the world," Sir Ralph promised him an increase of 10l. a year on his annuity, to be paid when he got there, and to cease if he ever came home again! The bribe had an agreeable sound, but by the end of the month Tom had abandoned his Barbados project, and craves his brother's consent "for spending this summer in a States man of warr. Noe damned bayliff, nor hellish sergeant can or dares disturb my abode there. A place secure enough and tenn pound will handsomely sett me upp, and I can begone out of the cryes of those cittye hell hounds, the next tide of ebb I have my money: ffor the place, where the states ffriggotts doe ride att anker, affords plenty of commodities that are for that my occasion. The desperateness of the service nor the justness of the quarrell, doth not att all discourage mee; for it is more honour to dye in the feild then in a stinking dark dungeon. My father and my brother shall be my patterne, if you say Amen to it, ffor I doe further declare unto you, that I shall not leave their service, unless extreamitye of sickness or desperate wounds, as the loss of any perticuler limb or the like, may call mee from it." After this outburst of heroics Tom condescends to discuss the other plan; soldier or trader—it is all alike to him. He is still willing to go to the West Indies if Sir Ralph will provide him with labourers and "such commodities to be delivered to mee there, as should be vendible in the countrey." Household utensils were apt to run short in the families of the English planters. From a schedule of the goods and chattels sold by Joseph Hawtayne in Barbados in 1643 we learn that he possessed "one jugge, one table-cloth, six napkins, one frying-pan, eleven musketts & twoe Bibles."

Tom had exchanged the confinement of the Fleet for a wretched lodging "in Lambeth Marsh," where he was "allmost choaked up for want of aire," but out of which he scarcely ventured to stir, except on Sundays, when debtors could not be arrested. "Deare Brother, Solitariness is the sly enimye that doth allmost seperate a man from well doinge: but your aptness in complyeing with mee in my desires hath soe infinitely oblidged mee, that Seariously I want language to express my self to the full. A heart, and a most true and faithful one I have, wholly devoted to your service. . . . I must owne you rather for a father then a brother. . . . I request you then to give mee as much holland of 3s. 6d. an ell, as will make mee a shirt or two; for in truth I have but one . . . & that hath been a fortnight on my back allready. I am as well able to endure the lyeing on a bed of thornes, as the life I now lead; ffor what with unwholesome smells . . . and most noysome stinks, which clothworkers use about their cloth, as allso being drowned with melancholy, my life to mee is a burthen."

"I doe know of a garment that would last mee to eternity, and it is to be purchased for less than forty shillings; which is a grave; and *that* I cannot have neither as yet; in time I shall, then I shall have a requiem sung unto my soul, and purchase a releas from this my miserable life to enjoy one more glorious; soe I thought to have made an end of this my sad complaint, but before I soe doe I make it my request to you, if I have either by writeing, or by word of mouth abused you, or spoken evilly of you (which to my knowledge I never yet did) as to bury it in the grave of oblivion, and to weigh those words of mine as proceeding wholly from a person drunk with passion, and overwhelmed with miseries."

Sir Ralph sends him shirts, but refuses to advance money, or to discuss his claims to enter upon a "glorious" life in a more appreciative world than here below. Tom writes again in his lofty style, being "much nettled" by his brother's coolness: "Mr. Lloyd, I am partly satisfied as being clothed by Sir Ra; but the reason that he gives for his not advancing the money I understand not; but am wonderfull desirous to know. . . . To fancye I still take ill courses, though I have for this half yearr in prison and out of prison lived hermitt like . . . my brother must delude children with such fancies. I understand him in that. I am too old to be caught. And when I have made my proposealls Sir Ra: will take an occasion then, to flye off, as he did when I condescended to goe to the barbados"!

Three days later he suddenly determines to resume the life of a soldier. "I am to be listed to morrow in Collonell Ingolsby's regiment, and to trayle a pike in his one company: but am to march with them on Munday or teusday next to Dover, where the hollanders have made many shott, which putt the inhabitants into a fright, and have sent for ayd. Now this regiment haveing been in Dover formerly there in garrison, it is ordered by the Generall and Councell of officers to march forthwith thither againe: therefore, Sir, I make it my request to you that . . . with all convenient speed you will send after mee, a cloth sute and cloak, a grey dutch felt, a pairr of gray wolsted stockins, a paire of shoes, a paire of strong bucks lether gloves, and 3 bands, 3 paire of petitt cuffs, and 3 hand kerchers; and to furnish mee with a slite sword, and black lether belt (all not exceeding 6*l.* 10*s.*) sometime this day. . . . I shall then most willingly list my self as aforesayed to morrow early in the morneing in Saint Georg his fields. One thing I had allmost forgott, which is, perewiggs are not to be had in Dover, therefore I must crave to have that with mee: and if you pleas to speak to Mr. Lloyd to goe to the three Perewiggs and 3 Crownes, in the Strand by Suffolk hous, and have but my name mentioned by the master of the hous, he being a frenchman, and knoweth the bigness of my head and what borders I usueally weare, he will by tuesday morneing next make mee one for ten shillings that shall doe mee service. . . . . I beseech you hinder mee not."

Another letter comes speedily on the heels of the former. "I am to advertise you that I entered my self into the States service on Satturday last. As for the coat you bestowed on mee, the heat of the weather commanded mee to lay it by against winter, but that my doublett injoyned mee to the contrary by reason it covers the patches of my doublett and britches; I cannot possibly march in it without much hazarding my health: And if I stay behind without leave, black will be my dayes."

In September Tom acquaints his brother with his "sudden & unexpected departure from England into Scotland." He requires 7*l.* for "the recruiteing myself with such needfull conveniences as the coldness and barrenness of that beggerly countrey together with my necessities doth require. Your refusall will caus mee to forsake my colours and in soe doeing I may be liable to a councell of warr, and even be punishable . . . thus leaveing the premises and my long and teadious marching a foot into Scotland unto your brotherly care of mee I take leave."

Sir Ralph, taught by long experience to be sceptical, takes advice. Mr. Gape, upon inquiry, "is confident there is no such matter." Tom, all unconscious that his brother was so well

Sir Harry Verney

an unnecessary expense in commeing to you to argue it out with you." The next letter was written on board the Lyon "in Lee Rode." "My over hast hath proved somewhat to my prejudice; for in the handing of my small parcell of goods out of the Lee hoy aboard the Lyon, one of my bundls broke, and I lost 3 new shoes." Would any shoes but Tom's have fallen overboard? "I have sent up my fourth to my ensigne to have that matched, or one forthwith made to it, and to send mee downe one new payre more besides my patterne; the which 3 shoes I begg of you to pay for mee, and if I live to make a returne, I shall see you repayed." As an alternative he asks for money for his "transportation to the Venetian Warrs, whereby I might appeare in some sort equall to my fortune tho' not my birth."

He writes "of the division of our fleet, some for the coast of Ireland, some northward, some for the straites, and the remaining part to plye to and againe upon our Inglish channell, to free the sea of holland free-booters." Tom had not been two months on board this "stately shipp of the states," and does not seem to have lost any particular limb, when he is back in town, and again plaguing his brother for money to send him abroad.

"To what part of the world am I most inclineable to repaire too? Give me leeve (I beseech you) to returne you this modest reply. Seeriously (for the present) I doe not well know. But be it either for Ireland, Scotland, fflaunders, Swethland, or Denmark, I shall give you notice where I am, becaus of haveing my annuitie returned mee, as it shall grow due. Moreover mee thinks you make an objection, and say, How doe I intend to imploy myselfe when I am abroad? Not in idleness I doe assure you: for experience telleth mee that that is the mother of mischief. A souldier I intend to be till better imployment proffer itself." His desire to be gone was quickened by hearing that "a citty sergeant" had been promised 40s. to arrest him, and was looking for his lodgings. "A missunderstanding between the king and his subjects," he writes magnificently to his brother, "hath been the ruine of himself and his three kingdomes: and I feare it will prove mine, unless you take in good part my letters, which hitherto have savoured of nothing but a reall and cordiall affection. I once more implore your aid that I may secure my self from the jawes of the devoureing lions." In April Tom shipped himself "in the Hanniball, it being a merchantman is since cleared with divers others in the fleet, soe in my expence of ten pounds I gained six and thirty shillings, a hopefull voyage."

In June his experiences were further varied, as the Government took notice of his eccentricities: "Upon Munday about noone I was accused of high treason and carried to Whitehall, where I continued till yesterday being then fetched off upon bayle: but am forced to give my dayly attendance till I am examined which I am promised by Liuetenant Collonell Worsley shall be sometime this weeke. . . . You will assuredly heare of mee nere the council chamber or else find mee walkeing in the inner court in Whitehall about 10 of the clocke." Nothing was proved against him, and he was soon discharged as an offender beneath the majesty of the Tower.

He had exhausted the patience of Sir Ralph's intermediary. "This day being Thursday," he writes, "I sent to Mr Robert Lloyd for my weekly allowance, whose brother being in the shopp would neither receive my letter, nor permitt my messenger to speak with him, he being, att that instant in the hous: but foamed forth some scurrilous language injoyneing my messenger to tell mee that I must send no more thither; for nothing that came from mee would be there received. . . . God in his mercy forgive them," says this injured martyr, "and cleans their harts from envy, hatred, and malice." The Lloyds refused to deal with him, even Roades had been "disrespective." "There is no rulinge of Beares," said Dr. Denton. "It is an easy thing for Momus," Tom writes, "to pick quarrels in another man's tale, to make his own the better. I supplicate to non for there good word: it doth not sute with my nature soe to doe. It is best knowne to God how I have desired an amicable compliance with you all, and it hath much greived mee of the ill retaliation I have received from you all, perhapps I may exempt yourself. . . . I have made choice of one, who hath found my dealings soe just, will, if you pleas, take the trouble on him." This admirable man was a Mr. Henry Palmer, whom Tom discovered later to be "an adventurer." He was most obliging in receiving Tom's allowance, but a little slack in transmitting it.

Genteel poverty in the seventeenth century had an additional burden to bear in that it required a wig. "Good Brother," writes Tom in October, "I shall begg but one poore favour more . . . and that is for a border to keep mee warme which will cost mee tenn shillings. This morneing it was my ill happ to walk abroad earlier then ordinary and being a great foggy mist, I received some little prejudice by it in my head, my haire being very thin."

"I shall acquaint you with a motion that was made mee, which I would gladly undertake. . . . It is to ride in the Protector his one troop, not in his life guard, but in his regiment of hors, which is now quartered in the west. . . . I conceive it farr better and somewhat more beneficiall to ride then to march on foot." He begs Sir Ralph to advance 20*l.*, which would put him into this employment, to be repaid by 4*l.* quarterly. "I am as well able to build Paul's as to rais it by credit or else how."

He has had a "tertian ague and a feaver (which through God's blessing and my uncle's care) I am recovered of; but to whose account the phisick will be put unto, I know not. . . . . I had only a vomitt, glister, a cordiall and breathed a vane [blood-letting—Ed.]." He is ambitious of adding a lawyer's bill to the doctor's. "My father-in-law entred into a penall bond of six hundred pounds for the payment of 300*l.* in 6 months after his decease to S*r* John Maynard (a trustee for mee and my wife). . . . My wife hath fooled mee of the bond, which drives mee to a chancery sute to prove it." The penniless debtor has engaged Sir Ralph's old friend John Fountaine as "my counsel." He writes importantly how he has to take out "two severall commissions for Hampshire and Southamptonshire for the gayneing the testimony of my sister Gardiner and my brother and sister Elmes," who were witnesses to the bond, "which when that is done and attested by some gentlemen in the countrey, I shall gayne an order for the executors to pay

mee what they and I shall agree upon." Sir Ralph promptly
declines to be responsible for the chancery suit, and Tom is
loud in his indignation. "Brother . . . you have not merited
a brother's esteeme. Sir, povertye may be blamed, but never
shamed," &c. He contrasts Sir Ralph's hardness with the
generosity of his ensign, "though he be noe brother nor any
wayes allied more then by a few yeares acquaintance; yet
pale-faced envye, mixt with hatred and mallice hath done
there best indeavour to sett us att variance; seariously they
have encountered with this my unmoveable freind, singly,
and allso alltogether, and yet they could not alter him in
his esteeme of mee. I could cordially wish I could say the like
of you. . . . I shall attempt to see you," though he is good
enough to add it is "not my desire to receive curtesye in a
compulsive way."

When Ralph himself is in trouble Tom improves the
occasion. "Sir, divisions in families are as much in effect as
in a state or republique. They are the fore runners of mis-
chiefs. God direct his judgements from us. Perhapps you may
imagine I rejoyce att your misfortune, and att your restraint.
Intruth I doe not." Tom is in his foul-smelling lodgings in
Lambeth Marsh, and again very sick; "Dr. could neither come
nor send, the river being well stored with ice." He has a furious
quarrel with Mr. Gape "in my sister Mary's chamber"; "shee
was not wanteing in her indeavours to palliate and pacify
us, which when she saw could not be done she wept." "My
wings are clipt, my troubles are many, yet (glory be to God) I
indifferently wage through them." Tom has accidentally met
with Mr. Hall, "who was once deputy marshal of the Marshalsea now Gaolor of the White Lion prison." The financial
matters connected with Sir Edmund's management of the
Marshalsea had been long under discussion between his
successor, Sir Edward Sydenham, and Sir Ralph; the Deputy
Marshal was still unsatisfied, and asked to submit his claims
to arbitration, in which case Tom would "gladly be an instrument of good." Sir Ralph next hears of him as having been
mixed up in a robbery. Tom indignantly asserts that his
brother's credulity "doth not only feed the fancies of deprave-

ing sycophants, but prompts mee to call your judgement and brotherly love into question. . . . Wee both had one father and mother, why should therefore our affections be soe alienated one from the other? An estate, perhapps, you may say: or that I have merited this strangeness from you by takeing base and unwarrantable courses, and in this my soe doeing the name and family is dishonoured by it. Admitt, Sir, this should be your reply. I hope you will not doe like the Mayor of Rye, when a malefactor was called before him, he sayd, lett us first hang him, then trye his caus. . . . You have beleeved severall things, as hath much intrencht upon my honour, fame and good name; as hath been as false as God is true . . . but I have a beleif that I shall as soone wash the blackamore white, as to alter your unmoved hatred towards mee."

Tom entered into mining speculations that autumn; in our day he would have written admirable prospectuses and have floated bubble companies; he was, however, disturbed in his "Mineral imployments to answer the malice of Sir Tho: Thinn at our assizes." "Sir, when Sir Thomas Thinn understood the sence of the Bench, and that I was acquitted, paying my fees, he cunningly arrested mee in the face of the court, charging mee with an action of 500*l*. . . . It will not be long till he hath lex talionis, and soe we shall make it a cross action. Some tell mee he hath putt my name in print and that it is in Mercurius Polliticus. Two pence will tell mee the truth of that, therefore I shall say noe further . . . in relation to malitious Thinn."

He is detained in Lambeth Marsh (and no wonder) by fever and ague; the kind Royalist physician Dr. Hinton is attending him for love of his father: every other day the ague "gives mee a visitt butt att uncertaine houres, which gives mee some hopes of its leaving mee. This day (being my well day) invites mee to putt penn to paper to impart unto your knowledge that my partners in the mines (hearing of my sickness) doe deal very unhandsomely by mee, by indeavouring . . . to work mee quite out. . . ."

He begs Sir Ralph to go surety for him. "A mine to you is of noe value becaus you understand it not, but I doe, and doe esteeme my interest in this my undertakeing to be worth to mee, before six months be fully expired, 600*l*. by the yeare. If I doe (beyond all your expectations) rais myself a fortune of 4,000*l*. or 5,000*l*., when I dye I cannot carry it with mee, somebody will injoy it, you or yours may have it; strainger things then this hath come to pass. The designe I am upon promises a greater fortune then I speake of." Sir Ralph drafts a reply for his servant to write to him; it is much to the point. "M^r. Verney, my Master desires you to excuse him for passing his word for money, hee is resolved against it and soe hee hath long declared, therefore you need not trouble your selfe any more in this kinde; this being all I have in command, I rest, your servant, Robt Kibble."

Soon after this Tom turns up at "Bottle Claydon," but after a talk with Roades is not encouraged to go on to the House. "Were the world in generall as unkind unto mee as a brother, I might well then complaine (like Job) miserable comforters are you all." Sir Ralph had authorised the steward to pay him 5*l*., and Tom extracted an extra 2*l*. from Roades' good nature. "If I dye before quarter day my hors which I left in one of your closes is worth his adventure."

"My mines," continue to be most flourishing on paper, and in the future, but for the moment ready money is urgently required. Tom is at "Sladburne in Yorkshire in the forrest of Bowland." "My minerall discoveries" have come to perfection, "which will augment my small fortune between foure and five hundred pounds the year," but a paltry sum is needed at once to "continue my repute with my workmen. . . . I hope you will not envye the prosperity of my fortunes but rather smile at my fortunate success. I am confident there be some that doth indeavour to make strife betweene you and I: but as for my part I doe here declare myself to be an enimy of all pik-thanks and insinueating people, and I take it as noe small mercy in these giddy and unstable times, that God hath raised mee a brother that hath afforded mee such a comfortable subsistence."

The poor wife who has long dropped out of the correspondence reappears in July 1657: she has returned from

Malaga in great want, and Tom desires Roades to send her 2*l.* They are evidently not together. Tom has been in Leicestershire "to the mine in Sir Seamoor Shirley's ground," but found all the ore disposed of: "Where money is wanteing unreasonable accompts cannot be well questioned." "I doe still follow my minerall discoveries at Sladbourne . . . but leave the success to God." Colonel Charles White, of "Bearall neare Nott^m," writes to Sir Ralph for 10*l.* he had advanced to Tom; his friend "Mr. James Hallam will attend him with the acquittance." Sir Ralph is obliged to reply that Tom had long ago desired him to pay that money to another creditor.

During the interregnum following Richard Cromwell's fall Tom runs into "a labirinth of troubles." "Where to abide in these times of danger I know not," he writes from East Claydon, "ffor in my travell through Lancashire to Darbyshire, I was taken by the Militia troop, & carried to Darby for a spye, & had not I been known in the towne, I should have fared much wors then I did; yet I was detained three dayes before I could be discharged; it was some more then ordinary charge to mee, I dare not lodge in any towne or village more then a night, least the like danger may befall mee. My present thoughts are for Sweden, there to abide till these dismall clouds are a little blowne over. Sir, I did promise (upon your granting my last request) not to trouble you till after michaelmass was past, in truth I . . . little thought of these grand mutations. God in his superabounding mercy, divert his wrath from falling on us."

He writes again to Kibble from East Claydon: "I ought to have taken shipping att Hastings in Sussex, but by reason Sir George Booth was att that time taken, they were soe strickt that I could not find out a meanes to goe; neither doe I well know where to take up my abideing place. Times are soe dangerous . . . Charity waxeth cold everywhere. . . . Yours to his power," etc. Kibble sends 40*s.* from his master, and Tom for once seems grateful. "By your meanes and brotherly affection I am inabled to travel somewhat further. God restore your charity an hundredfold . . . sweet brother yours most affectionately to serve you."

The next spring: "Mr. Palmer (my dayly tormentor) is in
hott persuit after mee with his bayliff barking currs, that I am
forced to be vigilant least I should be by him insnared . . . my
intentions are both for cheapness & privacy to journey into
North Wales into a place called Anglesey some 250 miles . . .
could you but spare mee one of your cast suits & my younger
brother a low prized horse." And so the forlorn wretch dis-
appears from view till the "grand mutations" are over, and it
is profitable once more to proclaim one's self a Cavalier.

After the Restoration he has thoughts of accompanying
the Earl of Windsor to Jamaica, but lacks a sufficient outfit;
and in 1662 we hear something of his domestic history in a
letter of Dr. Denton's to Sir Ralph. "I hope Tom will not be
such a clowne as offer to come to you without his new spouse.
I can assure you he & she were very fine & at a play on tuesday
last; . . . he had with her 4 or 500*l.* in money; 50*l.* a yeare
besides some expectations after the death of frendes. There's
your man Sir." Tom was not driven to so desperate a step without
cause. He complains: "I doe not love to trumpett out the great
paines & care I have (for 4 yeares last past) taken to rais a
lively hood, and if it hath not pleased God to prosper my
indeavours, my ingenuity is not to be blamed. It is a Scripture
saying, that Paul doth plant and Apollo water, but it is God
that doth give the increase. . . . Sir the ant reads mee a lecture
of providence & industrye which I have indeavoured to
imitate; the bee allso of witt and sagacity; for this little foul
when shee goeth abroad a forrageing, and is (perhaps) surprised with windy weather before shee returns back againe,
takes up some gravell in her fangs to ballance her little body,
then shee hoyseth sayle and steeres her cours homewards more
steadily." With such pious and scientific motives Tom seems to
have taken up a wife in his fangs as ballast, and now with a
more or less happy shot at the long Welsh name he announces
that he is "upon purchasing a leas of the King for all his
majestie's waste lands, lyeing in the parish of Llan vh=angell
croythin, in the county of Cardigan in South Wales: but I cannot
gett Sir Charles Herbord to make a report of the King his
reference on my petition till he hath received a certificate from

Mr. John Vaughan who is his majestie's steward in these parts; which hath occasioned my takeing a journey into Wales to make Mr. Vaughan my friend." He proposes to visit Sister Mary by the way.

Tom refers to his second wife as "a mayden gentlewoman, who is the eldest daughter of the Kendals of Smithsby in Darbyshire, of an ancient family, though of noe very great estate, yet her portion would be worth 1200*l.* if it were well secured." He is plunging into a lawsuit to obtain it, for which Sir Ralph is to provide the money. "I would not have my wife to be sencible of my wants becaus I have hitherto possest her with the contrary."

Lest Tom's correspondence should leave in our minds any doubt of his merits we have a testimonial which he gave himself on "St. Thomas Day, 1661: Sir,—Want is the greatest provoker to mischeif, experience telleth mee the same, I could wish the occasion were taken away, and you would soone heare of an alteration in mee, *ffor I am not natureally inclined to evill.*"

CHAPTER SEVEN

Sir Ralph Crosses Cromwell's Path
1654–1655

Among the Claydon thousands of letters there are probably more from Dr. Denton than from anybody else; all are short and to the point; all are grammatical and properly spelt. Curiously enough, though all look neat, signed Wm D, they are in fact difficult to construe, until one gets to know his handwriting. There is little to quote.

Yet Dr. Denton was the man who did more to keep the family together than anyone else. It was not what he wrote, but what he did.

He was the youngest son of the vast family of Sir Thomas Denton of Hillesden. The Dentons lived about 3 miles as the crow flies from Claydon House through Steeple Claydon. His mother was Susan Temple of Stowe and he was born on 14 April 1605. His eldest sister Margaret, much senior to him, married Sir Edmund Verney of Claydon, Standard Bearer to Charles I. So he could hardly help knowing every Verney, every Denton and every Temple, and in turn seems to have helped them all as required. It is not easy to realise what the huge families involved, but here is one figure worth consideration. Lady Denton's mother, Lady Temple, lived to see 370 of her descendants. So there was scarcely a family in Bucks who were not cousins and the Doctor had thus a good deal of social influence to start with, soon increased by his personal charm and, more important, by his up-to-date professional ability.

Socially he was known as "The Speaker of the Parliament of Women" for his polite conversation among women. There is a

very attractive picture of him at Claydon House, probably by
William Dobson, 1610–1646, possibly by Van Dyck.

It was during Sir Ralph's exile in France because he would
not sign the "Covenant" that Dr. Denton's invaluable help was
most conspicuous. He was the great link and adviser between
husband at Blois and wife at London and Claydon. To Sir
Ralph he would send constant letters often trying to minimise
squabbles and misunderstandings and sending as required
books and papers with the shortest of letters; to Mary Lady
Verney (Mischief) such sympathetic and shrewd advice as to
when and where to proceed with re-uniting Ralph to his
family and sequestered estate and all at the smallest possible
cost; as Mary wrote to her husband in 1647; "he is only a
little chargable unlike the lawers who are very dear and not
much use." At the same time the Doctor has absolutely forbidden her "to drink any wine at all noe not so much as to
discolour the water."

On Mary's death from overwork in May 1650 Sir Ralph
realises what he owes to the Doctor: "and yet I thanke my
God that I was not quite forsaken for hee was pleased to raise
upp you to be my true and faithful friend" and then "Ah Dr Dr
her company made every place a paradice unto me, but she
being gonn what good can be expected by your most afflicted
and unfortunate servant." Yes, what indeed.

But the friendship endured to the end, never was a friendship more perfect than that between William Denton and Ralph
Verney; the latter writes: "I confess meum et tuum divides
most men but by the grace of God it shall never divide us."
It never did.

In 1691 the end came; the Doctor's last letter is signed
"Yours body and bones Wm D." He would have laughed
over the shocking comment that at his funeral Sir Richard
Temple failed to appear in all the "blacks" he was in duty
bound to wear.

The epitaph in Hillesden Church is just right: "He was
Blessed with that happy composition of Body and mind that
preserved him cheerful easy and agreeable to the last and
endeared him to all that knew him."

Sir Ralph felt but little sympathy with the members whom Cromwell ejected from the House of Commons in April 1653; he had neither forgiven nor forgotten his own expulsion—indeed the Long Parliament, which he and his father had entered with such high hopes in 1640, had dwindled to a remnant "there were none to praise, and very few to love."

England was divided into eleven districts under as many major-generals, who exercised police jurisdiction and levied a 10-per-cent. tax on the fortunes of all who had served the King, to pay the expenses of keeping order. Bucks was under the command of the "Lord Deputy" Charles Fleetwood. Sir Ralph writes: "I confess I love Old England very well, but as things are carried heere the gentry cannot joy much to bee in it." Colonel Henry Verney's letters are a curious contrast to his brother's: "the gentry" that he lived amongst cared little for politics, but endeavoured by hunting, racing, and gambling to relieve the dullness of the Puritan rule; Cromwell's son and son-in-law seem to have been amongst them. Henry is visiting "my Lady Cuttings at Tustinge," and at "Sir Richard Shugboroughs, a good friend's house." He writes to his brother from "Thrusten": "I cannot send you any newse, more then what company came here, the last night unexpected, to hunt the fox for a weeke. My Lord Cro'well [Richard Cromwell?], my Lord Claypole, my Lord Sands, my Lord Deleware, Sir William Kingsmill, Sir Hue Middleton, and divers other gentlemen. It is soe darke that I cannot see to write a word more, then to tell you, wee keepe ill hours, and leade a lude life, which is noe way pleasing to me." "Tell Harry," writes Dr. Denton, "he had better keepe his money and lay it out on some of my Lord Duke [of Richmond]'s horses, then loose it to fooles and bunglers."

"I have bine att Stowe neere this weeke, and have waighted on Sr Richard daley to the forrest, and had good sport, but ill fortune with my dogg Hector, for the first course a did run their, a was spoyld in a battle with a bucke, never dogg gott more credit, the combate held neare halfe an hower, afore 20 of us, and all we could doe, could neither save dog nor kill the deare, though wee had severall times hold of him, it was

forty to one I had not let out Sr Richards gutts, loosinge his
hold att his hornes, my lord Claypoll seeinge the mettle &
greate couradge the dog had after recevinge five stuck deepe
wounds, would not bee deney'd the dog to breede one, soe,
much against my will, I was forst to present him, by his
lordship's surgons greate care the dog may live to run againe,
his greateness is more fond of him than ever I was, which does
not a little please me." Three weeks later he writes again:
"Our huntinge att the forrest is now done, and his lordshipp
gone, and my dogg Hector like to doe well again, Sr William
Farmer att the killinge of his three staggs entertainde the whole
company for tow dayes noblely, I dare say it cost him att the
lest £100. . . . My cousin Smith treated his honour att a dinner
hansomely; feastinge of late I have had plentifully but never
hartely merey for want of your company." Aunt Isham,
though she dearly loves a little gambling, is quite worn out;
Henry made them so late every night at Hillesden; "he will
never give one over as Longe as one is able to sit up." Sir
Ralph had presented her with "a paire of sable Brasletts, for
you may weare them at Play, which you cannot doe your
muffe, and these may possibly save you from many colds
this winter."

There was a report that Sir Ralph had been arrested, and
Dr. Denton writes: "This is to lett you know that you are in
the tower, gett out as well as you can, Verney for Vernham
hath caused the rumor & mistake." "Here is newes more than
is true in abundance. That that is most generally received is
that Sr Joseph Wagstaffe cum multis aliis is up in the West,
seized Judge Rolls & others & all theire horses & money at
Salisbury. That Sr Richard Mauleverer is upp in the north &
endeavoured the seizinge of York Castle etc. There is much
talking of risinge in divers other countries, wch I had rather
beleeve then goe to see. . . . I ghesse there will be a generall
settlement of the militia in all counties, & a generall securinge,
& though I dare be a compurgator for Claydon & Hillesdon &
Ratley that you have neyther head nor purse in the rebellions
designe, yett the names are malignant & that will goe far in
prudence."

During these public anxieties the trees that Sir Ralph had ordered from Holland kept arriving, much bruised in the packing but Dr. Denton hopes "the Abele Trees will make him an amends." Their arrival at Claydon is delayed, and Sir Ralph writes: "The advertisement came in pudding-time, for to morrow the cart was to set forwards but upon this I have stayed it till Monday."

Many of Sir Ralph's friends were supporting the Government: Fiennes had been made Lord Keeper, Sir Roger wished for a place as Groom of the Stole, Nat. Hobart was hoping for a Mastership in Chancery, and Sir Richard Temple for a place in the "Protector's Court." He also talked of going to Jamaica, but this came to nothing, as Dr. Denton had foreseen. "Sir Rich: Temple's purport of goinge for gold is 1,000 times better than holdinge of a trenchar, but I doubt he loves sleepinge in a whole skin to well to goe that journey."

Penelope Denton was in bitter trouble. A law-suite was pending between her husband and his mother. Sir Ralph took infinite trouble about it, for Pen's sake only, as he thought "The Squire" "a beast". In March John Denton is in prison in Oxford Castle for debt, and Pen is "almost brought to deths dore: . . . this 3 days I have not eate more then a mess of milk & an egg; my one seller beare is to strong for me to drink. I must sell myself to my sking, goods & all to defray this great chargis." . . . "The sheriff & gaolers' fees cost 8 or 10l. & their 2 cows have to be sold." "Brother no creatur that beggs from dore to dore can live in A mener condishtion than I do. Had my Good father or mother A lived I am confident it would A greved there harts to a sene or hard of my greate strats."

A man-servant of John Denton's was "a great vilin," Pen writes, "& had sayd that of me to his master that he could not mak good. The good lady at Ditchley & Sir Harry & his Lady was with me when I was ill, & I did one [own] soe much trouble to my Lady, which was no more then my looks did betray me in; that both herself & Sir Harry did tak upon them to tell my husband that if he did not kick the fellow out of dors, no gentilman but would scorne to keep him company, thos words of those parsons did work so much upon my husband that with my paying him his hold years wages, I thank God he is gon from us both."

The plots and the arrests continued; Mrs. Isham writes: "Moste of our Gentre is secured and took to Oxford. Sʳ Jhon: Bire Lase [Borlase], Lord Loues [?], Lord Folkle: [? Falkland] att Ox. all: ; Lorde Linesay thay have bine with, but the Lorde Camdine comeing a suter to his Dafter he is Lett alone a while, and whate to thinke of my Hus: I knowe not, Nothing they can have against him I knowe and wheather I had best sende him out of the way I know not, for none knowes whate these be had away for, itt may be all your cases. . . . My cays be all loste & I have no more paper."

In the midst of his quiet and useful life at Claydon, Sir Ralph was suddenly arrested, on 13 June 1655, by the Lord Protector's soldiers, as a suspected Royalist. His next letter to Edmund tells the story: "Yours of $\frac{18}{8}$ June I received this very evening at London being just now brought Prisoner to Towne with divers Lords and other persons of quallity, for wee know not what; our owne innocence is a Protection that cannot be taken from us; had you been heere, you had certainly beene in Prison too, for they tooke both father and sonn in many places, and though I must confesse the Soldiers that tooke me at Claydon on Wednesday last, used me very civilly, yet they tooke all the Pistolls, & Swords in the house, & carried me to Northampton that very night, and the next morning (though 'twas a fast) made us goe to Brickill, & this night they brought us heather. What shall be donn with us, and that multitude of Gentry that is secured in every counry, wee canot yet imagen, but I am glad with all my hart you were not heere, for you are yet unacquainted with the great charge, trouble, and inconveniences of a Prison, and I hope the times will grow so quiet that you may enjoy your freedome better then wee have donn. I pray husband your money as well as possibly you can, for these are not only very troublesome, but chargable times, and though I am willing to suffer first, yet if this contineu, you must thinke to suffer too."

Sir Ralph wrote to Mun again from "St. James His house. Childe, The letter I writ you on Friday last will fully informe you of my being brought Prisoner to London. That night late many were committed to the Gatehouse, & the next morning at lease eleven more of us were committed to Lambeth House, & that very afternoone my selfe with divers others were committed to this place, where every man hath a guard uppon him day & night, but wee are not kept upp close nor are our friends kept from us, I thanke god I am in good aire & good health & my innocency keepes me cheerfull."

Sir Ralph's friends were working for his release. There is a copy of a letter from Colonel Thomas Hammond to a person in authority unnamed: "Our ould acquintance makes me write to you about a cosen of my wife's, Sr Ralfe Verny, intreating you to stand his friend; he has by a mistake (I am confident) been delivered to you as a delinquent. He was sitting in the Parlement-house when his father was killed at Edgehill, & sent in volentaryly two horses into the Parlements army, tis true in the yeare 1643 he went beyond sea, it was for his wife's health, who about 3 or 4 yeares after dyed there, & he returned not long after for England. Now you know as much as I, I am confident you will be as tender in oppressing one well affected, as just against a malignant, I am far from pleading for a malignant, we in Surrey if men testify ther good affections (though malignants before) by our Commission are directed to spare them, I leave all this with you knowing you will proceed in righteousness."

Doll Leeke and Lady Hobart had all sorts of fine plans for Sir Ralph's release. Lady Warwick's name had been mentioned amongst others who might be approached, as she had more influence than ever in high places. Sir Ralph's reply must have fallen like a cold shower-bath upon these kind busybodies. "I earnestly beseech you," he wrote to Lady Hobart, "not to write to the Person you wott of, concerning mee, me, or my release. I came in with the crowd, and shall willingly attend to goe out with it. Heere are many that gett off dayly (& I am glad to see the dore open) but to say truth some goe on soe hard, & others on soe unhansome Termes, that I had much rather remaine where I am, then bee at Claydon, on those conditions, although my owne occasions did now as

much as ever require me there. Divers of our Lords (with your
Coz: Sir Fred:) have writ to the Protector & most of the Knights
& gentleman have petitioned him last Weeke, but as yet they
can get noe answere. Sir Justinian Isham & my selfe sit still &
are willing to see how they are like to succeed, before we
appeare too pressing upon our new Masters; but we have a
petition ready, which we hope may bee received at any time;
being we crave nothing in it, but what they ought to grant to
every Englishman in our condition, as well as unto him or me."

He writes to Mrs. Sherard that he is allowed to remove to
rooms belonging to her sister Susan Abercromby. "When I was
at St. James his Tennis Court, though I had a very good
chamber, yet I had noe place for a servant in the house; they
were forced, after I was in my bedd, to goe lodg neare Charing
Crosse, which was soe inconvenient that I desired to change
my Quarters; and my Aunts house being within the Jurisdiction
of the Garrison; she with her mayd resolved to pack away for
a considerable time." Mrs. Sherard is surprised that he should
be allowed "noe greater Liberty, for I her of many as aier
quite free, and com into the Countrey which was formerly
Deepely ingaged for the lat King."

Of good society there was no lack at St. James'; during the
early part of the time "new prisoners of quality" were "dayly
brought in." But Sir Ralph had not much heart to join in it;
he took his meals alone, and although Sir Roger supposed
"that your whole company keepe together and are as merry
as birds in a Cage," Doll Leeke heard from Sir Frederick
Cornwallis, who had just been let out of the cage, that Sir
Ralph was not at all sociable. "He was asked how you did, &
he ansred you never came amongst them, therfor he could give
no account of you."

Lady Gawdy ventures to remonstrate again with Sir Ralph
for refusing the conditions of release offered him. "I am apre-
hensive you will not let selfe interest have any power to sway
the lest part of that that lookes like honour. Pray only lay aside
singularity, for to bee vertuous alone will bee interperted
A vise."

Sir Ralph was not likely to be convinced by such feminine

E

reasoning; but with many apologies his anxious friends return to the charge: Doll Leeke hopes he will not "be perticular in the refusall, for Liberty is so presious (& the parsons you receve it from so indifirant whether you have it or noe) that you ought rather to court it, then to be nise in accepting, pardon me if I have said too much."

Cousin Stafford's men after hay-harvest have searched the hedgerows for elms for Sir Ralph. "I pray remember my Sweet Bryer," he writes; "if those that gather the setts use to come to Winslow market, it will cost nothing to bring them to Claydon, for I will appoint my man Roades to take care of it there, hee seldome misses a markett day, I thinke you told mee they were about halfe a crown or 3 shillings a thousand, which is cheape enough, & if they be to be had at soe easy a Rate, I would have 2000 gathered as soone as you please. . . . Charme them least they send ordinary Bryers, for sweet Bryers; & lett me know if I may have woodbines at the same rate." The very sound of woodbine and sweetbriar must have made Sir Ralph long to see the last remains of summer in his garden. Sir Roger, in despair, hopes at least that he may spend Christmas with them "if non bee before hand with me, as I trust they are not, especially St. James."

Wearied out at last, though not convinced, Sir Ralph felt that he would make himself too conspicuous by being the only prisoner who refused to be liberated on terms which even Sir Justinian had now accepted. He therefore entered into a bond to the Lord Protector for 2,000*l.*, together with Dr. William Denton and Mr. Thomas Leeke; Lieut.-Col. Worsley to deliver up the bond at the end of a year if it were not forfeited in the meantime. "Colonel Worsley then discharged Sir Ralph the next day out of prison." This is his own account of it: "On Thursday with the rest of the crowd, I sealed a Bond soe full of Barbarous conditions that I am ashamed to insert them here. All the Favour that could bee obtained was to get it limited for a yeare, but tis so untowardly penned that I doubt they will continue it longer on us. The Truth is if any one person of those I use to converse with all, had thought fit to refuse it, I should have done so too, but to bee singular in such a thing, at such a time, would have been interpreted meerly to be stubbornesse."

Cary Gardiner wrote on the anniversary of the battle of Edgehill, "The fatall day to Inglond & our family," to congratulate him "on his inlardgment."

There is a memorandum in his own handwriting: "The 26 Octob: 1655 I writ Mun word, I was come to Claydon uppon Bond."

Sir Ralph's satisfaction in his release from imprisonment was soon clouded by fresh anxieties. The year 1655 had seen Cromwell's protest and Milton's sonnet on behalf of the persecuted Piedmontese; all Europe recognised the power of the Lord Protector to defend English and Protestant interests abroad; the commercial and industrial classes at home were prosperous and, on the whole, contented; but in these triumphant days of the great Puritan's rule the little world pictured in the Verney letters was plunged in sadness. It was a world of "poor unknown Royalist squires," as Carlyle terms them, and of other squires by no means Royalist, who vainly tried to remain "unknown" to the Major-Generals, "Cromwell's Mastiffs," who had fastened on their estates. The dismal words, composition, compurgation, decimation, sequestration appear constantly in the letters, and the squires shuddered to be reminded that they had been classed as Malignants, Delinquents, Compounders, or at the best as "Disaffected Only."

Sir Ralph wishes to spend the spring in safe obscurity at Claydon, and Sir Roger writes hoping that he may remain "a fixed starr" in his own region. "I perceive you are shortly in expectation of a visitt from a person of quality: I shall longe to heare that it is well over."

"You doe not heare that I am sent for to Alsbery," Sir Ralph writes to Roades, "for if you did, you would certainly send a messenger to me with the summons, or a copy of it. But I trust in God they will let me Rest in quiet." There is a rumour of a warrant out against him, but perchance " 'tis but a Fable." Sir Ralph's fears, however, are soon confirmed. He receives a list of forty persons summoned to appear before the "person of quality" to whom Sir Roger referred, in which his own name appears; and a second list of the Bucks Commissioners sitting with Lord Fleetwood the Major-General, or in his absence with "Major Packer," as Chairman of the Court.

It is sufficient to read the two lists, in which the gentlemen of a county are pitted against each other, one set as judges and the other as delinquents, to understand the irritation caused by the formation of such tribunals. Dr. Denton, writing to Sir Ralph in December 1655 of an action he has brought before Quarter Sessions, advises him "to end it to-night before to-morrow if possible, & before any Major Generalls appear in your Quarters . . . for I believe many of your Justices will be coadjutors & informers. Verbum sapienti suf."

Sir Ralph applied to the clerk of the former Sequestration Committee, and received a certificate "that it doth not appeare (neither is there) any charge of Delinquency, Sequestration or otherwise against the said Sir Ralph Verney." He also obtained from the Haberdashers' Hall a note of the proceedings formerly instituted against him, and the subsequent entry "at the Committee for the County of Bucks sitting at Aylsbury the 29th of May 1647. . . . That the estate of Sir Ralph Verney was the 5th of January then last discharged of Sequestracion by order of the Committee of Lords & Commons." He had also "a note for the horses given by him, as a voluntary contribution to the Parliamentary Army, during the Civil War." Thus fortified, Sir Ralph appealed to Cromwell. The Doctor was of opinion that the petition would avail little. "Favour goes further than arguments." Cousin Smith helped Sir Ralph in drafting his petition, but he did not succeed in saving his own fortune from decimation.

It would have comforted the poor Bucks squires who rode away from "the George in Aylesbury" on that black Friday with such unpleasant documents buttoned under their riding-coats, could they have foreseen how soon the power of the Major-Generals was to be swept away.

Dr. Denton writes: "Deare Raph, I doe not thinke to make use of any Privy Councellor or any eminent person (who doe not love to be too much troubled) for my owne selfe, but will reserve them to spend their shott for somebody else. I have little crotchetts in my nodle & I will first try what they will doe. You will want Sir R[ichard] T[emple] to bringe you to the little officers, & to acquaint you with some little waies."

Sir Roger wonders "how any can possibly wind themselves into an estate that hath so much innocency to protect it, but my hopes are that your feares are more than your danger . . . trouble not your self, for an appeale to my Lord Protector, so noble & upright a person, I question not but will free you from such high inconveniences." Some of the agencies Dr. Denton alluded to were set in motion, but the "eminent person," Thomas Sandford, a cousin of Charles, "Lord Fleetwood," who was induced to write to one of the Bucks Commissioners was a good deal more anxious not to compromise himself, than to help on Sir Ralph's petition.

Sir Ralph "in greate perplexitie" went down to Aylesbury; the Protector had referred his petition back to the Bucks Committee, and he had prepared the "perticuler" of his property in case he should not get a reprieve. He returns his estate at Middle Claydon as worth about 711*l.* 12*s.* 6*d.* yearly, but states "that a greate part of it being in his owne hands, & other parts being never let neither by himselfe nor his Father but alwaies managed by a Bayliffe, he cannot set downe the yearly rent exactly." There are only "4 Dairy Cowes"; but there are "13 draught Bullocks; a coach and 2 coach horses, 3 Saddle Horses, 6 young steres, 1 yearling calfe; Wood, Hay, Peate & some Timber brought to be used about his house, worth about 150*l.*; his household goods his servants estimate about 300*l.*, but his debts amount to ten times more than this money." He mentions some "small Rents at Mursley, besides a cottage or two that never paid any Rent."

He writes to Dr. Denton from Aylesbury an account of his long and harassing day before the commissioners, when he argued his own case. "Deare D^r, I followed your directions & pressed all that could bee for a rehearing, soe they bid me withdraw, but being called in againe, they told me plainly though there were new matter, it lay not in their power to relieve mee, for they had only authority to charge all that were sequestered, not to acquitt them; they were not judges whether

I was justly sequestered or not, that belonged only to the protector & his councell, & therefore they desired my perticular. Then I acquainted them with the reference from the protector, & pressed hard for a suspension, soe they bid me withdraw againe, they told mee they would certify but they would not suspend, but they would give me till their next meeting (which would be about 3 weekes hence) to pay in my money, & if in the interim I could be discharged, they would be well pleased. Then I pressed very hard againe for a suspension, & lett them see how much harder it was to get a decimation [taken off] then to keep my selfe from being decimated. But when I saw there was no remedy, I desired that my name might not be entered into any of their bookes, nor any of their proceedings against me, for twas not the money I stood upon, but the mark of delinquency. Soe they bid me withdraw againe, & being called in they told [me] they would comply with mee in that, & cause the clerk only to take short noates of all that concerned mee, but not to enter it in any booke, till my Lord Protector's pleasure were knowne upon my petition. I urged that 'twas unlikely I should gett an answer before the time of payment of my money, & if it were entred into the Treasurer's booke, it would bee an evidence against mee, soe they told mee it should not be entred into any booke, though it were paid. Upon this I give them a perticuler which was read, & being appointed to withdraw the 4th time, they called me in againe & asked mee how & when those rent-charges & reversions were settled. I replied by my oncle Sir Francis, by my father many yeares since, & some by my selfe, soe they told mee if I did not gett the discharge, I must pay the Tenth, for what was mentioned to be in possession, which I gave in at 722*l*. 0*s*. 9*d*. per annum, & they told mee they would passe by that which was in reversion, & my personal estate also which I valued in all at 450*l*."

Sir Ralph's affairs are going badly. After some six or seven weeks' delay, "the Protector & Councell" deliver him over once more to the tender mercies of the Major-General and the County Commissioners. He writes to Lady Gawdy: "I am this day going downe uppon the business of my Decimation, but with soe little hopes of good successe, that were not Alisbery soe very neare to Claydon, I should scarce goe thether about it, unless it were to give an oppertunity to the Major Generall & Commissioners to make their injustice shine more clearly, which you may guesse to bee a needlesse errand being most men are already fully satisfied in that point. The coachman storms & vowes hee cannot staye a minute longer," and so Sir Ralph's complimentary ending is perforce cut short.

Some alternative having been given him which he was unable to accept, the decimation was finally confirmed; and he was forbidden to come to town for six months. "It is as well a marke of your virtue as of your misfortune," writes Lady Gawdy, "and such as are so accompanyed with honour may bee received with les regrett."

Public interest now centred in the coming Parliament, which would either confirm or destroy the authority of the Major-Generals. Dr. Denton writes from Overton, Cheshire, where he is visiting the Alports: "Here is a new Major Generall come downe, his name is Bridges, & I heere, labours to have a great influence upon elections, & that he hath laid a good foundation to his minde in Staffordshire as he passed. Its thought he will misse of his ayme however. There is like to be strong & stout canvassinge. The sheriff & justices at the last sessions pitched on 4, to which they will unanimously adhere. Sir Wm. Brereton he stands on his owne leggs & labours might & maine, & the Major he intends to prefer others. Bradshaw writt not to be nominated nor chosen. Steel was in nomination, but hearinge he is designed for Ireland he is laid by. . . . The High Sheriffe hath beene here these 2 daies, & we goe to his house on tuesday sennight, the knight will be chosen on Wenesday next & then you shall heare more. I heare Roles & Barcklay 'the last of the old judges' are both dead. Here hath beene a strange rumor of the securinge of Vane, Bradwshaw, Ludlow & others, but noe certainty, a little newes doth well here. All to all Vale, Yours Wm. D." He has seen a mountain ash for the first time. "Here is a fine wild ash (which the South yeelds not) which beareth red berries (now ripe & last longe on the trees) as pleasant to looke uppon as cherries trees, only the fruit little bigger than hawes, the usuall ornament of flower potts & windowes of these parts. I am promised setts of som; if I can gett them I will send som to old Raph the Provider General."

In September Sir Roger writes from London of the new House of Commons that "some were for the taking in peices the whole body of the law."

Penelope writes from Oxfordshire: "There is such breaking up of houses and binding the people in there beads that a maid Sarvant as usally did ly in my hous will not stay in it when I have Fawler, and I ever had a man that lay in the hous bysids, but that will not satisfy them the time to com."

Sir Ralph had also been visited. "My house was lately searched by a captaine and 12 Troopers who obeyed theire orders but I must needs say with civility enough." Lady Gawdy has not "bine yett so much considered as to have such potent viseters, & she hopes they may never return to his prejudice."

Sir Ralph took his decimation sadly to heart, and he was troubled by an eruption on his leg and thigh which would not heal. He was deluged with advice by his lady friends. Doll wished him to drink asses' milk while he sat in a bath of it up to the neck, for two hours twice a day; a less tedious remedy is a lotion "so violant a drop would fech of the skin wher it touched"; and a dreadful old woman is recommended who has an infallible "oyntment for yumurs." He wants to go to town to petition the House, but his friends think that "it is not safe for the foxe to come to the Court."

The Doctor has his joke about the Decimation Bill which the friends of the Government pushed on while their opponents were spending Christmas with their families. "Decimacon had but a poore Xtmas dinner no sweet plum broath nor plum pye, for they chose that day to bring it in when armiger was in patinis, & soe it gott the liberty to be entertained [by] the house, though Glyn yet spake stoutly agst it but was outvoted by 20^{ty} voices, if the house fill, much good may be hoped for, if not, actum est."

Doll Leeke writes: "I fancied you might have come this crismus but you have so totally forgot it that you do not compliment us so much as to wish your self with us. I wold be a littell severe

but that I wold have you beleve that I have altred that part
of my nature, and have resolved to be all my life kind, for now
I am so ould ther is no dainger in profising it." Moll Gape
thanks him for a chine; "variety maketh pleasure & therefore
your cold one is so well accepted."

Sir Roger continues to report the progress of the long debate.
"Tomorrow a fast is appointed to be kept, wher the prayers
but not advise of 5 Ministers are desired, for they are not to
preach but pray. The men are to be—Owen: Manton: Caroll:
Nye and Gelaspie a Scotchman: thus much for newes, for the
great feast & banquet with which the Parl^t was most sump-
tuously entertained at Whitehall on fryday last, I know the
whole kingdome almost rings of it." "The bill for Kingship
goes on," Dr. Denton writes, "notwithstanding Lambert is
highly against it, not without some passion, others say peevish-
ness; Wolseley & Fiennes for it."

Sir Roger continues his report: "As for the Major Gen^{ls} if
they were wounded it was thorow the sides of Decimation, the
bowells wherof were peirced by a Negative vote of the par^{lt}:
viz: that the bill which was brought in to confirme that peice
of Tyranny should not be so much as comitted, and positively
rejected. The Major Gen. were not so much as named, but
sublata causâ you know what followed. I suppose that the 6
mounths banishment is now expired . . . and that ther shall be
another house to give check to this I presume you are not
ignorant, the Maj. Gen: are as like Lambs upon this account
as they were Lyons upon the other, for they expect some
amends by this, expecting to be in the number of those that
shall be elected Lords by the Ld Prot. for that house. Diverse of
the Courtiers are pleased to absent themselves from the parl^t
upon this occasion, for they are ashamed some of them to
appeare for that cause against which they have been formerly
so violent."

Sir Ralph had no lack of congratulations, and we can almost
hear Moll Gape's loud voice as she leant over the apothecary's
shoulder and dictated her hearty message: "Molly rejoyceth
that the six months are expiring, and doubly rejoyceth
because shee shall then see Sr Ralph, all of him, his whole

tenne parts reunited, not a collop left behinde to feede y^r Dawes, yett shee doth not wish that what they have already may choake them & therein disagrees from S^r, Y^r true servant, Wm Gape."

The day of Cromwell's military tribunals were over.

CHAPTER EIGHT

John Verney,
the Industrious Apprentice
1653–1662

THE career of Sir Ralph's second son, John Verney, as portrayed in the old letters, gives us as complete a picture of the progress of the industrious apprentice of the seventeenth century.

Before his return from Blois, Sir Ralph had been pondering over the question of Jack's schooling. He was not in love with the new doctrines, and what we should now call a Church School was liable at any moment to have its light extinguished. By a stringent ordinance passed in 1654, ministers and schoolmasters "who are or shall be Ignorant, Scandalous, Insufficient, or Negligent," were to be ejected or restrained from teaching. It was hard indeed to find a schoolmaster with Royalist and Episcopal leanings who could not be brought under one or other of these categories. Under conditions so precarious, the Rev. Dr. James Fleetwood kept a school at Barn Elms in Surrey. His cousin, Charles Fleetwood, and his brother George were amongst Cromwell's strongest supporters, but he held firmly to the old opinions. It does not appear why Sir Ralph preferred a private to a public school; his brothers had been at Winchester, the Stewkeleys had a boy there, and the Doctor thought it "a very fitt place for Jack."

Two schools were recommended, at Hammersmith and at Kensington; "either of those places are very convenient, if the

Masters are good and carefull." The master at Hammersmith has "leave to teach," but Mr. Turberville of Kensington is finally chosen.

Jack's diligence in his studies, however, did not always come up to Sir Ralph's strict standard. "Truly Sr," Jack writes, "I doe mitily wonder how you should find me soe negligent towards my learning. I verily beleeve it was last Saturday when I came to London; but if you can afford a little time to riede on further you shall see . . . For that day I was at Winser and bake againe, a horse Backe with my Master's consent, and not onely me, but also 4 other young Gentlemen and our Usher, for my Master would not trust us alone, and I had done some of my Busenesse on friday night, Because I would not goe and lose all Saturday morning; now Saturday in the after noone wee doe alwaise playe, and therefore I doe straingely wonder how that negligence should bee soe found for to lye in my Bosome. Indeed I should bee very glad for to see you heere and also my most Dear Brother for to accompaine you along This pleasant Roade."

Music was a part of every gentleman's education, the Elizabethan opinion still happily prevailing, that it is the "natural sweeter of our sour life, in any man's judgement that is not too sour," and Jack had a real love and aptitude for it. His mother's singing and guitar-playing must have been associated with all his childish recollections of her, and he wrote to his father from school asking him "to bestow the gittarre which was my Mother's on mee: you did give it mee when you went out of France, and then when I came over, you sayed I should not have it because it would bee broken att schoole; that was a good reason, for wee lay 18 in a Chamber, but att this Schoole wee have but two to a Chamber, and wee keepe our Chamber doores loket and therfore noe body comes in but them which wee have a minde to lettin, nay and besides if they should come into the Chamber I have a Closet where I could putt it, but I am shoore there would bee noe nides; if there laketh a key unto it, I will have owne made. Heere is owne thing more is to bee putt in, that is if my brother would have it then I doe not petition it of you, but hee hath a very good owne of his owne [there were at least five guitars at Claydon], and I am shure hee would not bee my hindrance of it. That Gittarre which is in the wooden casse is of noe sound att all almost, and then it is very ugly; it is very corse and rude, and I am sure that you will not use the other which I demand if you please. . . . The Wioll hath putt mee in love with all sorts off musikes. My Master doth see mee proceede soe much of the Wioll that he hath promised mee to teach mee for to pleay of the Lute when the Deyes groe longer; hee hath also lent mee owne of his Wiolls this Christmasse for to practise on." Sir Ralph notes on the outside of this appeal, "I told him he should have it, or as good a one, but bid him let it rest till I come upp."

Jack himself was not satisfied with his schooling; he was fifteen when he wrote of his wish to be bound "apprintice unto some very good traydesman; and I doe know Lords sones which must be apprintices, and theire elder brother is worth 5 thousand pounds a yeare; as for example my Lord Cosselton [Castleton]."

Sir Ralph destined Jack for the bar, and was not desirous that he should have a purely commercial training; he had much else to occupy his mind, and at eighteen Jack is still complaining that he is taught little that is of any practical use.

It was not difficult to be taught classics, but arithmetic was a branch of wisdom to be dug for more than for hid treasures; Jack would willingly give all that he had to acquire it, "although it would bee but (as it were) a cromme or bitte in a loafe." Sir Ralph asks Mr. Wakefield of Edmonton to give him an opinion "With regard to an apprenticeship." He replies, "I doe nott know as these uncertayne tymes are, whom to advise you too, though I have very dilligently enquired of divers. The Spanish Trade att present you know is loste, wch was almost a 4th p^rt of our employment. To the east country and Hamburg trade you know I was brought up myselfe, wch is accompted the surest trade; Butt neither my Broth^r nor my selfe, could find any great good to bee done by itt; only some Auntient Rich-men, who followes itt as close as the Pack-Horses goes weekely; for the Barbados, New England, and all the Ilands, though many getts money by that trade, yet I should never advise any ffreind of myne to breed up his sonne too itt. And for the Turkey East and West Indian Trade, without itt bee some perticular men that have the knacke of itt, nott one in 3 of them thrives, soe that those wch doe itt makes them soe high that they aske and have 500*l.*, and sometymes more with an apprentice, wch makes mee conceave myselfe lesse able, and itt to bee of more hassard and difficulty than ever anything you putt mee upon before. Itt being high tyme, if you intend yor sonne for a merchant speedily to looke out for a Place for him; Hee being now very well growne, and 18 yeares of Age. For wch reason I have knowen some men to refuse the taking of an Apprentice."

By the end of 1659, Jack was rewarded by obtaining the long-desired position of merchant's apprentice. Mr. Wakefield, the pessimist, had failed to find an opening, but Sir Roger Burgoyne, who had a brother in the City, agreed, after careful inquiry, with Mr. Gabriel Roberts, a London merchant "trading to the Levant seas," to receive Jack, with a premium of 400*l.*, "the same sum my brother had from Sir James Harrington." Sir Ralph further bound himself to Mr. Roberts for 1,000*l.* A copy of the bond still exists, and the printed indenture, signed by Sir Roger, John Buckworth, and Gabriel Roberts. The terms of it are very quaint, stringent and minute. The agreement is for seven years. Jack is received at once for a fortnight on trial. "For his clothes," Sir Roger writes, "Mr. Roberts is to finde him after those are worn out that he carries along with him, whether on this side the sea or the other." Sir Ralph then came up to London, the seal was set to the bond, and Jack was really an apprentice at last. The choice of his master proved a very fortunate one. Gabriel Roberts came of a Welsh family, natives of Beaumaris, then so thriving a town that a proverb ran that men went to Carnarvon for lawyers, to Conway for gentlemen, and to Beaumaris for merchants.

His father, Lewis Roberts, a distinguished member of the Levant Company, had published in 1638, *The Merchantes Mappe of Commerce*—to give the result of "my own 12 years collections during my abode and employment in many parts of the world." Finding this knowledge too vast to be contained within the boards of a folio, "I was constrained," says the zealous Welshman, "with the wind-scanted Sea man, to cast about again and limit myself to a narrow scantling." The author's friend Izaak Walton, his cousin "Robert Roberts, of Llanvair in Anglesey," and others, prefaced the book with some complimentary verses.

In allowing Jack to be bound to a citizen of London, Sir Ralph rose superior to many prejudices of his age and his class. The tendency of the Civil War had been to bring the profession of arms once more to the front, as the only one befitting a gentleman. On the other hand such few apprentices as were "Persons of good Quality" gave offence to the City by affecting "to go in costly apparel, and wear weapons, and to frequent schools of dancing, fencing, and music." Proclamations of the Lord Mayor and Orders of Common Council were constantly directed against such irregularities. An apprentice was expressly forbidden to wear lace, embroidery in crewell or metal, any "cost of needlework, or any silke in or about any part of his apparel"; there was special legislation even for his nightcap. Jack was therefore bound to wear nothing except what his master provided; but if Mr. Gabriel Roberts shared his countrymen's love of music as well as of poetry, we may hope that he relaxed in favour of Jack's cherished guitar the rule which forbade an apprentice to own a musical instrument.

A few weeks later he is in the full tide of bustle and importance; his presence in the warehouse is so necessary that he can scarcely speak to Aunt Pen though she went up "unporpos" to see him. "As concerning the liking of my Trade I assure you that I never delighted in any play when I was at Schoole as I doe in this trade, and alsoe in hearing of Business both inland and outland." "Mr. Roberts doth not att all decline from his former kindnesse, but hath taught mee to keepe Marchants Bookes, which indeed is not ordonary. The Gentlewomen likewise continue in their former kindness unto me, And I still continue att Table with them, soe If you will be pleased (if you thinke fitt) this lent to send mee any sort of your pyes to Give unto them, I shall, whether or no, continue your most humbele and

most obedient son and sarvant." Claydon pies are duly sent;
the last "was a very good one," John writes, "but none can
tell what it is, some are of opinion of one thing some of another,
but most that it is Wild Bore." The fair, well-mannered youth
was no doubt a pleasant addition to the "Gentlewomen's"
society; and they showed their kindness in a practical way a
few weeks later by promptly sending for a "chirurgion" when
he had a "small mischance about 10 of the Clock att night; a
sckillett of hott Lye slipt in the fire, and scalded the hind part
of my right legg." Jack had frequent visitors, and if Mrs. Gabriel
Roberts and her daughters craned their necks out of the window
to see the young apprentice's fashionable relations, they
probably derived some feminine satisfaction in contrasting the
shabbiness of Aunt Penelope's attire with their own rich silk
gowns and riding-hoods; for the worthy merchant was pros-
pering greatly.

In the autumn of 1661 Jack went home, and Sir Ralph writes
on his return to Mr. Roberts, "I humbly thanke you for my
sonn's being heere thus long; truly hee had been with you at
your time appointed but that some of my friendes pressed mee
much to let him stay to goe upp with them, which I hope hath
not been to your prejudice. I confesse it was against my will
and his too in respect his time was out, but you know woemen
are importunate, and will not easily bee denied; therefore I
presume you will the more willingly excuse both him and mee."

Sir Ralph already made use of his apprentice son in a business capacity, and Jack provides with extreme care and minute-
ness for the transmission to Claydon of two cases of young vines.
With the near prospect of leaving England for many years, Jack,
that he might know something of his prospects, wrote to Sir
Ralph to ask "what estate you intend me first and last." Des-
pite the respectful tone of his letter, and that his son is of age,
Sir Ralph is annoyed at any such inquiries. "You must know
that children doe not use to chatechize theire Fathers what
Estate they intend to leave them, nor indeed can I tell you if I
would, for tis like to bee more or lesse as you carrie yourselfe
towards me and towards your Master . . . if you keepe lewd
company, and by drinking, gaminge, or your owne idlenesse

The unique inlaid main staircase in Claydon House

For our dear
Harry
with Aunt Florence's
love

And may each day
of this New Year 1893
be better & happier
than yesterday—

And may the young day
& the old woman make
of this a letter, & a
happier year than any
that has gone before.
So help us God!

New Year's Day
1893

In writing as her Florence N: this is made to her nephew, the present Sir Harry Verney loose your reputation, bee confident you will thereby also loose my affection, and your Portion too. Therefore as you tender my satisfaction and your owne advantage, carry your-selfe soberly."

Sir Ralph might write severely of a breach of filial etiquette, as he understood it, but his affection for the son about to be parted from him for twelve years was very tender and deep. He engaged Soest, the rival of Lely, to paint his portrait, and being dissatisfied with the first result induced him to "mend" it before Jack left England. In March 1662 "the King hath granted a Convoy to the Levant shipp upon those conditions, to depart with a Smirna shipp and all other shipps that can be ready, then to set saile." "Most Hon: Father," Jack writes, "this is to let you know that the Capt. of the shipp holds his resolution to be in the Downes by the 15th instant; so that now if you please to give order to your Cooke for a Pye, if it comes by the next weekes carrier it will not be to soone; alsoe if you please send me 2 or 3 winter cheeses wch I hope to carry to Aleppo, they being there in greate esteeme. The next week I shall send my things aboard. I suppose by ye 10th present ye shipp may depart from Gravesend towards ye Downes whether I intend to ride post to meet her. I have 3 Bottles belonging to a cellar of myne wch I thinke to send to Mr. Gapes, there to be fil'd with strong waters. I suppose they all hold somewhat above 3 pintes. Mr. G. Roberts a day or two since gave me 2 sheetes of paper of advise and some other particulars, which at your comming to towne, if it please you, you may see. . . . He intitles it on the backe side, viz. Commission given to John Verney now bound for Aleppo in Siria, upon the Dover Marchant, whom God preserve, Gabriel Roberts."

The journey to Aleppo was accomplished in 3½ months. Jack wrote home every few weeks as occasion offered. Having fallen in with a homeward-bound frigate off Cape St. Mary, he has time for a hurried note to his father. "On May the 6th we mett with the Queene [Catherine of Braganza] and the fleet her convoy, off of Faymouth."

The next is from Leghorn. "This is to advise you of my arrivall into this Port from whence I hope to be gonn in 8 or

10 dayse. I should have given you an account of my arrivall sooner but that I departed for Pisa, Florence, etc., to see those sights wch are at St. Jn's tide selebrated in the last city, where I have continued this 9 dayes. S^r it being very late at night and myselfe somewhat tyred having come post this day from fflorence (wch is 60 miles) notwithstanding the heat of ye weather and ye Badd horses I shall conclude, assuring you to write you somewhat more larger by some Gentlemen wch lately came from Aleppo and are proceeding for England over land in 40 Dayes." He comes across Dr. Kirton at Florence, who begs to send his old friend Sir Ralph his "most humble servis." Jack reaches Scanderoon on 26 July 1662, "having toucht noe where but at Cyprus." The 20th of August finds him arrived at Aleppo, whence he writes to his brother a string of requests; "the shipps being upon departure," he ends abruptly. His fair hair that Soest had painted so carefully "being already almost all come off," he asks for a wig, and he "must goe in the Turkish mode before it comes."

At home a certain form of fever and ague, known during the time of the Civil War as "the New Disease," swept over several counties in 1657–8, carrying off many familiar faces at Claydon and Hillesden, and uniting in a common death men who in life had long been foes and rivals.

The epidemic broke out in the Claydons at the close of a hot summer and soon spread to the House. William Gape describes how people are flocking up to town from the country districts to avoid infection. Sir Ralph, on the contrary, who is away on a visit, hurries back to Claydon to do his best for the sick in the villages as soon as he hears of the outbreak. Mrs. Westerholt is ill, and one after another of Sir Ralph's servants and workmen are disabled. "The Bay Mare is unable to fetch the bricks," she has been lent "to Roger Deely, to fetch a surgeon to his sonn, whose Heele is gangreaned."

The same epidemic is mentioned by Lady Fanshawe in her *Memoirs*, as "a very ill kind of fever of which many died and it ran generally through all families"; she and her husband and household fell sick of it: she ate "neither flesh, nor fish, nor bread, but sage posset drink, & pancake or eggs, or now and then a turnip or carrot." Lady Hobart had a more comfortable prescription. "If you have a new dises in your toun pray have a car of yourself & goo to non of them; but drinck good ale for tis the gretis cordall that is: I live by the strenth of your malt."

William Gape, the excellent apothecary, was also ailing in that sad autumn of 1657. "My voyse is lower then ever," he writes, "my throate more soare, and which is worst of all I have suffered a great difficulty of breathing this fitt. These are all alarmes to tell mee whither I must goe and that my winter quarters are preparing for mee. God almighty sanctifie all these signes to mee that I may make a right use of his mercyes et fiat voluntas Domini."

Edmund Verney was ailing also with "a loathinge of meat and queaziness of stomach," and Dr. Denton wrote quite anxiously: "We see younge men drop as well as old, and we cannot be too carefull one of another, our number decreasing soe dayly."

Cousin Stafford sends a queer story to Sir Ralph in November. "I heare Sir Arthur Haselrigg is fallen into a desperate nott, by defending a possession against the sherife and some troops of horse, which he did beate from a house and lande, which hee had recovered by law, and by a second verdict lost the same againe, and hee pursuing his opportunity upon the sheriff's recess for more aide, possessed himselfe of Newcastle upon Tyne, where in a hostile manner hee defends himselfe. This is Sir C. Packe's newes, which hee related something doubtfully ergo quer:" This letter was accompanied by "a bundle of Sweet Briar plants and fine Figg setts," for which Sir Ralph was to give him in return "a dozen young wallnutt trees, as many Chesnuts & Almons, fowre young firs and a pyne." Sir Ralph persevered with his improvements. Mulberry trees and red roses are being planted at Claydon; and "300 Asparagus Plants" arrive from a nursery gardener with some "Double violettes blue & white, 100 of goodlie July flowres, sweet Marjoram & Lemon Time, & some Althea Arborea essence." There are orders for "new stone seats, 6 feet 9 inches long and 17 inches broad, and stone stairs in the garden," and

14 feet of coping-stones for a balcony; and the house is beginning to look so comfortable again, and so well furnished, that Edmund writes in the summer of 1657: 'Of household stuff— I beleeve few gentlemen have so good or such great store." Lady Hobart sends down from London some gilt leather and a piece of "Pintado" for 5s. 6d. which she thinks cheap, with "fringe for the Pentado bed" and some Dutch tiles. Dr. Denton who is to receive some money for Sir Ralph, writes: "The gooses feathers will quickly be pulled, therefore be sure you have a Pegasus ready bridled, sadled & plated, & your Jockey ready stript; to carry the enclosed the next day & receave L'argent, but not to bury in Brick & mortar."

Sir Ralph's next project was to have a deer-park, and the negotiations begun with Lord Monson in the Fleet Prison for the purchase of deer stretched over several years. Doll Smith writes of some deer offered to her husband: "From my Lord Gray's park . . . but non but dows, & fawnes, and prickets [two-year-old bucks—Ed.] & prickets sisters . . . twenty shillins a peece for all thees, one with another, & that he must be tyed to take twenty brace of them for else they will not bestow the making of a cops to take them . . . if they be not honest they may send more fawnes than any other deare." Cousin Smith, who is to divide them with Sir Ralph, says, "Male Deere are my principle aymes." Thomas Stafford writes about some " of the wild beastes" he is getting Sir Ralph from Mr. Dodesworth, "of Harrold Park, 4 or 5 miles beyond Owlney."

After an infinite amount of negotiation Lord Monson is ready to accept an offer for his herd of deer at Grafton Park, Northamptonshire; Sir Ralph intends to buy them all, and then to divide them with Cousin Dick Winwood. The latter writes: "Because you desire to know what price I can be contented to give, I doe as in all cases of purchase, grounde myselfe uppon the markett, which is twentie shillings for every Deere above a Fawne . . . the purchaser being att all the charges of taking and bringing away, & thirtie shillings a piece to have them delivered to me att Quainton. I shall expect the full indevor of the Keepers to holpe me in the taking of them, and to paie my money when I receive them." But even this trans-

action could not be carried through without political compli-
cations. Sir Ralph heard "that Homan of Paulers Perry might
doe good service in taking the deere"; but "because he had
sworn as a witness against my Lord, he knew not whether my
Lord would like him." Lord Monson's agent gave permission
to "bring in whom we pleased." Upon this Sir Ralph felt
himself authorised to employ this person of heretical opinions
to catch the deer, but he did not escape "my Lord's great
wroath" for this "indiscretion."

The deer themselves prove to be as delicate and as easily
hurt as my Lord's feelings, and give occasion for many remon-
strances and explanations on both sides. Two drown themselves
in the park at Claydon, others sicken in the winter. "It is an
extraordinary trouble to me," writes Holmes, the new steward,
"because my master delighted in them so much, I know not
what to doe in the busnes but feed them, as well as may be."

William Smith, who had narrowly escaped in 1657, was
arrested now. He writes to Sir Ralph from his own house: "Sir,
on Wednesday here came souldiers with a warrant to search
for and seize horses and arms and to apprehend me, I desired
to see the warrant, which was under Sir George Fleetwood's
hand. I was in Phisick but they would not lett me stay untill
the next day, there were many in the warrant besides my selfe,
but not you, but since I came home I hear that my Brother
Alex. Denton should say they were att your house. Sir George
Fleetwood came the next day to Allisbury, and told me he had
a commission and instructions to imprison all that were of the
late King's party. I am confined to Mr. Kilby's house, and
Mr. Stafford is my bedfellow. Sir John Burlaiy, Mr. Tyrring-
ham, and many others are confined to other places, and some
are put in the Gaole. We have liberty of the gardens and
orchards of the house, and may goe into the towne or fields
with a souldier, which I doe not trouble. Sir George gave me
leave to come home this day with a keeper with mee, but I am
just now returning againe to my old Quarters: where I desire
not to see you, and from whence when I shall be delivered or
upon what termes I know not. God's will must bee donne,
under which I am patient. If the souldiers have not been as

yett att your house it is my opinion that you goe to London and stay there till this business is over." "It is said that the High Court of Justice will suddenly sitt to try those who are thought to be guilty, and till then I believe the goates and sheepe must keepe Company together." Sir Ralph upon receipt of this news sent to inquire after Sir Justinian Isham, who when Royalists were to be "clapped up" was ever the first to suffer. "Sir, I write now only to know both how and where you are, and how you have beene, and are like to bee, for in these wretched times a man must bee alowed to bee a little inquisitive after his Freinde. For my part, I am yet at home, and soe I hope to bee unlesse some new and stricter orders ishew out. That very day the gentry were taken heere, I went to bury Sir Roger Burgoyne's Lady in Bedfordshire, little dreaminge of such a businesse. . . . I presume the heate is already over, for in these parts wee have had none taken of late, which makes me almost confident that this time shall bee escaped by Sir, yours etc., R. V."

Sir Justinian replies: "Sir, With divers other Gentlemen of these 4 Counties (under M^r [Major-General] Butler) I am at present under guard at Northampton, nothing hath bin yet declared to us, nor Major Butler yet seene amongst us; some particular men have laboured their freedom & hope to obtain it from above, but I cannot yet say who have it. It hath bin intimated to some that some declaration or acknowledgement is expected, but I heare no farther of it, & tis probable a great part may remaine here for some tyme, where most of us are visited with extreame colds and many taken with vomiting and purging. I am glad 'tis yet so wel with you, endeavor to keepe your selfe soe, none have bin brought hither since the first taking, and Sir L. Griffin hitherto excus'd by reason of his indispositon, your old Lord Brudenel heere, Lord Camden, Lord Cullen intra multos alios."

Cromwell himself was full of trouble. Four months after the wedding celebrated with so much joy, his daughter, Frances, was left a widow, while still in her teens; and a few weeks after Lord Warwick had replied to the Protector's affectionate letter of condolence, he followed his grandson to the grave. The news reached Sir Ralph in one of Nancy Denton's childish scrawls. "Sir I am forced to give you this trobill becas my father was sent for to my Lady Wharton's unexpectedly istardy . . . and my mother is sick a bed . . . truly I thinck that there was never so sickly tim this-mani years as it is now for truly all ouer house is sick, I think thar is not 5 that is well . . . all the newes I can wright you of is that my Lord of Worik is Ded & died on munday morning." There is a hurried line from Dr. Denton at midnight, having just returned home: "My Lord Wharton beinge dead, & soe is my Lord of Warwick, I can say no more, nor advise you what to doe, but to eat & sleepe in quiett. Stow is the fittest for Harry [Sir R. Temple being in favour with the Protector]. Its thought many heads will fly, sound discoveries having been made."

Lady Hobart urged Sir Ralph to come up to town, where he was wanted to swear to his father's handwriting, but it was the eve of the day he always kept holy, the anniversary of Mary's death. "It is impossible for me to be there soe soone," he wrote, "for tomorrow I never stirre wherever I happen to bee."

The Protector was at the height of his power in the summer of 1658; a new parliament was to be summoned, and the Royalist plotters were at last thoroughly discouraged. Henry reports the fate of some of them: "The good D^r, & Sir Harry, are both executed & this day the high court doth sitt again to trey Woodcock and another knight, whose name I have forgott." Though the Royalists mourned Dr. Hewitt as an "excellent preacher" and "holy man," most people felt that he and Sir Henry Slingsby richly deserved their fate, and even they would probably have been spared but for a second plot which came to light while their trial was actually proceeding; of those concerned in it Dr. Denton writes: "2 were executed yesterday & 1 reprieved when rope was about his neck."

Henry also gives us the other side of the picture in the honour paid to Cromwell by foreign Powers: "On tueday last here arrived a parson of greate honor, whose name at present I have forgot [the Duc de Crequi] with a complement from the kinge of france to the Protector, & for the honor of our nation like to be nobley entertained by his Highness, for I dare say no imbassador whatsoever had soe greate an alowance as this courtier; 200*l*. a day for his table and other expenses, & logd at Brookhouse."

Henry keeps up his racehorses, and the Doctor is not averse to a little quiet gambling. "Harry and I have had this day a smart bout at Tables for colt Peterborough & my dun mare that is at Stow; & he gott but 2 games of the 21. Soe I have won ye mare though happily in ye sense I may loose by the match. . . . 100000 (I can allow you cyphers enow) thanks to Chesnut it is best to send her on Satterday [to Stowe] least Sir Rich: should be gone to the Assizes on Munday. . . . If my coach horses be out of tune, Kate will scold me into an Augure hole. Mal & Will are for Cheshire [Madcap has volunteered to go with them and to take Claydon on her way home], Kate is for Surrey & Wm. D. must be left all alone."

The new disease is rife again in the autumn of 1658. "Lady Fiennes cannot recover," Dr. Denton writes; "I have given her 2 vomitts but it profits little. I shall have a wonderfull losse in her, sed fiat voluntas Dei." The precious colt and "his keeper" are also ill at Claydon. The Doctor finds his materia medica within the limits of the old court-yard; the colt is ordered "a groundsel purge," and the man "a stone crop vomitt" in repeated doses. By the end of the month Cromwell was himself struck down. No alarm was felt at first, and Cromwell had an intense belief that he would recover. While the life-and-death struggle was going on in the sick-chamber, a terrific storm shook the south of England, and the Royalists said that the Devil had come to fetch his own. The quiet chit-chat of the family letters contains no allusion to this event of supreme importance

The expectation that there would be "no show" was emphatically falsified; there was a public funeral, magnificent and costly. The coffin lay for more than six weeks "in open state" in Somerset House, and there was a wax effigy of Cromwell standing robed in crimson velvet (or, according to another account, in black), a sceptre in his hand, and a crown on his head. "We are all a whist, no newes stirring," writes

Sir Roger Burgoyne, "but that the old Protector is now gott upon his leggs againe in Sumersett House, but when he shall be translated to the rest of the Gods at Westminster I cannot tell. Pray, doe you come and see."

"It is supposed that the great funeral will be about All Saints," writes another contemporary. "Henry the Seventh's Chapel is being cleansed." But though Cromwell died on the 3rd of September the funeral was not till the 23rd of November, the oppressive ceremonial being rendered still more hollow by persistent reports of a secret burial. Some believed that his had taken place immediately after death, others that the corpse had been hastily buried a week before the funeral upon an alarm that the discontented soldiers meant to seize it as security for their arrears. Evelyn watched the "superb" procession pass with the "imperial banners, atchiements, heralds . . . guards, soldiers, & innumerable mourners . . . but," he adds, "it was the joyfullest funerall I ever saw, for there was none that cried but dogs, which the soldiers hooted away with a barbarous noise, drinking, & taking tobacco in the streets as they went."

Though Evelyn looked on with hostile eyes, it was doubtless true that the procession evoked no reverent sympathy from the crowd. The profound lull that had followed the shock of the Protector's death was already giving way to intrigues and discontents. The French Ambassador, also an eye-witness, gives us a vivid picture of the close of this dismal pageant. The starting of the procession was long delayed by altercations in the Corps Diplomatique about precedence. The service was to have taken place by daylight, this delay not having been forseen: but darkness fell upon the short November afternoon. "There was not a single candle in Westminster Abbey," he writes, "to give light to the company, and conduct the hearse into a sort of 'Chapelle Ardente' which had been prepared; there were consequently neither prayers, nor sermon, nor funeral oration, and after the trumpets had sounded for a short time every one withdrew in no particular order."

In the gloom of that winter afternoon the Westminster boys were marshalled to witness the ceremony. Less than ten years before they had voluntarily gathered themselves together to pray for King Charles as he was led to the scaffold, and all the Puritan governors, and the Presbyterian and Independent preachers in the Abbey, had been unable to extinguish the chivalrous loyalty of Westminster School. Robert Uvedale, whose family had been conspicuous for services rendered to the fallen dynasty, sprang forward through the legs of the guard, snatched from the bier the little satin banner known as the Majesty Scutcheon, darted back again, and before anyone could recover from the shock of the surprise was lost in the crowd of his schoolfellows. It would have been highly inexpedient at such a moment to arrest and search the Westminster boys; so the bit of crumpled white satin remained in Robert Uvedale's pocket, to be displayed in after years, and preserved as an heirloom in his family.

CHAPTER NINE

After Cromwell
1658–1660

WITH Cromwell dead, Richard, the Lord Protector, ruled in his stead.

But there are mutterings of the coming storm when Dr. Denton reports, in October 1658: "The souldiers are not so quiett as I could wish, they would fayne a generall distinct from the Protector."

In marked contrast to preceding years, the Verney letters are full of references to the state of the country during Richard Cromwell's protectorate, and the confusion that followed it; public anxieties once more taking precedence of private interests. Sir Ralph was eagerly watching every shift of the wind, but he was not too busy to write a charming letter to the ladies at Croweshall when Doll was planning a visit to town. "Deare Cozen, I would not interrupt your London pleasures at your very first coming . . . but Cozen is it possible you should take a journey of 4 score miles in this season, through such wayes & Waters, to visit London, & then stay but 8 or 10 dayse there? it cannot bee, for though almost all the World is changed yet you are still the same D: L: that dwelt at Claydon, & cañot bee guilty of such a crime soe highly prejuditiall to all your Friendes, kindred, & acquaintance, & soe absolutly contrary to your owne knowne Humour, & affections too; this were to forget your owne People, & your Fathers house indeed, if you lie under such a vow, tis better broke then kept. I must confesse when my Lady Gaudy is at Croweshall, the seate is good &

pleasant, & that old House (in my conceit) excells the Louvre, & Escuriall; were her Ladishipp here, this House would doe soe too: her presence is able to consecrate all places where she comes; but I presume she is still at Hewzon, with her beloved sonne & daughter, delighting herselfe in her new acquired Title of a Grandmother."

On 22 April 1659 Richard Cromwell, yielding to the dictation of the Council of Officers at Wallingford House, dissolved the Parliament that had met in January. But the difficulty of raising money forced the soldiers to have recourse to another, and on the 7th of May, to avoid fresh elections, the fragments of the Long Parliament were pieced together and set up again at Westminster, under their old Speaker, Lenthall. In the meantime all authority was passing out of Richard Cromwell's hands. The Rump announced that they were to "endeavour the settlement" of the Commonwealth "without a Single Person or House of Peers"; but for eighteen days he lingered on at Whitehall. On the 25th of May, however, his Highness the Lord Protector sent in his abdication, which the House instantly accepted without demur, and "Mr. Richard," shorn of all his titles, was requested to retire from Whitehall and "to dispose of himself as his private occasions shall require." So easy is it to fall!

The bills for Oliver's State funeral were still unpaid, the country could hardly throw them upon "Mr. Richard" now, however unpopular this outlay had become, and matters were no further advanced by the order of the Council of State for "the demolition of the chapel in which the late Protector's effigy was exposed." The House of Commons had to be appealed to, and Lady Hobart writes in July of an Act "to mack all pay for the morning my Lord protector gave." There are "rumours of many troubles but noe certainty of any."

Public anxiety is growing, a terror of a new civil war seizes upon quiet people; but the troops of the Parliament are successful. Massey, who is leading the Royalists in Worcestershire, is defeated and taken prisoner. Dr. Denton relates how he subsequently made his escape while riding in front of the trooper who guarded him: "The horse stumblinge threw them both, by which meanes he escaped into the wood, & is not yet found that I heare of." There is a warrant in August requiring Sir Ralph to send a horse to the George at Aylesbury, or 10*l.* "to excuse horse & armes."

The Doctor next writes to Sir Ralph after the Parliament had despatched Lambert to crush the insurrection in Cheshire under Sir George Booth, and the greatest anxiety was felt in London. "I hope you will be soe wise as to put the horses in the woods. I pray let your Favoritt's shooes be pulled off that she may goe for a colt. We all wished ourselves with you last night; this place was never so neare aflame, bussell, confusion which you will, as last night by the Judgm^t of all, & what will be the Issue a few more houres I ghesse will declare. We have all a mind to be out of the towne, but yett hopes feares, & jealousies doe soe distract us, as that we can resolve of nothing. I wish my papers & other things were with you, for we doe not thinke ourselves at all secure here. . . . The face of things may alter in a mom^t, the battle not beinge alwaies to the strong nor the race to the swift etc; but the open face of things at this present appeares thus, viz. noe considerable force, if any at all, up anywhere but with Sr G. Booth, who with others are now proclaimed traitors, & agst whom there is gone a strong force. Desborough gone into the West to keepe all quiett there, with power to arm all 5th monarchy men & the like; new militias raisinge in every county: The only thinge that lookes like countenancinge Sir George, is the intended peticõn of the city for a free parl^t as they say. This finds soe great opposicõns that for my part I thinke it can come to nothinge. I doe not heare of any one Cavalier in all this affaire, but that it is wholly on the presbytery, & those that fought & engaged for what they call the good old cause; the result out of the premisses is this, that if warrs continue the debt must encrease; taxes, free quarter, militia horses, besides the casualty of plunder must & will dock the revenew, & interest as bad as all these will eat like militia horses whilst you sleepe."

Sir Ralph is obliged to suspend payment of interest to some of his creditors. "I never yet fayled paying within the time, but if warres come God knows what we shall all suffer."

A new Constitution was proclaimed by the Council of Officers, and Parliament was to meet in February. Sir Roger writes: "The comon councell satt yeisterday from 10 in the morning till 6 at night, and the result of all was not very acceptable to the generallity of the Citty; they have not yet according to the petitions settled a militia of their own. What a few daies more may produce God only knowes: God fitt us for the worst of times." "Several horses have been taken & when to be restored I am to learn. Lambert is reported to be at Newcastle and his men reduced to some straits, being not supplied according to expectation with shooes & stockins, for if report be true a friggott that was bound for Newcastle with that kind of ware & arms, most unhappily mistook the port and sett in to Leith in Scotland, so that Monk's army have mett with them. Monk they say is at Barwick, a good distance from the other, yet its said that Major Creed had an encounter with a party of Monk's & had not the better of it. Sir H. Vane is return'd and Salloway; severall of Rump, with Lawson [Admiral of the Fleet in the Thames] who for the present declares for a Parl'; I suppose the Rump, though some doubt it. Sir Arthur Hasilrig & Morley are still at Portsmouth."

Meanwhile, the uproar in the City increasing daily, and the Council of Officers in Lambert's absence being less and less able to cope with it, the old Rump showed fresh signs of life. On Monday the 26th the Members reassembled at Whitehall, marched with Speaker and Mace to Westminster Hall, made a House and began upon business. Lambert's army had melted away in the northern snows without waiting for the enemy.

Neither Sir Roger nor Sir Ralph could so far forget their old fight against Charles I in the best days of the Long Parliament as to feel any enthusiasm for promoting the return of Charles II, and they would not swell the crowd that waited upon Monk at every stage of his progress to London. Margaret Elmes writes to reproach her brother: "I wonder one soe exsackt in all thinges as your selfe is, should let soe greate a person as Moncke is to pas by soe neare you, without your invitation, or att least your going to complyment him with

sum of your Neighbors; I see nothinge can make you stur
from your beloved Claydon."

"Lord Fiennes is gone to Broughton," writes the Doctor,
"& would not sitt because they act on a Commonwealth
Bottom. If a free election come & he be chosen, he will sitt,
or if this sitts & the Lords called in (of which there is some
hopes) then he will sitt as two houses. I can say noe more but
that if you are not a member, I misse of my aime."

Sir Roger writes on the 8th: "Monck was at the house on
Munday last who expresst himself so obscurely that most
men know not what construction for to make of it": Sir Roger
was not in love with the Sphinx. He adds a postscript the next
day: "The Common Council was very stiff yesterday & will
not submit to taxes, & would not own the Parl^t. Souldiers are
gone this morning into the Citty, I suppose to reduce them,
they will only make addresses to Monck." Dr. Denton gives
some further details. "Just now newes is come that Monke &
all his Army is marched into the Citty, on the occasion of the
Common Council beinge mighty high last night in giving the
Warwickshire gentleman great thankes (volens, nolens the L^d
Maior) promising to live and dy with them. It works apace
now." Monk was ordered by the Council of State to repress
by force what was in effect a Royalist pronouncement by the
City: he obeyed, and the City was overawed. "Bristol for
certaine," Dr. Denton continues, "standes on theire guard &
will admitt noe souldiers. They that desired to passe through
the other day, were dismounted at the gate leaving their
horses & their Armes, & marched 10 & 10 quite through, with
10 & 10 of the city guard betweene each 10 of them; & when
quite out of the citty had then delivered to them, theire horses
& armes again. There are your men, Sir."

Monk's attack upon the City nearly wrecked his own
reputation as well as its gates and portcullises, but he saw his
mistake, and retrieved it in a moment. Dr. Denton tells the
story: "13th of February, 12 at night. . . . As soon as Monke had
sent the enclosed letter to the house [requiring them to fill
up their numbers at once, and to dissolve on the 6th of May
to make room for a newly elected Parliament], he presently

drew his army into the citty beinge Satterday & complied with the Citizens, which was quickly spread, & uppon which there were bonefires circum circa, & from one end of the city to the other, Westminster etc. & with such joy & acclamation as was never yett seene. The Speaker (who sate late) in his march homewards affronted, his men beaten, his windowes broken. A Rumpe in A chayre rosted at his gates, & bonefires made there. Never so many rumpes rosted as were that night. What this will produce nemo scit. About 12 A clock this day at noone, it was generally beleeved it would prove Ignis fatuus, for that Monke was strongly looked for to dine with some Grandees at White Hall, but did not. . . . If you goe to Twiford tell my Lord he lost much sport by going out of towne that he is never like to see the like." It was evidently hopeless for Kate to get her doctor away.

The news is running like wildfire through Hampshire, where several private letters have been received. John Stewkeley rejoices that General Monk "hath declared for a single Person (you may Imagin whom) and for a Free Parliament. . . . We may all soon meet if the Wind blow from Flanders: wch I pray for, pro Re: pro Ecle. Ang: pro reg: as a Subject, as a member, as an Englishman."

The streets are full of soldiers. Pen, looking out of the windows of her London lodging, writes: "I wish Munke may be so happy a Parson to this poore distressed Land, that he may merritt Applause from all parsons, as yett I am not so much taking with him, as to delight my self with aney sight of his men."

Sir Roger sends his version of the reconciliation between Monk and the City and "of the great joy that was conceived by inconsiderat persons (which were very numerous) by reason of his letter, which they pleased themselves with those constructions their phancies made of it, & no expressions were wanting to it. The bells & fyres fully discovered rather what they would have, then what they had: out of the same mouths proceed blessings & curses, for they who cursed him the day before for pulling down the gates, blesst him this day for coming into them. On Sunday thousands resorted to St. Paul's Church, to get a sight of him.

He hath continued there ever since & severall of his forces
at the Citty charge, who entertaine them with much seeming
contentment. . . . What Monck will do to answer the expectations of all parties, I am to seek—though very many may be
deceived, I shall be non of them. . . . Addresses are still made
to him, people will not be quiett. Lambert summoned to come
in by this day, which if he refuse to doe then to be sequestred.
This morning I was told that he was come in, which is contrary to what I heard yesterday. . . . There are nothing but
riddles asked."

The Doctor writes: "You may longe to heare of the fruits
of the Bonefires, I can only in briefe tell you this, that all sides
ply Monke with warm cloaths & he like a prudent person
would fayne reconcile. I heare that he offered the secluded
if they would only promise not to bringe in the King, that he
did not doubt but to procure their sittings. Dick Norton told
him that Freedom of Parl^t was the just right & interest of the
nation & if they thought it fitt to bringe in the Turke, they
ought not to be imposed on the contrary. Last night 10 & 10
of Rumpers & Secluders met before the Generall; the result
of which I cannot yet learne, but I doubt nothinge but
wranglinge."

Sir Roger announces the vote which would enable Sir
Ralph to take his seat again, after sixteen years of "seclusion."
"Sir, without the least preamble to it or giving you an account
of what pass't in order to the last and most unexpected turne:
you may by this understande that the secluded members, by
the assistance of Genl Monck, were readmitted this day into
the house in which place he was voted Capt Genl of all the
forces of Eng^l Scot^l & Ire^l under the Par^t, Lawson to continue
vice-Admirall."

Dr. Denton writes the next day: "Monke brought in the
secluded members who act & vote as formally as before, &
take noe notice of anythinge. Our Cozen Greenvile hath lost
himselfe most wonderfully amongst his countrymen in refusinge
to doe as other neighbours did, noe man dissentinge but himselfe. Sir R. Piggott hath done little lesse. Sir R. T[emple]
carries it plum on all sides; he writt to Dick Winwood by coach

F

yesterday, he havinge notice over night that it would be. We knewe nothinge till about 9 A clock. I have sent to hasten Dick W. to his duty, they are all earnestly desired. I wish my Lord Wenman were in a condicion to come up."

Penelope rejoices "above all that by this new & great chang" she has lived to see her brother "onc more in a Capacitie to sarve the Country." "It would vex me to the hart to have us both out," writes Dr. Denton, eager in the general excitement to add to the duties of his over-busy life; "but if Cavaliers are to be excluded we shall be mumpt." There is also a talk of Sir Ralph standing for Westbury, Bedwin, or Malton. He at first fights shy of election expenses, as the parliament is expected to be a very short one.

Kind congratulations pour in. Sir Henry Lee has just heard "of the great news at London": "I assure you," he writes to Sir Ralph, "it is the best wee have had this many years & trewly I am very glad Sir R. Var: entends to serve his Country & friends in that Honble imployment." He offers to use his interest on Sir Ralph's behalf, and desires to see him "at Ditchley, though I confesse it has nothing that deserves an invitation from Cladon, though I can promise no person to be more wellcome then yourselfe." His mother, Lady Rochester, at once sets her agents to work, and writes to Mr. Thomas Yates to secure seats for Sir Ralph and her son in the elections for what was emphatically called a Free Parliament, though the electors seemed amiably ready to submit to the Countess's dictation, and to acknowledge it as "their duty to their Country & their younge Lande-Ladyes to serve Sir Ralph therein."

The rush for seats in the parliament of 1660 was in marked contrast with the difficulty of getting candidates to stand under Cromwell's rule; the great interest and importance of the crisis was fully understood, and the part the House of Commons was to play in it. Edmund Verney has "a very greate desire to serve in Parliament. . . . to advance my understanding unto a higher piche, by learning the intrigues of my owne native contry, whereof I am wholly ignorant." Dr. Hyde encouraged his ambition while advising him to "expect the qualifications now hamering here. Every day produces such vanitye of

Contradictions, it is not possible to write any certaintie as yet. . . . but certeynly I shall never advise you to hazard your Fortune, much lesse your Honour or Conscience for a little improvement of your experience."

Dr. Denton writes that it is generally believed the Parliament "will dissolve this weeke; the sooner the better, for under the Rose I have noe faith in Rumpe Major."

"Rumpe Maior begins to smell as ranke as Rumpe Minor, I knowe noe man pleased with their proceedings, here are great feares & jealousies that they have a mind to establish themselves, & to re-establish Richard . . . which is all at present, & enough to burne. . . ."

Doll Smith, sending for money, writes: "I sent too barrors becaus I was afrayd to venture one of them alone now the souldiers are about."

The last show of armed resistance came from Lambert, and he was routed by Tom's old Colonel, Dick Ingoldsby, a regicide whom the "turning wheels of vicissitude" had brought round to the Royalist side, though he cheerfully declared that the King would probably cut his head off as soon as he landed.

When the Convention Parliament met on 25 April 1660, England was in a frantic hurry to fetch the exile from over the water, and, as in another great revulsion of popular feeling, the sole question men asked their neighbours seemed to be, "Why are ye the last to bring the King back to his house?"

CHAPTER TEN

London Life: the Plague and the Fire

1662–1666

Sɪʀ Nᴀᴛʜᴀɴɪᴇʟ and Lady Hobart, the "Sweet Nat" and "Sweet Nan" of Sir Ralph's early days, were still, in middle life, the truest of friends and the most delightful of correspondents. In 1652 Sir Nathaniel was made a Master in Chancery "in Sir Ed. Leech his dead place," and in 1658 the family removed from Highgate, that he might live near the law courts. Lady Hobart gave as her address "A greate house in Chancery Lane, over against Lincoln's Inne, near the Three Cranes, next dor to the Hole in the Wall, within two dors of Mr. Farmer's and one dor of Judge Ackings." The house was further distinguished as being "nigh to the Pumpe" and as having "a very handsom garden with a wash hous in it." The rent, 55*l.* a year, was considered a heavy one, and as there were more rooms than they required, Anne Hobart set her wits to work to reduce expenses, by letting part of the house to relations during the London season. Her first experiment of taking in her married daughter, Lady Smith, was not a success, and her next overtures were made to Sir Ralph, who since his return to England in 1653 had kept a *pied à terre* in Covent Garden or in Russell Street.

Sir Ralph liked the idea, but other relations, who were accustomed to lodge near him, made indignant protests against his removal to so remote a quarter. "Uncle Dr. and self

mander most greviously att it," writes Peg Elmes; "I wish it
a thousand inconveanyantis to you, & them moare as temted
you to it." On the other hand, Lady Hobart, with her hospitable
anxieties, was not always easy to satisfy. "You were not kind
to me," she writes one evening that Sir Ralph had dined out,
when she had been "busy all the morning buying a banquet,
and in the afternoon at my Lady Bartley's to tech her to do
paist, wich are all at your sarvis . . . but you not coming I
intend to send my swetmeets into Iarland." But on the whole
Sir Ralph was free to come and go as he liked, and the evenings spent with Sir Nathaniel were most congenial to him.
Thus, the winter of 1662–3 found Sir Ralph with Edmund
and Mary Verney settled in their own suite of rooms in
Chancery Lane, to Lady Hobart's intense satisfaction. Her
daughters "Frank" and Nancy, whose strong wills sometimes
brought them into sharp collision with their mother, were
fond of cousin Mun, and gave his bride a kind welcome.

Mary Verney's health and spirits had been variable; when
she first arrived she was popular with them all, but she became
subject to fits of moody silence or of hysterical excitement
during which she was a torment to herself and others. She vexed
her husband with unreasonable suspicions and grievances, or,
as Dr. Denton expresses it, "Zelotipia [jealousy] is gott into
her pericranium, & I doe not know what will gett it out."
So disturbing an element in the house completely destroyed
Sir Ralph's comfort; he suddenly left for Claydon and "frightened them with his sad looks when he went away."

Undeterred by former experiences, Lady Hobart was happy
in her hospitable preparations. Sir Ralph's quarters must be
quite to his liking. "I have whited the room, & stars hed, &
clened the bed and hanings. Pray send me word whether the
chamber shall be paned at the full bigness or no. If it be, it
will be Ligheter at the chimny, but then your beach box must
stand in one of the closets. The dor must goo in by your man's
beds fet. Now fur the stabels. i have my chos of 2, one in
Magpy Yard. Thar is a pond in the yard to wash the horses and
very good water. It will hold four horsis, and the hay loft will
hold 4 lod of hay; ther is bins for ots. Thay say they ar very

honist and sivell people; judg Ackings coach has stod thar this 14 year. Now that is another at the Red Harp in Feter Lan; tis one turning mor beyond the Magpy, but it has the same convenency. The Magpy is 16 pound a year, if thay Log a man; the other i can have for 14 pound." A little later she has "paynted all the windows and mayd all clen. You may come when you will, but you sayd you will Ly on a quilt, thar fer I must beg you to bring on, for i have non. I have mayd all my hous better than it was for clennes, but i am very wrought in my stomack. Pray send me som grens to set agans my new wall & som Jeseney and hunicuckells."

For Edmund and his wife she has prepared the "gret chamber. I now want a bed; if it be not to much trobell to you to send up som curtans & valanc, for at presant I want som. If it be your wroght ons, or any other, it will be much mor convenant for them, & thay shall hav the Low room at thar sarvis to set in, & to bring all compeny in to, for we did want that very much Last year. Hur mayds shall have a very good Login to thar selfs whar hur truncks shal stand. . . . Pray tell Bes King she must Leve tiling storys; my mayds dred hur, thay Live quietly senc she went. But for what she sayd to me, I forgive hur, & wold have her com to dow thar worck; it will be very convenant for me. She may wash all thar clos here. Say nothing to hur master, & pray Let them bring up 2 par of shets for thar on bed. I will have on hundred of fagets Layd into your wod hous redy against you com. My mayd shall Ly in all the beds, & all shall be well ared."

Mrs. Abell hopes her dear Mary may "inioy the pleasures of the towne, which God be blessed, you have all the reasone in the world soe to doe. I am troubled with that illness at my hart that I was when you left me. I have often wished my selfe with you since you went from hence, that I might in some part partake of your pleasure, but that is a thing that I have bine weaned from a long time, & the onely comfort that I have now left me is your Deere selfe. I have soe great a tye & oblygation upon me for my Dearest of frinds sake, as allsoe for your owne sweet deportment allways towards me, that it hath for ever obliged mee." But these lovable qualities were again to be sadly overclouded. The noise and bustle of town life probably affected poor Mary's nerves, and she had not been long in Chancery Lane before the distressing symptoms returned with increased violence.

The degree of moral responsibility attaching to actions on the borderland of sanity was a problem far beyond the medical science of the day; and Sir Ralph took a severe view of Mary's want of self-control. As she grew worse, the slovenliness of her person and attire, and the indecorum of her conduct, aroused in him nothing but disgust; her screams, and her still more terrible laughter, so irritated his nerves, that his only wish was to fly from any house in which she might be. All Lady Hobart's plans for him were overthrown; the old opinion once more prevailed, that he would be driven to marry again, and that his choice was likely to be Vere, Lady Gawdy. Another version of the rumour reached that lady, and she hastens to congratulate him: "I heare you are not farr from inioyinge A Considerable pleasur, if our sex might procure it you; if it bee so, may all that renders women less worthy then Men bee exempt from the Parson you shall make happie." Sir Ralph let them talk, and left town for Claydon in January, making the journey in one day.

The best side of Mun's nature was brought out by his wife's sad condition, much as she had tried his patience; the terrible symptoms which so repelled Sir Ralph only made him more constant and pitiful in his attendance upon her.

In a few days Sir Ralph was back in town; Mary, having recovered from the measles, fell much more seriously ill with small-pox, but recovered "without any inconveniency to her complexion," and by the advice of the whole family Edmund went to Claydon with his father, for rest and change, after his arduous nursing.

The news of Mary did not improve. "We have had a sad day with your dafter," writes Lady Hobart. "She now hats us all but thar to mayds, & this day she has bin kind to franck wich dos ples me much, for she must not be out with all at once. I have no mor to say but Love your self, & mack much of honis Sir Raphe, for when he is gon, his frinds will not find

shuch another. I am suer por me shant, thar for Love hur
that is Sir your sarvant to command A. Hobart." "Tusday our
cosen was very ill all day, and hyly discontented. At night thay
had no way but to give hur a sleping pell, & she slep all night
& till ten in this morning, & wacked very tame but sulen. We
had much adow to get hur to eat a bet, but with much in
trety at Last she did eat a leg of a rabit, & had a mind to goo
a brod & i did goo with hur as fur as Kensington, & as we
cam back she wold goo in to the parck, & if she will she must
and did, & was very well but sayd very letill, but as we cam
hom she wished she had never com to London, but stayd
with dear mother, for nobody dos love hur but she and por
Jan. And tould the gerls and me she mought have lived if
she had had som about hur, & raled on us all, & begon to
gro very bad. So at last I did pursuad hur to wright to hur
hus to let hur Live with hur mother. So she is now a writing
in gret wroth. She says he shall hear a pes of hur mind. Bats
[Dr. Bates] is out of town," but Dr. Denton at night "gave her
dainty ease, & soe she continued all Wenesday, and marcht
abroad."

The improvement is not sustained, and Lady Hobart's
mind misgives her: "Pray dow not stay to Long, nor kep your
son, for i am so full of fears that i dar not stur, for fear she
shold have a freck of running out . . . in earnes she is very
disablegin. I fear you have played the arant Theife with me
for all my fine seeds, I have bin starck mad for them; it was
ill don to tack all. Send me som of them agan, or your wig
shall off. As the weather is windy and stormy abrod, we have
had our shar with my cosen with in. She has bin very ill
yuemered, by fits i may tell you mad. She has cryed & scremed
& singed & raled on us all, & por docker tow. Now Bats is
all & all with hur; she says she thinks in hur hart he is not
yet corupted, but thar is nothing but hur mayd Jan, but longs
for hur deth. She dos says such things as flesh and blod never
hard. To days i kept from hur, only morning and night Locked
in to see how hur to mads did order hur.

"She has tacken ephsome waters this thre days. I fear her
ill yumer will never be quered [cured]. For two days she did

cry send for hur hus, but now she is off from that, but she dos hat us all. O dear sur raph i feare she will never be well; hur por hus will have a sad tim with hur."

Edmund returned soon after his wife's birthday; he had only been gone a fortnight, though his absence had seemed so long to Lady Hobart. He wrote to his father telling him of his poor wife's extravagances; two nurses are constantly with her.

The perplexed husband hears of a woman named Clark, who undertakes to cure his wife in two months for 20l.; but he dares not trust Mary to her without consulting her uncle Gale. Edmund will not consent to put her in a public institution, or in any house where they would be free to take in other patients; he thinks of taking a private lodging, observing exactly all that the doctors prescribe for her treatment. Sir Ralph replies: "I know not what to say to the Woeman more then this, that unlesse her owne friends desire & advise it, twill not bee fit for you to put her to bee cured, for if any ill accident should follow, all the world would blame you for it. I confesse divers Woemen have very good receits, & good successe too, & frequently have cured those that the Drs. have not; but all that will not excuse you from a just censure."

Mary's health improved, however, beyond expectation, and by the middle of August she was moved to East Claydon accompanied by "the woman Dr."

Edmund expresses in every letter his joy in his wife's recovery; both were taking pleasure and interest in their home and its plenishings. Frank Hobart is to send down curtain rods; Sir Nathaniel is to order a frame for what his wife calls Edmund's "gibbonish Whimwham"; while Mary at her own pace writes a number of epistles to Lady Elmes about feminine shoppings. "Sr Ralph & my cosen Leke both teles me, as you ded before, that gimp is out of fashing; tharfore i shall quit my sellf of the troble by taking your advice to worke a dimity bed in gren cruells. For a drawing-rome i should have 2 squobs, & 6 turned woden chars of the haith of the longe seates. Be pleased to by a tabel & stands of the same coler; & for the same rome a pair of andirons, doges, fire shvl, tongs & thre bras flours with irnes to fasten my glas. I have yet my closet to furnish, & I beg your asistanc in it. I think to hange it with peregon, but the coler, & whether it shall be watered or no i leve to you. If goodnese might merit honor, thar is none could be greater then dere Aunt Elemes; my self only hapey in being alied to a person so truly vertueus." Aunt Elmes can find no tolerable chairs under 7s. apiece, and the squobs 10s.

Edmund asks Sir Ralph's help in organising his Christmas entertainments; Michal Durand has become head cook, and he wants to borrow him. Sir Ralph entered heartily into their hospitable plans. "Sir Richard Temple tells mee the newes at Buckingham is, that you will keepe the best Christmas in the Sheire, & to that end have bought more frute and spice then halfe the Porters in London can weigh out in a day. I have writ to tell the Cooke that hee shall doe my businesse about the Beefe at such times as you can most conveniently spare him from East Claydon; and soe hee may very well, for hee hath nothing to doe for mee but to make 2 collars of Beefe, & bake some in Potts. I am very glad to heare your Wife is so well, I pray remember mee to her, and tell her I wish her a Merry Christmas." Plaistow the carrier expects a Christmas box of 10s. for the delivery of letters, which is what he receives at Claydon House.

The country is surprised to hear of the "monstrous sum" of 2,500,000l. granted to the King. Edmund thinks Holland might be conquered with half that money. A postscript of Sir Ralph's contained the bitter news which had just reached London. "The Duch have beat us out of Cape Verde at Guiny, taken the Marchant Shipps, put our men to the sword for resisting them. De Ruiter did it with his Fleet, & tis feared hee will do us mighty mischeifes in the streights."

Meanwhile the festive preparations were being hurried on; the presence of the Claydon cook ensured the success of the joints and plum porridge; but the drink caused Edmund some anxiety. He flattered himself that he had brewed a good store of strong ale, but he had no common white wine, and his best claret was too good for the occasion. Sir Ralph believes that he may get "Claret of 6 pence a quart . . . & good enough for the use you intend it, and twere pitty to cast away better in that way . . . I will look out some for you . . . twill be ready enough to drinke in two dayes for it shall have no Lees, & you may draw it out of the Runlet without Bottleing it, if you have no time to bottle it."

Before the wine arrives, this unthrifty host discovers that he does not require it, because the best claret will not keep and may as well be finished; later he is glad of it again, when the strong ale proves to be no better than it should be. Mary sends loving messages to Sir Ralph, desiring his blessing, and rejoicing in the prospect of his speedy return to Claydon, where his presence will add to all their Christmas joy. He desires her to thank Heaven and be careful of her diet. Her East Claydon tenants were feasted on the 27th, Middle Claydon tenants on another day, and their third and last entertainment was given to 50 of their poorer neighbours with their wives and children. Wine and ale, good, bad and indifferent, flowed in streams; Edmund reported that the 6d. claret had served its purpose well.

Edmund's lavish hospitality had reinstated him in the good opinion of his neighbours; he was at length settling down in his own home, with some prospect of domestic happiness, and had been able to increase his estate by one or two judicious purchases; as Cousin Jack Fust expressed it, "you must needs be my Lord of East, West, North and South Claydon." The plague so often referred to in the earlier Verney letters had been for many years in abeyance. "During the Civil Wars London had been the safest place of residence and had grown fast while other towns were languishing."

The fresh outbreak in the spring of 1665 is noticed at first merely in joke: "Tis plaguey newes that the plague has come to Southwark." In May Sir Ralph writes from Chancery Lane: "Tis an ill time to put out money for the feare of the Plague makes many willing to take their Estates out of the Goldsmiths' hands, & the King's greate want of money makes many very unwilling to lend any money to these that advance greate summs for him. Mr Kempe came to my Lodging on purpose to desire mee to helpe him to dispose 3 or 400*l.* on good security. . . .

Coals [which come by sea from Newcastle] are not only excessive deare, but are not to be had, wee heare of a hope for greate Fleets hereafter, but we doubt tis but discourse." He is thankful to have the Claydon woods to fall back upon, but must cut down more timber than he desires. It is a hot and dry season, and Mun must see that the young mulberry trees are well watered.

The plague is spreading; in June "tis suspected to bee at the Black Swan in Holborn where the Alisbery & other coaches stand"; a little later all the carriers are stopped, "the sickness is not far from Lombard St. & if it should visitt the Goldsmiths twill be hazardous to have too great a stock there." Sir Roger Burgoyne, whose children are at Clapham, is afraid either to leave them there or to have them home; but eventually they return to Warwickshire, Sir Ralph entertaining them by the way; Sir Roger has received them "safe & sound, but so full of the good dainties that Claydon afforded, that the best we have at Wroxall will hardly goe down with them."

The men of Sir Ralph's generation still considered smoking a nasty habit, and Sir Roger Burgoyne, in planning a new wing at Wroxall, designs a door into the Oval Garden "to make it serve instead of a withdrawing room for tobacconists & such goodfellows & to free the house from all such unwellcome parfumes." But it was rapidly becoming fashionable, as a preservative against infection, and the Eton boys were ordered to smoke in school daily. They still do.

Sir Ralph has to confess "the Sicknesse is strangely increased & that several houses are shut upp in Chancery lane & severall neare it, but I trust God in Mercy will preserve mee & this family from that violent disease. I have been ill of late, soe that the Dr. hath purged & blooded me, & now I hope to get home within few days."

In August, Buckingham "is soe sorely afflicted with Small Pox, suspected to be worse for there are blew spots with it," that Sir Ralph is advised to send to Bicester Market; Edmund cannot deal with his butcher at Winslow because the butcher's man, Hogson, comes from an infected house. Squire Duncombe "pensa mourir ce matin et cette après diner il alla au Cabaret se boire bien." Hogson's sister dies, and the plague spreads to their relations at East Claydon where Edward Cox and all his children die of it, the wife alone recovering, and falling ill later, after the birth of her posthumous child, of what is again supposed to be the plague. Edmund remains at his post, and Sir Ralph returns to Claydon as soon as the plague breaks out, that they may do what they can for the villages; it does not spread in the Claydons, but through that terrible September when the mortality in London reached its highest point, there were plague-cases at Stowe, Stony Stratford, Fenny Stratford (where the market was closed and the highway diverted), Bletchley, Lavendon (where fifty died in the village), Winslow, Hardwick, Aylesbury, Wendover, Marlow, Wycombe, etc. A wandering dog was said to have carried the plague from Wendover to Ellesborough, where the Rector, Thomas Emery, died of it. A pest-house was set up in the fields outside Aylesbury, whose wretched inmates burnt "the sheep-racks & gates" of the adjoining farm, being forbidden to wander in search of fuel. The Aylesbury Gaol, "so decayed that it was scarce fit for a dog-house," had long been a centre of infection; at this time it was crammed full of miserable Quakers and Nonconformists.

Men hardly dared to leave their homes for fear of bringing "the sickness" back with them. Thomas Stafford speaks "of the sad confinement of all fathers of families in this time of contagion." In Hampshire, Cary deplores the fate of a poor family three miles from her own door, where the plague was brought down by a brother from London, and all died of it; "for two months past here have been fifty deaths a week in Southampton."

Court, Parliament, and the Law fled to Oxford; the Chancellor with my Lord Manchester is taking orders for the King's accommodation there. Sir Nathaniel Hobart writes to Sir Ralph: "If the Plague continue at the rate I feare it will, what a madnes would it bee to have such a confluence of people as the Terme must bring into such a place as Oxford, but in regard we are uncertaine what will bee resolved on by them that sit at the Sterne, our humble request is that you will bee pleased to use your interest to procure us lodgings, a lower and an upper chamber would bee sufficient. . . . S^r if they can be had neere the Schooles where they say the Court will bee kept it will bee the better but beggars must bee noe chusers."

Lady Hobart is ready to disregard all sanitary considerations if she can but be with her "Nat." "There goo non but my husband self and Mayd and man and it may be my boy. One rom for us and a plas for my hus to sit in, but tou roms shall sarve all we will mack shift . . . my son dislicks that the new Colag shall send to ofer him logins for he will mack no requist to them . . . my husband writ a leter to docker Bate to see if he cold help him, but my son says the toun Logins are so dear that thar is no deling with them. I hop we shall see you to morow or the next day for I have no pashans to be so long from you, I wold be glad to have a lon rom for my husband any shall content us."

Sir Ralph lays the case before his Oxford friends. The Principal of Brasenose, Dr. Thomas Yate, hospitably responds: "Sir, —I have had Sr. Nath. Hobart's name in my list, ever since mr Cary told me your desires for him, and I hope I shalbe able to serve him as you desire, with a lodging chamber and another chamber below staires, if those that now take upon them all power here doe not attempt to doe more then hithertoo they have done, Mr Attorney Gen: lies in my lodgings, and hath desired me to provide for his two sonnes [one or both members of Parliament] some where also in our Coll: I have designed where to lodge Sr Nath. and I hope I shall hold it, I will not easily be beaten off, though I had a ticket this morning from my Lord Chancellor's Secretary to desire I would provide for 4 knightes but I hope it is but a thing he assumes, and that it is not by my Lord's Command. But be assured I will use all the power and friendes I have, but I will have a lodging such as you desire for him, but what his servantes will doe I cannot at present tell you, though I will thinke myselfe obliged to do all I can in some place or other to fitt them also. Wee heare the Duke of Yorke wilbe here to morrow, his children came on Thursday last, and though some cariages of the kinges are come already to Christ Church, wee are not assured the king wilbe here on Tuesday next, but most say that Ev^g he wilbe

here. The great trouble Sr. Nath. Hobart wilbe put into wilbe
for his diet in a Colledge if his lady comes along with him:
otherwise those that are members of the House have names in
the Booke, and dine and sup in our Hall, wch they seeme to
be pleased with, but wherein I may serve them therein also I
shall, and if Sr Nath. Hobart could give me notice 2 or 3 dayes
before his coming I might be enabled to serve him the better,
that he might not be to seeke when he comes, as many maybe
(for the Court hath so enlarged themselves having Christ
Church, Merton Coll: Corpus Xti Coll. Pembroke Coll. &
Oriol Coll. assigned wholely and solely for them) that it putts
many to straites and many to seeke, for if I provide for Sr Nath
(as I hope to do) in our Coll. I must remove a fellow and some
furniture and they must have some tyme to doe it."

Mrs. Sherard writes from Whitsondine: "I am in a daily
fere, we had a market town about 4 miles of us that bureyed
about 9 or 10 in a hut, just as I cam ought of the North, and
wee hoped all would have bin well, but about 3 wickes since
it brake out in that town affresh and non knows how it cam.
A child of 3 years old dyed first, and 5 more since in that same
hous, and it was in one hous more which sold all sortes of ale;
he conselid his dead wife tow dayes, and ther was 40 in the
hous after shee dyed both Jhentry and others, my Ld Sherard
told me that non in his hundred coold say thay wair free, &
severall of that town stole into our town & brought in ther
Goodes in the night. My hus. hearing of it armd himselfe with
his pistoles & went about 9 at night & saw them all shut up
with thos as resived them; it is a great blesing that all plasis air
not infeckted considoring the carlysness of the common sort
of people." Six months later the plague is still in "the market
town" and likely to last through another summer, "the town
being full of poore & very unruly." Sir Justinian Isham is
driven from home, the sickness being all round his house in
Northamptonshire.

Betty's fears are confirmed: "The sickness is at Chelmsford
a litel mile from me which coseis me to be veri fearfull, so
many of our town goes that way to Markit, thos which bee
shut up would run About did not sum stand with guns redy

to shoot them if they stur." By December there are fifty houses infected; she is the "joyful mother of a fin girl," thankful for her recovery "in times when wee hardly dare visit one another if sick." As soon as she can sit up in her bed she writes to Sir Ralph a list of benefices he might apply for. As Tom had found balm in the thought that creditors were not plague-proof; and Jeffereys, a lad in his teens, profiting by the havoc the plague had wrought among the lawyers, "put a gown on his back & began to plead" before he had been called to the bar; so Betty reading with some complacency of the "many ministers dead in thees times of Mortoloty," thinks it strange indeed if her brother cannot get them one of the vacant livings; "the taxis here is so hi & the plas so smol that we know not what to doo, this with my praiers to God for our hapy meeting I rest that am Y^r most affec^t Sister & sarvant."

Oxford, crowded as it is in every corner, is not exempt— "the porter of Lincoln is dead of the plague," and other cases are mentioned; the saintly Bishop of Salisbury, Dr. Earle, is dying in University College, but of what illness does not appear.

Pepys could rejoice with the opening of the New Year at the plague's decrease in town; shops were opening, porters bowing and beggars begging at the sight of a nobleman's coach come to town again; but in many parts of the country the sickness raged all that year. Cary writes that Winchester was "never near so bad as now, ther died 11 in one day, for all the town is emptied so much into the countary a bout; poor Milly, the pretty made as sarved my daugter Grove, is shut up and her husband and 3 children, last tusday her made dying of the plaug, so my littell scolar is like to continue with mee who presents his humble sarvis to you tis a sad los of time to him. In Southampton, I thinke, have died almost 1000." Winton College remains closed for above half a year; "so that for that time," writes John Stewkeley, "I have been Jack's Tutor; after Xmas the school opens again, if the sickness doe not breake out again which is much feared, by reason that one fell down dead there last week, as he was going to grinde mault."

Bad news of the war with the Dutch contributes to the

Detail of a door in Claydon House

The Chinese Room in Claydon House

general depression. There are riots amongst the plague-stricken wretches who are shut up in their houses; the plague is still "so violent in Winton and Petersfeld and Porchmouth as tis sad to relate, and last week the sick brok out, not for want, as wee are told, but to visitt the houses of the better sort and opened the jale and 17 prisoners escaped, bot 15 are taken againe, the royal white trained bands ware left in town and soprist them with the lose of one man and 3 hort, of that party as did mutiny, wee are afraid of all wee meet thay ramble a bout . . . our assises is kept next wensday at Andovour so the Sherrif is come into this sickly countary how long to stay I know not, I pray God send peac and helth."

A more terrible blow than any that had yet fallen was to "crush the weak fortunes" of the Stewkeleys, and of many other members of the family, whose incomes depended on London property. Lady Hobart, in her beautiful house in Chancery Lane, writes in an agony of fear, while the Great Fire is blazing: "O dear Sir Raph,—I am sory to be the mesinger of so dismall news, for por London is almost burnt down. It began on Saterday night [she is writing Monday morning] & has burnt ever senc and is at this tim more fears than ever, it did begin in pudding lan at a backers, whar a Dutch rog [rogue] lay, & burnt to the bridge & all fish street and all crasus stret & Lumber Stret and the old exchang & canan stret & so all that way to the reaver & bilingsgat sid, & now tis com to chep sid & banescasell [Baynard's Castle, to the east of Blackfriars Bridge] & tis thought flet stret will be burnt by tomorow, thar is nothing left in any hous thar, nor in the Tempell, thar was never so sad a sight, nor so dolefull a cry hard, my hart is not abell to expres the tenth nay the thousenth part of it, thar is all the carts within ten mils round, & cars & drays run about night & day, & thousens of men & women carring burdens. Tis the Duch fire, thar was one tacken in Westminster setting his outhous on fier & thay have atempted to fier many plases & thar is a bundanc tacken with granades & pouder, Casell yard was set on fier, i am all most out of my wits, we have packed up all our goods & cannot get a cart for money, thay give 5 & 10 pound for carts. I have sent for carts to my Lady Glaskock if

I can get them, but I fear I shall los all I have and must run away. O pray for us for now the crys macks me I know not what to say, O pety me. I will breck open the closet and look to all your things as well as i can, I hop if it come to us it will be Thursday but it runs fearsly, O i shall los all i have, we have sent to se for carts to send to higat & cannot get one [for] twenty pounds to go out of town. Viner and Backwall have saved all, and so has all Lumbert Stret, all Polschurchyard cloth is saved. Mr. Glaskock is com & says we shall have carts tomorrow. God bles us & send us a good meting." Two days later she writes again: "O dear Sir, we are all undon, the holl sety is down, my hous is not yet burnt, but all I have turn'd out, & som saf & the rest in the felds." Among the distracting rumours in the crowd a report ran that the French and Dutch who had planned the fire would sack the town, and with this "dreadful outcry we did look to be kiled every hour, I have all most lost my wits & my por gearls. It has cost me 20*l.* to remove my goods in porters & carts if you can sen me som money you will hyly obleg me, you shall have it again at Micklmas dear sir send me but 10*l.* & love & pety y^r Ser^t A. H."

Lady Hobart has lost her wits in good company; the Lord Mayor, Sir Thomas Bludworth, running about "with a hand-kercher about his neck, cried out like a fainting woman to the king's message—Lord what can I do, I am spent, people will not obey me, I have been pulling down houses, but the fire overtakes us faster than we can do it!" It was evident if the fire did not reach Chancery Lane "before Thursday" it would not be thanks to the City magnate, who, flurried and worn out by the unwonted exertion of running about all night, had gone home "to refresh himself," leaving London to burn. The rapid spreading of the fire "bred a kind of Distraction and stupidity in the Inhabitants and neighbourhood near it." The pipes had been destroyed in a few hours, and the water supply, such as it was, failed entirely. Men were clamouring for General Monk, but he was out of town the first days, and the fire was even more hasty and unreasonable to deal with than Saints and Levellers.

Friends wrote at first to tell each other what streets were

burned down; then they count up "those that are yet standing."
Dr. Denton writes: "Whether this will find you or noe I know
not because I know not where the carrier doth inne, the fire
being now come as far as Holborn Bridge or near it. The short
account of the fire is that more than the whole city is in ashes,
wherein W. Gape & my selfe have great shares in St. Sythes
Lane, and in Salisbury Court in reversion & I & wife in possession, & to render our condition more deplorable, the de-
population is so vast that it cannot afford us a livelihood so
that I want the advice of all my friends to advise what I had
best doe. Our persons I thank God & our moveables are saved
but at a vast charge, 4*l.* for every load to Kensington. The
frendes in Chancery Lane are safe, but the fire was neare
them behind the Rowles where it gott a great check soe that we
hope it is stopt, I think they are still in towne. We had sent
away all but my bookes soe that we were fayne to ly only on
blanketts. It came so far as to burn the King's Bench office &
the Alienation Office, but not so far as Nelly's chambers. Our
Navy lies at St. Ellen's point & the Dutch on the Coast of
Bretaigne. This fire stops all trade & traffique & posts, the sad
consequences of which may easily be ghessed att. Since I writ
this the fire broke out at the Temple again next to Nelly's
Chambers, & his chamber the Duke caused to be blown up &
it hath burnt now the Inner Temple Hall & I have not heard
how much further. . . . I give you many thanks for your invitation, but at present am in such a distraction that I know not
how to make use of it, we are neyther safe here nor you there,
for it is generally beleeved, but not at court, that the Papists
have designed this & more, many & strong presumptions there
are for it, as gunpowder, & balls & wildfire taken about many
of them, that if they destroy them there are more left behind
to doe the business; send them to Whitehall they are all dis-
missed. Here nothing almost is to be gott that we have not in
possession, bread, bear, meat, all in scarcity & many want it.
The fire broke out vehemently again last night about Shoe
Lane, & as we ghesse about Cripple Gate, but we ghesse by the
smoke that it is well-laid againe. I wish 2 or 3 trunks with you, but
they are at Kensington & I know not how to convey them. . . ."

"Clothworkers' Hall is now on fire but in a fair way of being stopped. Justice Godfrey behaved himself so well at the Temple, that the King would have knighted him, but he refused it, so the King has ordered a piece of plate of 50*l.* for him with his arms upon it, & with ex dono etc. Betty Adams sent this day purposely to us to invite us to her if in distresse, and my Cozen Turbervile sent to proffer men, carts & horses. we are in such a confused condicion that we know not w^t favour of frends to make use of, though we have need of them all." "The very very sad misfortune of poor London is an unexpressable troble to us all," writes Lady Elmes from Stanford; "sure soe sad a sight was nevor seen be foare as that sitty is now lying in ashes, besides the unimmajanable loos the hole kingdom receives buy it." Her own things have suffered much in removal, and those who have paid heavily for having their goods carried into the fields are half provoked when the fire stops short of their houses. Aunt Isham is terrified at the stories that reach her "that there is dayly taking of Men, & some in Woman Clothes with fier bals."

A surveyor's report sent to Sir Ralph states that the fire burnt from 1 or 2 a.m. on the 2nd of September until the 6th, consuming 373 acres within the City walls and 63 acres 3 roods without the walls; 89 parish churches besides chapels, and 13,200 houses were destroyed. Aunt Isham writes of a hurricane near Lincoln in which the wind blew fifty houses over with "Hay-ricks, Corn-ricks & all trees; hailstones fell as big as half-crownes & the inside was like to Butter vele & one had little things like maggets, thes be great Judments, the Lord make every one of us mend one." After describing the desolate look of the country with all the trees torn up by the roots, she says it was "as naked a place as the Citie of London," a surprising expression, until the date reminds us that the letter was written by an eye-witness during the month of the Fire.

CHAPTER ELEVEN

The Squire of East Claydon

IT WOULD have been nice to know the good-natured and incorrigible Edmund, universally known as Mun. His dates were 1636–1688. He was Sir Ralph's eldest son and seemed to have had most of the characteristics his father specially disliked. He was unbusinesslike, untidy and badly dressed; he was much too fat, could not manage his household or anything else, and he had a mad wife. But there was nothing he would not do to help others; so everybody loved him.

"I beeleeve you know that Capt: Blarkes is dead. His company was in Alisbery, & Burnham Hundred, certainly hee died of Fatt, for hee would not bee perswaded to rise early, nor to use much exercise, nor to drinke any thing but New Beere, soe that hee has growne very Bigg, & choaked; the Surgeon assures me all his parts were very sound, & that hee verily beeleeved hee died with Fatt, hee being between 30 & 40 years old. If you know any gentleman that does the very same thing in all points, I wish you could prevaile with him to doe otherwise, least hee kill himselfe by it"; thus did the anxious Sir Ralph preface a moral lecture to his eldest son on his "ill howers, greate Lazinesse and general course of Liveing."

The good-humoured and incorrigible Edmund was wont to join a little grimly in the laugh against himself; "I am weary of this deepe Dirty Country life," he writes on a wet November day, "for want of such a strong Horse as I may depend upon; yea 'tis safer for mee to foot it, then to Ride any Beast of an ordinary Strength, Neverthelesse that is More irksome & dismall to mee, then all the Irish Boggs or Lincolnshire Washes, for I can never Walke, but I sinke so deepe in the Earth (such a heavy Burthen thereof am I growne) that it puts mee frequently in mind of Korah's, Dathan's, & Abiram's Fate: soe that without the Convenience of a very lusty Good Horse, I am like to stick fast in this Ugly Clay."

He is a big, tall man, weighing twenty stone at the age of thirty-seven and growing heavier, but he has a certain air of refinement which marks his foreign training, and a wider acquaintance with the world than the country squires about him. He drinks French wines at home, and is not of those who conclude the evening repast under the table. He acquires a slouching gait as he grows older and stouter, and he can only get on his heavy boots now with "much ado & greate helpe." His tailor is constantly rebuked for not taking sufficiently ample measurements. "My Coate is too scanty in the circumference, a fault a man should not have committed that had ever seen me." He wears a large grey beaver hat with a loop and button on one side, and a knot of ribbons to match the colour of his suit, where the brim is turned up. He orders his "stirrup thredd stockins" from the hosier near St. Dunstan's Church; they are to be of a "bignesse & length wch is greater than ordinary." Mary Verney is tall too, but very slight; we hear of a "black thread bodice she wears at home" and of "ribband Knots for her head of sky collor, or yellow, to go with it." When Edmund wishes to pleasure his wife he has a pair of stockings made for her in "very fine worsted, the colour of scarlet Bow-dye, as good as can be gott. The Feet must be very extraordinary smale, but the Leggs must be very long though very little likewise." He also buys her "a twelve penny Black Orange Necklesse." He is very particular about his sword and "his carabine, his pocket-pistols and screwed pistols," and has a suit of light armour, though the fashion of wearing it has almost gone out. He plays the lute and guitar, and has generally a book on hand; the story of the Siege of Buda, the last French treatise on the Art of War, Mr. Dryden's Verses, besides sermons, political squibs, pamphlets, and News Letters which come down by carrier. On his study table there is "a very little brass mathematicall instrument about the length of a Pen to draw lines with ink, & also an Ebeny Ruler."

He writes excellent letters, keeps copies of them, and dockets those he receives. But while sharing many of Sir Ralph's tastes, he fails where his father excels, in the management of men and in the maintenance of his personal dignity. His disorderly household is the constant theme of local gossip. Nurse Curzon, his head servant, is "old, crazy and decayed, and hath more need to have one to look to her, than to look after others." The village nursemaid has been chosen, in Sir Ralph's judgment, "very unadvisedly, & tis greate odds his child would be changed for one of the Nurse's Sister's children." Every one about him imposes upon his good nature; entangled in a network of debts he puts off or ignores, his rents are in arrears, his horses fall lame, and when the ill-written letters his man sends out in his name are complained of, he replies with a shrug of his broad shoulders, that it is as impossible to make the man a better scribe as to wash a blackamoor white. The lads in his employ turn out no better. "I caused my little boy Thom Warner to be whipped againe this morning for more faults than this sheet will contain, viz picking pockets, opening Boxes that were lockt, picking locks, stealing, lying etc."

Edmund pays Cousin Woodward a visit to arrange for his wife's confinement: "touchant une sage-femme nous parlâmes de cette demoiselle Kent, ce Quaker de Reading, et elle la loue grandement, d'être tres habile dans son art et le mesme faisait aussi la vielle mad^{elle} Woodward, laquelle fut, il n'y a gueres, dans un lieu ou ce Quaker exercoit son office, & elle dit qu'elle n'avoit jamais veue une si cognoissante & adroite sage-femme, et que chascun se croit bien heureux s'il peut l'avoir, & qu'on luy donne 20*l.*, 10*l.*, et au moindre 5*l.*, pour sa peine, & que cette femme ne veut rien prendre des pareins et mareines, & qu'elle ne se mesle jamais à parler de religion a ses patientes, qu'elle eust esté la sage-femmes de la Reine, & que si elle promets de venir qu'elle est parfaitement fidele à sa parole." Edmund finally decides, however, on religious grounds, not to engage the clever Quakeress. Mary is in better spirits when she has a baby to look after, and takes pleasure in the adornment of the cradle and the "peencushion." She wears a "white satin Mantle" for the christening of her little Ralph, a white

satin waistcoat, a white summer gown lined with white silk,
and a white mohair petticoat; there is also a fine white mantle
to lay over the head of the cradle, and a smaller one to match,
to wrap the child in when taken out, or to form a quilt.

But happy days such as these were too soon overclouded, and
Mary's fits of madness made the house at times almost un-
bearable, though in her worst attacks she was more amenable
to her husband's influence than to any other. He was assidu-
ous in his attendance upon her, and was nervously anxious to
conceal her condition from outsiders. When in health she was
gentle and amiable, full of sympathy for her poorer neighbours,
and she was still "my beloved wife," and "my darling Moll";
but at other times his bitterness of soul overflowed in letters
to his father. He is up with her night after night, no soldier in
a campaign gets less sleep, while he complains that he reaps
none of the honour which at least rewards the soldier's toil.
The poor woman takes knives and scissors to bed with her,
and, in default of instruments of offence, swallows her silver
thimble and a piece of glass. She assaults her husband with
blows and kicks, and with a torrent of bad language which
hurts him much more; he is afraid to leave her with her maids
as she might injure them, or with any other man lest he should
use the necessary force with less than the necessary gentleness.
When his father implores him "not to tie himself to so strict
an attendance," he accepts an invitation from Sir John Busby
to go out hunting with him, and to dine at Addington. On his
return he finds the house upside down, the maids crying and
screaming, and his wife's hands bleeding from her successful
efforts to break every pane in the latticed windows. On calmer
days Mary haunts the churches and churchyards, and must
have been no small trial to the preacher on Sundays. When
Mun takes her to Middle Claydon, she waxes restless under
the number of headings to which Mr. Butterfield's texts lend
themselves, and goes out of church, but just as the worthy
divine is reaching the application, she comes in again to wander
round the font and distract the attention of his hearers.

Mun is tormented by the infallible cures recommended
for her; and "would go from Dan to Beersheba to get her ease"

though nostrums abound at his own door. The tenant of the Lawn Farm, Widow Scott, boasts of "a secret powder that sends people to sleep for 3 or 4 days and nights in succession, after which they awake cured." Old Judith is sent for, and her master conjures her to tell him "whether she uses any manner of Charmes Sorceries, or Magic whatever," but she "giving devout assurances to the contrary," is allowed to try her experiment, "which is only the head of a Jack Hare, wrapt in something, & hard bound about the Patient's Head for 3 or 4 days & nights together, and then to be taken off and put into the feathers of a pillow whereon the partie grieved must lye as long as they live." Mun asks "What sympatheticall vertue there may be in a melancholy Hare's Braine to draw away all Melancholie out of that hayre-brained People?" but he adds "it would be very pretty if so slight a thing should cure." The woman desires Mary "should be prayed for during six Sundays successively," and Mun arranges "to send bills to some bychurch remote from all her relations, That a Person of condition who labours sorely under a melancholy distemper desires the prayers of the congretation," but so sensitive is he on this point, that "the partie" is to be nameless.

The children who are "very hopeful" are their father's chief consolation, Ralph (b. 1666), Edmund (b. 1668), and Mary (b. 1675). But as "the two little Esquires" become more and more capable of mischief they add heavily to the burdens of the waiting-gentlewoman as soon as their father is out of sight. Even his threat "to be about their eares when he comes home" fails to secure that they "stirr not abroad without Cosen Bestney's leave."

A sadder widower than Sir Ralph, he has to supply the place of both parents to his little ones. "Mis wants a nupper Coate," his servant writes by his desire to a relation, "and I have heere Inclosed a measure taken by a Tayler. She also wants a Petty Coate or too, and a Copple of frockes, my m^r Understands not the fashones of Coller or stuff Therefore he Leaves those things to you, but he doth not think Silck so Proper for soe Little a Child, and therefore is unwilling to goe to the cost, he soposes Tammy or sum such kind of stuff most fitt for her and

Genteele, my M^r desires you to Enquire what sort of Linen
Sutes such Children ware and send him word." He is very
sensitive to kindness shown his little Molly; she has an "his-
torical pack of cards" sent her as a Christmas present at the
discreet age of four, when Lady Hobart describes her as "handsome & witty," and she is credited with still more severe tastes
at seven years old.

Edmund Verney holds his Court as Lord of the Manor of
East Claydon, and attends the Sessions regularly and the
Assizes. He has generally a law-suit in hand about boundaries
and rights of way with the neighbouring squires, whom he
considers "very malicious & stomachfull," when they disagree
with him. To prevent Mr. Chaloner making "an Inclosure"
he buys up half a yard of land in Steeple Claydon at a high
price, and "the Halfe Cowes Common," that he may be able
to sell it again very dearly, if he should hereafter "find cause to
consent to the enclosure of the Common." He is seen at militia
levies, county elections and race-meetings, and—when he can
find a horse to carry him—in the hunting field. He is a pillar
of the Church, and prosecutes poachers and dissenters, as in
duty bound, but he signs the Presentment of Papists and Nonconformists "very unwillingly, hating to do anything like
an Informer tho' never so legally." He farms some of his own
land at a loss, opposes the importation of Irish cattle with other
squires whose estates are in "the breeding counties," entertains
his neighbours with a lavish hospitality that he can ill afford,
and generally supports the character of a country gentleman
of the period. So absolute are the claims of the most distant
cousins to the hospitality of a country house that when Mun is
unwell himself and has decided not to keep Christmas, he
consults his father as to whether there is any polite way of
declining a noisy party of youths who announce that they are
coming from town to spend that season with him. Sir Ralph
ponders the question, but writes at last "How to put off these
young men is utterly unknown to me."

There is much eating and drinking in Mun's correspondence.
Dr. Denton has a picturesque banquet: "All ye gange was here
last night drinking Sir Ralph's health & preying on a goodly

formidable beast out of ye Fens called a Bustard, wth was more then a whole round table & by standers could devoure, When will Barley yard or Knowle Hill produce such a Beast?" "I pray, good Mun," writes Sir Ralph anxiously, "keepe goode Howers, both for eating & sleeping, & bee very Temperate, for many dye of Pleurisies, after a fit of Good fellowship . . . & the excesses of last Christmas have sent many into another world." Mun agrees: "me semble que le Monde dans ce Temps icy se haste grandement d'aller à l'Autre," but he does not mend his ways; though he is severe upon other people's imprudences: "Lady Hobart might happily spinne out her Thredd of life a long while yet, if she do not cut it off by quality & quantity of Dyet."

This is his account of a Bucks wedding: "I dined at Stow yesterday Nelly Denton & Jack Stewkeley went wth mee: Wee met Sr Harry Andrewes, & his Lady & Daughter his only Child There, as also Cosen Risley & his Lady & Jack Dodington, & 3 Sisters of Lady Temple, & Mr. Stanion, Husband to one of them, & Nedd Andrewes and Grosve his Father in Law, & Thom. Temple & an other old Temple with 3 or 4 Very Drunken Parsons, wch made up our Company, Lady Balting-lasse was invited & promised to be there but ffayled. Wee saw Sr Richard & his ffine Lady wedded, & flung the stockin, & then left Them to Themselves, and soe in this manner was Ended the celebration of his Marriage à la mode, after that, wee hadd Musick, Feasting, Drinking, Revelling, Dancing & Kissing: it was Two of the Clock this Morning Before wee Gott Home." Sir Ralph thought Mun's news "so pleasantly related I have read it over & over."

Sir Ralph exacted in his own house a strictly modern standard of sobriety, but Lady Gardiner, in giving a servant's character, thought it high praise that she "could not hear that Tom was given to drink more then whot natur requiared." In Mun's household, "Nature" always made large demands on the cellar. When John, after his return from the East, owned land in Berkshire, the brothers compared notes: Mun writes: "Y^r Arrabian Deserts as you call Them, are much More Cleanely than our dirty Country, & if you knew our

People here as well as I do, you would ffind Them ffull as Irreligious & Brutish, as y^r People of Wasing, & perhaps more savage then the wild Heathenish Indians, For a Tenant of Myne, an old Man, at an Easter Communion drank up all the wine in the sylver Callice & swore He would have his Peny worth out of it: Being he payd for it. By which you may see what manner of Men wee are in these Parts. I do not Think that among the Infidels, this story can be Matcht."

But in spite of times of depression Edmund took an interest in his country life. He and his wife rebuilt the village inn, which with its high-pitched roof is still so picturesque a feature of East Claydon, with their shield and initials and the date over the door. Vines imported from Blois produce grapes in Sir Ralph's garden and Edmund is laying out "a little Viniard but not to do as Noah did afterwards"; he has a small pack of beagles who turn the kitchen spits when nobler sports fail, and we hear of pheasant-hawking in Runts Wood. He knows every man and boy about the place, visits the old women who are sick, and sees to their funerals.

Like his father, he has a great capacity for taking trouble, and writes numberless letters to get his men places, or to help on the village boys. One of these he has apprenticed, paying 5l. and giving him a good outfit of clothes. "Nedd is so thick-sculled a fellow without any apprehension, & so indoseble, a cook is the easist trade he can think on for him," but he proves "very wavering": "now that Nedd hath bin with Fosket he hath a mind to be a barber, then if he should smell out Will Scott's sweet shop his mind will turn to be a perfumer, & so as oft as he spyes any new trade, whereas God watt his stupiditie will find it a hard Taske to learn one, therefore seeing he is such a Nass, he must be drove to understanding of it—& that if he doth not stick to sum thing he will com to nothing." The master cook suggests that if the boy "can neither write, read nor cast," these three things might be useful to him, and offers to share with the Squire the cost of having him taught; meanwhile the boy refusing to scrape trenchers till his articles are signed, Edmund can only wish that the cook would baste him soundly with his ladle, he must be taught something "be it butcher, cobbler, tincker or gold-finder, . . . if nothing of all this will doe, he must down in the Contry & be doomed to be a perpetuall hewer of wood & drawer of water & so ware a foole's coat & collars if he can yarne it."

When we turn to the comments Edmund makes on public affairs, we find his knowledge of them to be far more intimate than anything Macaulay is willing to allow to the "rustic aristocracy." He discusses with Sir Ralph the campaigns of Louis XIV, the advance of the Turks against Austria, the politics of Denmark and Sweden, the articles of peace with Algiers, the condition of the West Indies, the Levant trade, and our relations with the Dutch, whom he detests. Sir Ralph gets him the latest published map of the seventeen provinces.

The year 1670 opened with the death of Monk, whose name for ten years had been in all men's mouths as the man to help in any crisis: "On Mounday morning my Lord Generall died," Sir Ralph writes to Mun, "& left 1,200*l.* per ann: in land, & 18,000 Pounds in Money besides what the Dutches hath in Plate, Jewellery, & in her Privy Purse. tis beeleeved she will never come out of her chamber, being so farre Gon in a consumption. Hee desired the King to give his sonne after him, the Lord Lieutenancy of Devonsheire, and that hee might bee of his Majesties in his Roome, and enjoy his Lodgings at Whitehall. . . . The King sent a Garter to the Young Duke, as soone as his Father was dead, and will burry him at his owne charge, hee is to lie in State at Somerset House, and there is a committee appointed to consider of all things for the Funerall . . . hee was cured of his Dropsie, but had something like an Anchois growne in one of his Arteries which stoped the Passage of his Blood, wh: the Phisitians call soe many hard names, that I can neither write, nor remember them. Mr. Gape was present when the Body was opened. . . . The Young Duke being married on Thursday last to my Lord Ogles Daughter, & grandchilde to the Duke of Newcastle, is not like to bee so thrifty as his Father. . . . The King, Queen, Duke, & Dutches, have made theire condoling visits to the Widdow Dutches."

The most interesting event of the year 1670 is the arrival of the fascinating Henrietta, Duchess of Orleans. Edmund could not estimate, as we can, the political importance of her visit, but the fame of her goodness, her beauty, and her charm of manner reached East Claydon. "The King," Sir Ralph writes, "sent to invite his sister, Madame, to London; but tis impossible she should come, for she will not yield the Place to ye Dutchesse of Yorke, nor can it bee allowed that the Dutchesse of Yorke should yield it unto her." This difficulty is solved a few days later in Henrietta's favour. "The King & Duke are at Dover with Madame theire Sister, & this morning the Queen & Dutchesse goe thetherwards, to Visit her, all the Towne is gonn, & the Kings Musicke, & Duke's players, & all the Bravery that could bee got on such a sudden. The Dutchesse is to give the Place to Madame in this kingdome, because the Duke of Orleans alwaies gave it to the Duke of Yorke in France." . . . "I heare the King sent the Earle of St. Albans to the K. of France, to get leave that his Sister might stay a few daies longer in England, & that she might come to London, & I beeleeve tis granted, & that they will all bee heere from Dover this Evening or to morrow, for the whole Court is weary of that place. Heere will bee all the bravery & Jollity that England can well afford, & more then will bee payd for, in hast. Just now a friend came in, & tells mee all is crossed againe, & that there is noe leave granted, soe that our Bravery is like to bee at an End, but tis certaine Lady Castlemaine hath farre exceeded all the French Ladies both in Bravery, & Bewty too."

Dr. Denton writes: "The Duchess of Yorke died on Friday, opened on Satterday, embalmed on Sunday & buried last night. I know y^u longe to be satisfied whether Pro: or Pa: of wch ye towne speakes variously. by ye best & truest intelligence she did not dy a Papalina, but she made noe profession or confession eyther way. Her last acts were these, she dined hartily att Burlington house on Thursday before, and that night accordinge to custom she was about ¾ of an houre att her owne accustomed devotions and at her returne from Burlington house she called for her Chaplyn Dr. Turner to pray by her, ye Queen & ye Duke were private with her an hour or more on friday morninge & noe Preest, but Father Howard & Fa:

Patrick were attendinge accordinge to theyr duty on ye Queene in ye next roome. Ye Duke sent for ye Bpp of Oxon out of ye Chappell, who came, but her senses were first gone, in ye meane time ye Duke called 'Dame doe ye know me,' twice or thrice, y^n with much strivings she said 'I' after a little respite she took a little courage & with what vehemency & tenderness she could she said 'Duke, Duke, death is very terrible,' which were her last words, I am well assured that she was never without 3 or 4 of her women soe that it was impossible a Priest could come to her." The Duchess had been nursed with "extraordinary sedulity" by a young maid of honour, Margaret Blagge (afterwards Mrs. Godolphin), who had been from her childhood in the Duchess's service. She sorrowfully contrasted this scene with her own mother's devout death, who "ended her life chearfully, left her family in order & was much lamented." "A princess honoured in power, with much witt, much money, much esteeme, was full of unspeakable tortur & died (poore creature) in doubt of her Religion without the Sacrament or divine by her, like a poore wretch. The dead Duchess none remembered after one weeke, none were sorry for her, she was tost & flung about, & every one did what they would with that stately carcase."

Two years later "the Duke has gone and many Popish Lords with him to meet the new Duchesse at Dover, Crow Bishop of Oxford went to marry them, they come to Whitehall by water, & so there will be no show in the city." Sir Ralph remarks, after Mary of Modena has been a few months in England, that the new Duchess is better looking than he ever thought she would be; and thus is Anne Hyde, the mother of two English Queens, quite forgotten.

In 1672, the Dutch War has broken out, and Edmund is fretted by his own inaction. He had always been attracted by the Navy, and he seemed to know by instinct the names and tonnage of our ships, and their stations. Being very wroth at our naval disasters, and at what he deemed the cowardice and incapacity of our officers; unwieldy as he was, and more likely to sink a boat than to fight her, he suddenly resolved to volunteer. He had spoken to his father on the subject, but he makes an earnest appeal to him in writing; he feels the war a righteous one, and is ashamed to be out of the Fleet now that the Heir-apparent is engaged in it. He remembers the services of his grandfather and his glorious end, and that he was pleased to bestow his own name upon him at his baptism; he would seek deliverance in active service from all that he feels unworthy in his present life, and he earnestly begs his father's assistance in this—a turning-point in his life. But it was a wild project at best, an attempt to wrest out of the hand of Time the years of youth that had slipped away from him, and to the reasonable and unwarlike Sir Ralph it seemed too preposterous a plan for discussion. "Mun, I pray say noe more of your desires to goe into the Fleet, unlesse you have a minde to render mee & your children miserable." To make amends for his curt refusal he writes Mun a longer letter than usual, with all the news he specially cares to hear; he does not think "the Hollander soe easy a bit to swallow" as some do; "the little Victory, a shipp of 38 guns and 250 men was unhappily taken by the Dutch fleet. Capt. Fletcher commanded her & is very ill-spoken of, for hee yielded without shooting one Gunn. . . . Tis beeleeved the Dutch will fight under decks, that is only with cannon, for they want men & are affrayed to lose those they have. . . . Seamen & Watermen are daily impressed, there are 400 Men now sent out of the Guards, to supply the shipps, till the Irish come upp, whom we hear are now landed." There is a further story of the Kent frigate of 50 guns, "lost within 3 leagues of Harwich. The seamen beleeve she was bewitcht, they tell stories of a crow hoveringe over them 2 days togeather in stormy weather &c. only ye captaine & 11 men saved."

The letters meant to daunt Mun's ambitions, only roused them the more, but he bows to his father's will: "je choisirai d'offrir violence à mon genie, et ainsi passer ma vie comme un Faisnéant plus tôt que comme un fils desobeissant"; he pours out his pent-up wrath on Capt. Fletcher, whom he longs to see shot, and then relapses into the ordinary routine of his life in the heavy clay of his native county, "ou je suis empestré parmi mes yvrongues de Paisans."

There was a good deal of paternal government in the cottages, carried out by squire and parson, with a firm but kindly hand. We get glimpses of the village life in Edmund's letters to Sir Ralph.

"Last Satterday Night There Beffell a most sadd and lamentable Accident unto yr Tenant William Taylour, His House is Burnt Downe to the Ground and very little saved that was in it. He Hadd a Calf and a Cow Burnt, this Mischance Happened by Heating of their oven as They conceive. I sent my Man Wood This morning to see in what condition They are, and his children have never a rag to cover them. I sent them in my Cart a ffull Barrell of Beare & Gave Them my Barrell also. This misfortune makes me Apprehend some Mischeif from our Church House, wherein There are ffoure ffamilies That make ffires without a Chimney against wattled walls only Daubed over with Mortar, There is one Common Chimney in the sayd House, but None of Them will use it, because Every One will Be private: yet my ffather-in-law Abell made Them use ffire no where but in their common Chimney, when There were as many ffamilies in the Churchhouse as there are now."

One of Edmund's men sends him "some very good lace" which his daughter has made. He gives the lace-worker a guinea, Betty "makes it up into a cravatt" of the new mode, and he intends to "make himself fine with it at Christmasse."

Edmund rejoices in the detection of the "Cooper who hath stole a great many of the best Pales from Sr William Smith's Park, to make Coopery ware," and of other sturdy vagabonds, "who comes with Dogg & Gunne, Perching, Poching & killing Pheasants in yr Woods & mine. Sir John Busby told me How He committed one Smith of Oakely to the Goale. Twas He that cheated young John Hicks. He is a Very Rogue I believe but whether any thing can be proved against Him sufficient to Hang Him Time must Try, it is sayd That He Hath maliciously Killed a World of Cattle & perticularily above 100 Cowes in the Oakely Parish where He Dwelt with one Eustace a Butcher There, who divided the advantage thereby with Him: it is Reported He Hath stollen Horses too." The rough justice the squires administered sounds

G

harsh to us, but when a servant of Edmund's is ill he can always command "the best the house can afford"; at East Claydon a sick man is moved into the guest-chamber in order to have a fire. In London his footboy "Dick is ffallen sick, and in all liklyhood will Have the smale Pox, I sent Him out of this House yesterday in a Chayre (& that a Sedan) to a Good Nurse-keeper who Tended my Lady Gardiner's Children: my uncle Doctor Denton Hath Been with Him and is his Physitian, if He were my owne Child I could do no more for Him, He shal want for Nothing."

Sir Ralph takes a deep interest in his little grandsons, and keeps one of Ralph's first letters, endorsing it "from Little Master with a basket," when the child sends his "humble dutys" and "A few Puddins."

Ralph at sixteen is to go to Winchester. He is to live in the College; the outfit required is large, and "Gentlemen Commoners wear very costly gownes"; "Kersey's Arithmetic" is one of his books. Edmund had settled to take him: "My Boy Ralph having lost his ague, keepes a great deale of Begging at me to go on Horseback, pretending that he is alwaies sick in a Coach." So the father and son ride from Claydon to Winchester with two servants on horseback. Ralph seems to have been there only two terms, when his father wrote as follows to the Headmaster, whose name is unfortunately not given on the copy kept of the letter dated 5 September 1682: "Sir, I Received yr Civill Letter, for wᶜʰ I Returne you my Very Hearty Thankes, as also for yr paynes about my Sonne & care of Him: I Didd ffully Intend to send Him Back to you (or Mʳ Usher which of you I know not) But Hearing you Gave a very Ill Character of Him Here before a great deale of Company at Table openly at London, Since he left Winchester I Didd not Think it Decent in me to Trouble so accomplisht a Gentleman as you are nor yʳ Schoole with such a Block Head any more, for I Know ffull well, that Ex quorvis Ligno non ffit Mercurius, and am sorry that my Sonne should Be composed of such substance that nothing can shape Him for a Schollar. But it is his ffault and None But His, and the worst wilbe his owne at long Runne, for William of Wickham's

ffoundation is I Beleive the Best Nursery of Learning for
young Children in the World, and perhaps never was Better
provided with abler Teachers then now at this present, yr selfe
for a Master, Mr. Home for an Usher and Mr Terry for a
Tutor. I have another Sonne, whom I ever Designed for
Winchester also. I Do not Despayre But That He may Regaine
the lost Reputation of his Brother, But untill the ill impression
wch my Eldest Hath Left Behind Him in Winton Be utterly
eraced and Worne out, I am ashamed to send Him Least the
impression should prove a disadvantage to Him in yr Schoole.
I understand that my worthy ffreind Dr Sherrock Hath payd
All my Sonne's scores within and without the Colledge in
Winchester. I pray Deliver this Enclosed Letter from my
Sonne to Mr Terry his Tutor and you will oblige yr Humble
Servant Edmund Verney. . . . Things may (I hope) Be so
cleared that his Brother may appeare There with Credit and
Honor Hereafter: if I should send Him." Ralph's note to his
tutor does not suggest that he considered himself in disgrace:
he writes affably as one gentleman to another, and makes a
present to Mr. Terry of his green carpet. Mun was probably
writing under "the horrible smart" from a bad leg which
tormented him in later years, for he shows as much irritability
to little Mun, who had just earned for himself the title of "as
goode a childe as can be" after a visit to his grandfather.

"Childe, I Received a Letter from yr Master Mr Blackwell,
who complaines of you in yr Businesse, & That you are Idely
& Evilly inclined, and particularily That you jointly with
some other, as Badd as yr selfe, Have lately Mischeifed a
Tablet or two of his, and That you Rise in the Nights which
was made to Rest and Sleepe in . . . you Have much Deceived
me, yr ffather, who Blinded with Love to you, Thought you no
lesse then a young Saint, But now to my Greife perceive, That
you are Growing very fast to Be an old Devill." He "designes
forthwith to choose a place for him of extreme severity such as
he had never felt nor seen"; a threat which fell lightly on this
hardened offender, who doted upon his father, and infinitely
preferred his wrath and bluster to Mr. Blackwell's favours.

Mun is anxious to get Molly away from so sad a home,

much as he will miss her, and at eight years old he takes her with him to London. "Tomorrow I intend to carry my Girle to Schoole, after I have showd her Bartholomew Fayre & the Tombs & when I have visited her & a little wonted her to the place, I'll come home." She goes to "Mrs. Priest's school at Great Chelsey," in Mrs. John Verney's chariot with her father, aunt, and brother. She learns to dance gracefully and "to Japan boxes," but more solid acquirements seem to be wholly left to Mrs. Priest's discretion. To Molly he writes: "I find you have a desire to learn to Jappan, as you call it, and I approve of it; and so I shall of any thing that is Good & Virtuous, therefore learn in God's name all Good Things, & I will willingly be at the Charge so farr as I am able—tho' They come from Japan & from never so farr & Looke of an Indian Hue & Odour, for I admire all accomplishments that will render you considerable & Lovely in the sight of God & man; & therefore I hope you performe y^r Part according to y^r word & employ y^r time well, & so I pray God blesse you." To learn this art "costs a Guiney entrance & some 40s. more to buy materials to work upon." Edmund hopes to put her later into the household of a lady of quality, paying her board and giving her a maid, and then to marry her to a country squire of good character and moderate income.

CHAPTER TWELVE

Under Charles II
1675–1683

THE reign of Charles II was—on the surface at all events—a time of coarse wit and loud laughter, of clever talk, of dancing, duelling, dining, theatre-going, card-playing, and horse-racing, and of amusement raised to the dignity of a fine art.

This is Dr. Denton's account of "Beauish Pembroke's" dinner party; he was Lord Lieutenant of Wiltshire and a favourite at Whitehall. "James Herbert lost his cause. Pembroke treated ye Jury, where every one was affraid to sitt next to him, but att last S^r ffr: Vincent did, my Ld began a small health of 2 bottles, wch S^r ffr refusinge to pledge, dashed wth a bottle att his head, & as it is said broke it, they beinge parted S^r ffr was gettinge into a coach & alarm arisinge y^t my Ld was cominge wth his sworde drawne, S^r ffr refused to enter, sayinge he was never afraid of a naked sword in his life, & come he did, & at a passe my Ld brake his sword, att wch S^r ffr Cryed he scorned to take ye advantage, & then threw away his owne sword & flew att him furiously, beate him, threw him downe in ye kennell, nubbled him and dawb'd him daintily & soe were parted. A footman of my Lds followed mischeivously S^r ffr into a boat & him S^r ffr threw into the Thames, two more were cominge wth like intentions, but some red coats knowinge S^r ffr., drew in his defence & I heare noe more of it." A little later "My Ld Pembroke being in a Balcony in the haymarket with other Gent^n, some Blades pass^d by and fired at him but mist him & kill^d another."

A still more outrageous scene is enacted in the room of a lady of quality. "Two exchange women (to whom Lady Mohun owed a bill, and to whom payment was promised with Michaelmas rents, wth wch they seemed satisfied,) after drinking brandy, came with 4 braves to my Lord's lodgings: the women went up, spit in my lady's face &c. the men staid below and cried where is my L^d &c. My Lord at this alarm went upstairs, took his sword & pistol & one of his men the like, and after some passes, shot, miss'd the man but shot thro' his hat; that not doing shot again, but the pistol would not go off: the hubbub increasing they retreated, my lord having rec^d a slight wound on his hand; they were 3 Irish & one lifeguardsman." The guardsman, when wanted by justice, is screened by his officers, though perfectly well known ("one Sutton of Laxington's family"), and takes occasion to beat Lord Mohun's footman next time he meets him. My Lord himself dies of a wound received in a duel the following year.

Sir Ralph rejoices that a tax of twopence a quart is put on wine to pay the King's debts, "for if the People have noe Minde to pay this Tax, let them bee drunke with Ale and strong Beere. I beeleeve Brandy will be forbid, or soe greate a Tax Layd on it that none will import it: for since Labouring men have got a Trick of drinking Brandy, tis evident it hath hindred the Brewing of many hundred thousand quarters of Mault in England."

"The Citizens are most noble feasters." John describes the "Great Wedding made by y^e Widdow Morisco for her Eldest daughter (who had 10, or 11,000$^£$ portion) married to Ald^n Fredericks son & kept at Drapers Hall, the first day there were 600 dishes, & the second & third dayes were alsoe great feasting at ye same charge, And then S^r J^{no} frederick entertained them with 400 dishes, And this day the six Bridemen (for so many there were & six bridemaydes) Entertaine the company. . . . Today is another great Wedding kept at Coopers hall, between Kistings son, & Dashwood (the Brewers daughter) both Anabaptists, I intend to be there in ye evening."

Child marriages, with consent of parents, are still solemnised; Sir Ralph speaks of "a young Wedding between Lady Grace

Grenville, & Sr George Cartwright's Grandson, which was consummated on Tuesday by the Bishopp of Durham; she is 6 yeares old and hee a little above 8 yeares old, therfore questionlesse they will carry themselves very Gravely & Love dearly." . . . "The E. of Litchfield is married to the Dutchess of Cleveland's daughter, who is 11 years old, & the earl 12." Sir Ralph is his trustee.

Sir Ralph hears that "The Kinge is soe delighted with his jorney to nuemarkett, and with the sport a saw there that a is ressoveld to spend the mounth of March att that place and for his better incouradgm^t divers persons of quality did make afore their breaking upp severall maches to bee runn att that time." Dr. Denton describes the amusements that had been so congenial to Royalty: "Neighbour Digby did uppon a wager of 50l. undertake to walk (not to run a step) 5 miles on Newmarkett course in an houre, but he lost it by half a minute, but he had ye honor of good company ye Kinge & all his nobles to attend & see him doe it stark naked (save for a loincloth) & barefoot," and he adds that "the Queen, for a joke in a disguise rid behind one to Newport (I thinke Faire) neare Audley Inne to buy a paire of stockins for her sweetheart; ye Dutchesse of Monmouth, Sr Barnard Gascoigne & others were her comrads. Kate Tate is married to a man of 3,000l. pr Ann: Y^e Queen sent me word^e y^t she did it to justify ye Sultan."

Mun writes: "The King & the jockeys met at supper at Ned Griffin's where were made 6 hare-matches for 500l. a match, to be run at Newmarket next meeting." On another occasion the King "has been hawking in Bucks, but walked soe much, he took cold thereon, soe that he fell ill that very night & was unwilling to be blouded, but severall Physicians coming from town persuaded him to it & likewise to take some Manna . . . he is now said to be pretty well again, which God grant."

Ursula Stewkeley illustrates the manners of a fast young lady of the period. Cary writes to Sir Ralph, her husband being in London: "I wish he had stayed at home, Bot yr sex will follow yr Enclynations wch is not for women's convenincys. I should bee more contented if his daughter Ursula ware not heare, who after 8 months plesure came homb unsatisfied, declaring Preshaw was never so irksome to her, & now hath bin at all the Salsbury rasis, dancing like with Mr. Clarks whom Jack can give you a carictor of, & came home of a Saturday night just before our Winton rasis, at neer 12 a clok when my famyly was a bed, with Mr. Charles Torner (a man I know not, Judg Torner's son, who was tryed for his life last November for killing a man, one of the number that stils themselves Tiborn Club), And Mr. Clark's brother, who sat up 2 nights till neer 3 a Clok, & said, shee had never bin in bed sinc shee went a way till 4 in the morning, & danced some nights till 7 in the Morning. Then shee borrowed a coach & went to our rasis, & wod have got dancars if shee could, then brought homb this crue with her a gaine, & sat up the same time. All this has sophytiently vexed me. her father was 6 days of this time from home, & lay out 3 nights of it, & fryday she was brought home & brought with her Mr. Torner's linin to be mended & washed heare & sent after him to London, where he went on Saturday, to see how his brother Mun is come of his tryall for killing a man just before the last sircut, And sinc these ware gone I reflecting on thes actions, & shee declaring she could not be pleased without dancing 12 hours in the 24, & takeing it ill I denied in my husband's absenc to have 7 ranting fellows come to Preshaw & bring musick, was very angry & had ordered wher they should all ly, shee designed mee to ly with Peg G, & I scaring her, & contrydicting her, we had a great quorill."

The disorderly state of the London streets is constantly referred to. In the winter of 1670 Dr. Denton relates that "betweene 7 & 8 aclock, 5 or more horsmen dogd ye Duke of Ormond, who went home by ye way of Pal-mal & soe up James' Street & just as his coach came to ye upper end thereof, on of them clapt a pistoll to his coachman y^t if eyther he spoke or drove he was a dead man, the rest alighted & comanded him out of ye coach; he told them y^t if it were his money they should have it, soe they puld him out of ye coach, forct him on hors back behind one of them, & away they carried him, my L^d havinge recollected himself y^t he had gone about 30 paces as he ghessed (& as he told me himself for I went yesterday morninge to see him) & finding he was hinmost, his foreman havinge his sword & bridle in one hand, & his pistoll in ye other wrested ye pistoll out of his hand, & threw ye fellow downe, fell with him & upon him, & gott his sword & gott loose of them not wth out some other hazards, one pistoll beinge shott att him & two more fired. He is bruised in his ey, & a knock over the pate wth a pistoll as he ghessed, & a small cutt in his head, after all wch he is like I thank God to doe well. This makes all ye towne wonder, if money had beene their designe they might have had it, if his life, they might have had y^t alsoe. Some think & conjecture only, y^t their malice & spite was such y^t they would have carried him to Tiburne, & have hanged him there. They cannot Imagine whom to suspect for it. The horse they left behind. It was a chestnutt, wth a bald face, & a white spott on his side. He y^t was dismounted gott off in ye dark & crowd." Dr. Denton reminds Sir Ralph, "if Ormond do chance to come to you a byled leg of mutton is his beloved dish for dinner." Sir Ralph Sydenham is known as "the man that loves barley broth."

Mr. St. Amand is attacked in his coach between Knightsbridge and Hyde Park Gate, robbed of two guineas, some silver, and his periwig, and so much injured that prayers are desired for him in Covent Garden Church, where his assailants may well have formed part of the congregation.

Tom Danby, who had married Margaret Eure, was killed about this time in a London tavern "by one Burrage, an affront at least, if not his death," being planned beforehand. Mun Temple in a similar brawl was knocked on the head with a bottle, and died of his injuries. Sir Ralph had to use all his interest to save Will Stewkeley from the consequences of a drunken quarrel in which a man was murdered, though not by his hand, and he had to retire to Paris for a time. Duels are of daily occurrence: John's letters to Mun are full of them. Mr. Scrope, sitting by Sir Thos. Armstrong at the Duke's playhouse, struck him over the shins twice; both men wished to speak to "Mrs. Uphill, a player, who came into the house masked. The gentlemen round made a ring, and they fought, Sir Thomas killed Scrope at the first pass; not the first man he had killed, said the bystanders." The sudden quarrels between intimate friends that end fatally are most startling. Sir William Kingsmill's cousin, Mr. Hazelwood, "came of a visit to see him, they fell out, & it ended in yᵉ death of Mr. Hazelwood, nobody was by but only them two; tis to be hoped yᵗ his sister being at Court may help to save his life."

Lord Cavendish and Mr. Howard disagree about some proceedings in the House; Lord Cavendish sends a challenge which Mr. Howard, being sick of the gout, cannot take up at once, and my lord posts him at Whitehall Gate for a coward and a rascal; it needed the combined efforts of King, Lords, and Commons to put an end to this absurd quarrel. Young Lord Gerard, aged fourteen, takes his mother to see New Bedlam; the drunken porter and his wife are insolent to him, whereupon the lad draws his sword and "runs the porter into the groin"; the rabble fall upon Lord Gerard and nearly pull him to pieces, thrust him into prison, and then break the windows to come at him again. The Lord Mayor rescues him and shelters him in his house all night. Meanwhile the Countess of Bath driving past "has her coach broke to bits & her footman knocked down, being taken for Lord Gerard's Mother." The plucky boy rouses one's sympathy, but there are worse stories than these.

John Verney writes of Cornet Wroth, who dined with Sir Robert Viner at his country-house, "and after dinner going an airing with him, drew a pistol on his host, and having six or eight troopers to assist him, carried off Miss Hyde in a coach, a wheel broke and he laid her across a horse, and rode off to Putney ferry where he had a coach and six; the country was roused and the girl was recovered speechless, but the gallant Cornet escaped." Some of the doings are tragic, some merely foolish. John tells Mun how "a Quarrell happened at Islington Wells, and swords were drawn, but noe blood, & indeed the falling out between 2 friends was soe silly, that it lookt like an agreement between 'em beforehand. I was present at the sport, which happened in a room where were at least 30 Ladyes very much frightened & most of 'em underfoote, soe that there was fine speaking and squeeling for a minute or two." Edmund relates "a pleasant Passage that Happened t'other day in Barkshire: viz my Ld. Ch. Just: Scroggs Being upon the Roade in his Coach, two Gentlemen on Horseback overtooke Him, and perceiving Him a sleepe, One of Them sayd to the Other I will Rowse Him with a Trick: and so Having Such a Baston in his hand as I use to Ride with, smote the Toppe of his Coach with it mighty Violently, & Cryed out with a Loud Voyce A Wake Man severall Times, and so Galloped away with speed."

There were problems enough to occupy the minds of thoughtful men: the price of food was rising, and the poor were sinking into deeper poverty. Sir Matthew Hale, amongst others, was occupied with a scheme for giving work to the unemployed, when he died on Christmas Day, 1676. Edmund writes: "That incomparably Learned & upright Man & Just, Judge Hales it seems is dead to us, & gone without question unto a better Place, though He will be more missed then any man in England except His Majesty, for he hath not left his fellow behind him. Therefore I cannot choose, but condole a Losse so considerable & universall to my Country, for the Newcastle Duke & Lady Duras & Latimer's still-born sonne, They are nothing to you or I, or any Body Else besides a few private friends of their owne. My Cosen Greenfield of Wotton I heare is Dying also & that signifies as little, & so the death of Cuff Emerson is as inconsiderable, he was father to young Mistress Hide's husband & lately died of the small-pox."

In the summer of 1677 Mun was seriously ill in London; as soon as he could be moved he went with Sir Ralph and John to the Stewkeleys. "Preshaw Ho. puts me in mind of the loaves & fishes," writes Dr. Denton, "it increases & Multiplies with the company." Lady Smith had arrived with two daughters, a chaplain, two maids, three in livery, and six horses; "if rightly informed there was but one guest-chamber & how to provide roome for 65 is next to Miracilous. I doubt not of the mirth & entertainment, but I am sure I could not be contentedly merry in any crowd." Lady Gardiner is so happy in the good company of her brother and his sons, "which made up a most pleasant harmony," that when they leave her, she writes: "Our naighbours lament our soden chang, for all heare looks like the novesis when thay put of ther gorgeous cloths, and put on ther nun's habits." Sir Roger wrote one of his affectionate letters, inviting Sir Ralph and his sons "once more to come together & visit poore Wroxall, where I think to spend a good part of the next summer if we are not by some cross providence prevented"; he was staying with Daughter Guyon at Yeldham on his way to Sutton for the winter. He is very unhappy at the conduct of public affairs, which has left "the enemie at liberty to come & cut our throats at our very doors."

A new figure appears in the letters this autumn; William of Orange arrives in England, and has been with the King at Newmarket; and with the Royalties "incog. to the revels at Lincoln's Inn." Dr. Denton writes: "Ye match wth Lady Mary & ye Prince was Concluded last Sunday night; on Munday ye Councill, Ld Maior, &c went to congratulate her, & y^t night of Bells & Bonfires good store. . . . Dr Lloyd of St. Martins goes wth Lady Mary for some few months to settle her chappell. A Greeke church hath beene long a buildinge in St. Giles feilds, it goes on slowly."

The old jealousy of a standing army is warmly expressed, yet when troops are wanted for the war with France in 1678, Edmund writes: "The Drums beat up last Saturday at Alesbury for Volontiers, but not a man came in to list, altho' they might have been under [Capt.] Wisedome's conduct, whereby it playnely appears, the spirit of the nation is down, or elce we are not the Men we fancy ourselves to be, for I have heard Many say if we had war with the French that vast Multitudes would go against them, but for my part I see no such thing, if people in other parts of Eng^d are as backwards as in our Country & Wallingford where I myself frighted most of the young fry into Holes & Cellars, with only walking up & down the streets, being taken for a Presse-Master. If there is a shower of blood at Orleans, it is a sign of Much Effusion of Blood in France, those prodigies sent from Heaven never come in vaine."

"I think Collonel Legg Hath made a good Choyce in Crad-

dock the Butcher for a Captaine in his Regiment. I know the
Man and Have sene Him ffight Prizes, He is a stout Man and
a Neat Gamester: when I am a Collonell I will also Choose
my Master Druse a Gladiator of Alisbery, who Hath ffought
with Craddock and Worsted Him, for one of my Captains."
He laments that "the overflowing scum of our nation is listed"
and that "the better sort of Men will not come in voluntarily
unless they like their officers very well. In Northamptonshire
men come in pretty thick to be enrolled under Lords Brian &
Peterborough. Capt. Wisedome can get none at Ailesbury but
'Gaolbirds, thieves & rogues'."

Edmund has no doubt that he could raise "both Horse &
Foot for his majestie's service as good men number for number
as any he hath"; he is willing to serve "provided he has his
own terms not otherwise." When the troops are paid off the
following year there is still more discontent. "The troopers
of Buckingham were disbanded by Sir John Busby, Sir Harry
Andrws, my old Cozen Stafford & Captain Lovett. My L^d
Latimer was also there & the Troopers were extremely angry
with him & swore they would never serve under him again,
nor fight for King Charles & a many of them sayd they would
robb, for home they durst not goe. The King & Dukes Guards
15 in number that passed & repassed here the other day carryed
the money to pay them off. Theyr fire armes are sent up to
London by one Webb a caryer." The men are selling their
"very good buff belts for 18^d a peece." "I never remember
this country so infested with rogues as it is now, last Thursday
3 or 4 of them stood with theire swords drawne in my Ridge
way wch leads to Buck^m, they were on foot yet very fine in
apparell & had Cloakes . . . they meant to robb H. Scott's
house but the market-folkes passing theire hearts failed them.
. . . I Heare Sr John Busby Doth ffancy Himselfe a great
Commander, Having Gott two smale ffeild peices of about 3
inches Bore, wch were Sr Anthony Cope's, and are to be
discharged often against Stow & Claydon: These are Thunder-
ing Peeces of Mortality wch Do no wayes affright nor can
possibly Daunt Y^r most affectionate Kinesman & Servant,
Edmund Verney."

No two figures in the society of the Restoration could be more typical of the old influences and the new than Sir Ralph Verney and his ward Lord Rochester.

Anne, widow of Henry Wilmot, 1st Earl of Rochester, had been accustomed to depend upon Sir Ralph for advice ever since her first marriage with Sir Francis Henry Lee of Ditchley. When her second husband died (in 1659) she claimed his services as guardian to her boy of eleven; and for her sake he had filled a difficult and thankless post. The names read strangely in conjunction, the grave Sir Ralph with his austere morality and fastidious tastes, and the handsome young peer, courtier and poet, with his wild genius, defying all authority human and divine, "for five years together continually drunk," leading the mad revels at Court, or practising physic as a mountebank on Tower Hill, with equal "exactness & dexterity." Sir Ralph had been summoned in haste by the Dowager on the occasion of "my sonne Rochester's suden marage with Mis Mallet, contrary too all her frinds' exspectation. The King I thank god is very well satisfyed with it, & they had his consent when they did it—but now we are in some care how too get the estate, they are come too desire too parties with frinds, but I want a knowing frind in busines, such a won as Sr Raph Varney—Mas: Coole the lawer & Cary I have heare, but I want one more of quality too help mee."

Old John Cary still transacts their business; he writes, when Sir Ralph is invited to Rycote, "I pray do not thinke of trouble to my Lord Norreys, for he will be very glad of your company & bidd you very wellcom, & so will his good Lady: You catch me with a why-not still: Indeed my memory growes bad, very bad, & things go out as fast as they come into my head now, I am walkeing (as well as others) apace towards the land of forgetfullness & cannot help it, it must be—Happy are those who are fit for that day."

Fourteen years of a wild life had followed his marriage, but Lord Rochester's reckless self-indulgence had been unable to quench his lovable qualities, and those about him accepted his repentance with eagerness when "he came to himself."

In 1680 he is very ill, and is advised to drink ass's milk. Sir Ralph is, of course, to find the ass. Mr. Cary writes: "I much feare my Lord Rochester hath not long to live, he is here at his lodg & his Mother my lady dowager & his lady are with him, And doctor Short of London & doctor Radcliffe of Oxon. Himselfe is now very weake, God Almighty restore him if it be his will, for he is growne to be the most altered person, the most devoute & pious person as I generally ever knew, & certainly would make a most worthy brave man, if it would please God to spare his life, but I fear the worst, at present he is very weake & ill. But what gives us much comfort is we hope he will be happy in another world, if it please God to take him hence, And further what is much comfort to my Lady Dowager & us all in the midst of this sorrow is, his Lady is returned to her first love the protestant religion, And on Sunday last received the Sacrament with her lord, & hath bin at prayer with us, so as if it might please God to spare & restore him, It would altogether make upp very great joy to my lady his mother & us all that love him."

"He is like to dye," Sir Ralph writes; "his mother watched with him last night; he hath been a most penitent and pious man in this sicknesse."

A week later Mr. Cary reports that "My lord we hope is on the mending hand, but many changes he meets withall, pretty good dayes succeed ill nights, which help to keep upp his spirits, but he is very weake, and expresses himselfe very good, I hope God will spare him for his owne service for the future."

"My lord Rochester continues very weake, he is sometimes a little lively & gives good hope of his recovery, but anon downe againe, which makes us much to feare the worst." A week later he is dead; his young widow and "my little Lord," the last of his line, follow him to the grave before three years are out; and Sir Ralph lives to see his very name granted to another.

Shaftesbury's success in getting up petitions to the King to allow Parliament to meet, drew forth a host of counter petitions, expressing abhorrence of the design to force the

King's will. The address of the Town of Wycombe "presented by Dr. Lluellyn to his Maj^tie at Windsor upon Bartholomew day 1681," is a type of the abject loyalty and the flowery language of the Bucks Corporations. They speak of "the late defeated Politicians," as "disappointed of their dark designments by y^r Majestie's profound wisdom & divine prevision," and protest that "wee have alwayes detested & rejected them, togeather with their now exploded scanty & forsaken abettors. We have ever incerted o^r loyall selves amongst the resolutue, grave, & deliberate p'sons. And wee doe most highly applaud the stout fidelios, the strenuous, brisk and valiant youth of this your now much undeluded nation. We therefore, Yo^r Mat^ies most dutyfull & most devoted subjects entirely p'fesse: That we will to the utmost stresse of o^r sinews, to the latest gaspe of our lives, & the last solitary mite in o^r coffers adhere to your Matie. . . . Many have out stript us in the wing but none shall exceed us in theire wishes; we envye much their more earley apply, but none shall ever appeare more faithfull . . . God preserve yor Matie from all rebellious Machinacions. Amen."

The King repaid this adulation by an attack on the municipal charters, which placed the representation of the boroughs in his hands. The names of the Petitioners and Abhorrers were soon changed into those party titles which have lasted to the present day. Two years later Mun writes: "Tho: Smith went with Cosen Denton to Holson Race: where There Happened a Contest Betweene Wigg and Tory, the Later would not contribute to the Plate in case the Duke of Monmouth Didd Runne for it, and the Wigges offered to Make up the summe for it, in case the Toreys would not."

When Shaftesbury is tried, Dr. Denton writes: "Our friend Sr W. Smith is of this grand jury, where you know his pregnancy of parts will justly entitle him to be *Dominus fac totum*."

The Rye House Plot again disturbed the peace of the kingdom and cost two lives. Close to the lodgings where Betty Adams stays when she is in town, a scaffold is being erected "right against the Marquis of Winchester's House, where the wrestlings are used to be in Lincoln's Inn fields," upon which Lord Russell must suffer on the morrow. And so closely do tragedy and comedy jostle each other in this unhappy time, that while Algernon Sidney is being tried for his life, some mad court ladies, "The Lady Mary Gerrard, & others, had a frolic to putt on men's aparell, & walke the streets attended with some Gentlemen. In Leicester fields they mett wth a fidler, & I know n^t on what provications, but ye poore man was killed amongst them, tis said they are in ye Gate house."

John writes a few days later: "Here is no newes but that Coll. Sidney is to morrow to dye & tis said ye Whiggs have talkt him out of his life by talking the plot to be at an end & no more should dye for it." He writes again when the deed is done: "On Friday Coll Sidney was beheaded on Tower Hill, he dyed a great hero, shewing all the Indifferency Immaginable, he made no Speech, but delivered a paper to Sheriff Daniell (which he hath given to his Majesty, but tis said twill not be printed), He made a very short prayer to himselfe, & was beheaded at one stroke, before the horse Guards came, who were all with ye foote Guards, ordered to encompass the scaffold, & I think the foote Guards were but just on the hill." "He met death with an unconcernedness that became one who had set up Marcus Brutus for his pattern."

CHAPTER THIRTEEN

The Highwayman and the Undergraduate
1655–1688

IT IS said that the romance of the road was buried with Claude Du Val in 1670; when, having been "hanged a convenient time," he was conveyed to his grave by persons of quality, with a fashionable train of the weeping fair, and laid under a white marble stone curiously engraved with the Du Val arms, in the middle aisle of St. Paul's Church, Covent Garden.

The Verney letters offer little enough of romance in the life of a gentleman turned highwayman; and he was likely to spend more of his days in dunning his friends from a stifling cell in Newgate, than in galloping over breezy commons, or lying in wait for dowagers' coaches in tortuous lanes. There were doubtless brave spirits, who, in a simpler age, might have "stopped the mouths of lions," or, in our own, would have found vent for their energies in African deserts, or in Arctic snows; but like Dick Hals, weary of risking their lives in being defeated by the Dutch, and sick of waiting for arrears of pay, they threw themselves into reckless and desperate courses, making war against a society which had refused to receive them as allies.

Even the sensible and prosaic John Verney felt his blood stirred by tales of their valour and resource. "A couple of highwaymen," he writes in 1679, "having robbed a country-man & leaving him his horse, he pursued 'em with hue &

cry which overtook them, but they being very stout fought their way through Islington & all the road along to this town's end, where after both their swords were broke in their hands & they unhorsed, they were seized & carried to Newgate. *T'is great pity such men should be hanged.*"

The Verneys were not behind other persons of quality in owning relatives among these gentlemen of the road; and the correct and austere Sir Ralph did his best to get his highwaymen cousins out of scrapes. He gave them money; lent his wig, even, on occasion, to assist in a disguise and an escape; and used all his political and social influence to procure reprieves and pardons. Lady Hobart, living among the Judges, in the high places of law and order, threw her sympathies into the same scale, helping with all her might to baffle justice, and to promote adventure.

Whatever might be public opinion about the highwayman's career, his sentence never failed to evoke a burst of compassion. A rowdy gathering of good fellows accompanied him to the foot of the gallows, and laughed at the devil-may-care courage with which he met his doom; kind women, like Frances Hobart, shed hot tears of wrath and pity over his execution, while they prayed Heaven to have mercy upon his soul.

On less tragic occasions, those who had not themselves been robbed or frightened treated the adventures of their friends as a good joke; and a man like Colonel Henry Verney, when charged, half in jest, with an attack made on his old uncle's coach, was in no hurry to clear himself of an accusation conveying a distinct compliment to his pluck and horsemanship. Men applauded just as heartily when a traveller of unwonted courage stoutly defeated the gentleman who meant to rob him; in short, the risks of the road gave rise to a number of capital stories which had this spice about them, that the man who in his armchair laughed at the highwayman's audacity and the traveller's alarms, did so with the strong probability of having to experience both, the next time that his occasions called him abroad.

"Richard Dawson, whose family intermarried with the descendants of Mary Verney and Robert Lloyd, is remem-

bered for the courage with which he and his servant Christopher
Fogwen successfully fought the highwaymen that infested
Kennington Common and the neighbourhood. Mr. Dawson
and Kit were famous characters in their day. They would
sometimes drive out disguised as old ladies, in bonnets and
veils, and, when attacked, would rush out at opposite doors,
take their assailants in the rear, handcuff them, put them into
the coach, and drive off in triumph with their captives."
Mr. Dawson was worth robbing, being as wealthy as he was
capable and determined. He was at the head of the Vauxhall
glass-works, established under the patronage of the Duke of
Buckingham in 1670.

In 1657 Dr. Denton's coach was stopped on the highway
by "St. Nicolas Clarks . . . who rob'd him and his Lady."
The whole family cracked their jokes upon the Doctor;
Lady Hobart hears that "he has recruted his self of Hary
and others at play; let him tack heed he be not met with
agan." Sir Roger Burgoyne tells them that if they will but
undertake a journey to Wroxall, he will secure them from
such kinds of vermin, and return them laden with thanks
into the bargain. "When you see the doctor let him knew,
I goo nowhar but I met with his news," writes Lady Hobart,
"and never any man was so lafed at, for ever body macks
mearth at it: tis said he knos the thefs, and my ant Varney
vows Hary Varney one, and mayd por Pen mad; let him
knou what a repitason he has with hur." Good Nat is sarcastic.
"You doe well to make yourself merrie with the storie which
goes of my cosain Hary Verney; it seemes he is pleased with it
too, but I am persuaded he would have liked the money
better then the jest."

Frank Drake is coming to pay Sir Ralph a visit. "We
shall take it as a favour if you please to account us so farr
strangers uppon the Way, as to send a Guide about nine
aclock to the George in Alsbury, to direct us the best way
for the coach by my cosen Winwood's gronds, or any other
cleane way to Claydon, and my wife particularly intreats
you if my cosen Harry Verney be at home that you will shutt
him up, for fear he meet with us as the Dr. was mett with,

for whose Lightnes I am very sorry." "Harry is heere," Sir Ralph replies, "and I will shutt him upp for once, but for future Clapps, looke to yourselves for hee is a dangerous fellow, and wherever hee thinks any money may bee had, you know a protection will not be within my power."

Each neighbourhood had its own legends of highway robberies; Bucks abounded in them, and Fuller has preserved for us a proverb of the county, "Here if you beat a bush, it's odds youl'd start a Thief." An adventure in Buckinghamshire lanes befell Sir George Wheler. He was courting a beautiful young heiress, Hester Harman, who eventually refused him, and accepted Alexander Denton. When Sir George recalled in later years how he had been saved from the thieves who sought for him, he never omitted to thank Heaven that he had failed to gain the wife whom he had sought.

This was, however, a later development; at the time of his ride through Bucks, "in the summer of '72 or '73," he carried about his person a jewel of great price to be given to the fair Hester, as well as a gold watch, 20 golden guineas and some silver; he had providently bargained that if he himself were to be rejected the jewel might be returned; in either event it was important that he should not be relieved of it by the way.

Sir George Wheler had spent some days with his tutor at Lincoln College, Oxford; and was sensible, he says, "of the risque I were Like to Run in my Return to London.

"To conceal the Time of my Return I knew was scarce possible among so much acquaintance; all that I could was to conceal the way I designed to Returne which I did, ffor I went downe the town as to goe by Beconsfield Road but as soon as I was out of East Gate turned Nor'wards, and went to Sr. Ralfe Varney his house in Buckinghamshire, where I was kindly entertained all night. Sir Ralfe Varney was a worthy and ingenious Gentleman, I came to be acquainted with him at my Uncle Dentons, where I frequently met him.

"The next day Sr. Ralfe obliged me to stay and dine with him, and Staying after Diner too long, night overtook me before I could reach Alsbury. Within a mile or two of this town I came into a deep and narrow Lane, covered over with the trees in the hedges, so close that I could see neither way before me, nor skie above me, nor anything about me. Having Pistols before me, I drew one and held it in my hand, So that I could Span it in a moment for ffear of a surprise. I was not, I suppose, above half way down this Lane but on a suddain two or three men cald out Stand! Stand!! Stand!!! ffearing them to be Robbers I Blustered also &c., til we came to a Parly, and I demanding what they would have, they told me they were the watch sent to Stop all Passengers, ffor that there had been Robberies committed that Day upon Uxbridge Common; That every body had been Robbed that past that way from nine or ten in the morning til one or two in the afternoon, which was the time I should have bene there from Beconsfield had I gone that Road. So I desired these men to conduct me to the towne and shew me the best Inne, and I would Reward them."

John writes: "Last night about 6 miles from London the Dutch mail was robb'd by 2 men, who gott a purchase of 10,000*l.* in gold and Jewells, the letters are allmost all lost. There was one Passenger rode with the Post Boy, and a Trooper was so kind as to accompany them, but not to defend them. Sir Robt. Knightly and his son in the day time last weeke was robb'd just by his country house, by 3 highway men, who commanded them out of his Coach; and tooke neither Rings nor Swords but money, they were very well mounted. One of his servants, a woman, lookt on all the while and thought they had been of Sir Robert's friends. They calld him by his name, his and his son's loss was about 5*l.*"

When we turn from highwaymen in general to the special worthies belonging to the Verney family, we find two cousins, Hals and Turville, who earned the crowning distinction of the gallows; they were both connected with that strong woman "ould Lady Verney," mother of the Standard-bearer. Richard Hals was Sir John Leeke's grandson, and nephew to Anne Hobart and Dorothy Leeke. Robin Turville had served with Sir Edmund Verney the younger, and Fred Turville claimed cousinship at Claydon; Sir Ralph writes for him to his trustee, "John Ashburnham to the care of Capt. John Walterhouse, governor of Garnsea Castle," about some money Turville wants to spend "to put him into a capacity to live. I heare hee hath been represented unto you under a very ill carracter, & soe hee was to me, which made mee the more narrowly observe him, & truly I must needes doe him soe much right as to assure you, that since I knew him, I could never justly Tax him with any manner of crime or vice, and yet hee hath spent some part of his Time in my owne house, and my Cozen Natt Hobart's, & with other of my neare friends, where hee hath gayned much Love and affection, & had hee misbehaved himself, I must have heard it." Turville did not justify this good opinion; just after the Restoration, Sir Ralph is concerned to hear "how matters went with Fred Turville at his triall, for really I should be very much troubled if hee should suffer, but his own groundlesse confidence made him too carelesse, & may cost him deare."

He escapes on that occasion, but a few years later we learn his fate amongst other sensational items of family news sent by Edmund from East Claydon to John at Aleppo; "Cosen Jack Temple, Sir R's Brother, was tryed for having fourteen wives at once, and escaped the gallows. I think I have sufficiently spoken of marriages. Now for hanging, which also goes by destiny according to the opinion of some. My cosen, Fredd Turville was hanged at Hertford for burglary, and other crimes. But I'll speak no more of such ignominious ends, though these ensuing may be as deplorable; for my cosen Thom: Danby was basely murdered in a tavern in London by one Burrage; Cosen Reade killed in France; Cosen A. Temple, lieutenant in a ship of war was slayne before Algiers," etc., etc.

Frances Hobart, who had a special place in her heart for the black sheep of the family, refers to the catastrophe in a very different tone, in writing to Sir Ralph Verney: "I receved a letter from my poor coussin Frederick Turville the day before he was executed, where he made a request to me to send you this inclossed which he did ernestly desire might be conveyed safe to your hands. I know you have had soe much kindness for hime that I fear his death has given you some troble, for though he was guilty of many crimes in his

Life, yet he died as we are informed a very good christion, with a most undanted corage showd nothing of conserne at all, but told all thouse persons that where with hime at the place, which where divers gentlemen of great quallity, that he did not fear to die, but the manner of his death trobled hime; he aded that he would not troble them with a formal speech only desired there prayers, and after he hade read some prayers which he hade in wrighting he weept, and made noe confestion there, he told them he hade don that to God, he died a chatholick, he had a priest with him a weeke, who wrought a great reformation in him. Noe gentleman was ever more lamented both by his friends and strangers, only by thouse barborous unclles that did make it apeere by there jingling proceedings that they designed his death all along, which I beleve will light hevie upon them; and Walker with his servants declar it was their will he should die; and for his sister it ware to tedious to tell how unnaturall she had bine. He expressed some troble that in all the time of his affliction she never once came or sent to him; it is too late to wish, but sertainly had you bine in town I doe verily beleve he had never come to this, but there was an ill fate hung over him, for there was many designes for an escape, but he neglected them. . . . They did not take any care at all for his buriale, but that woman that was continually with him till his death did bury him in the church yard. I know not what she is, but never any woman had a greater kindness for any man than she, and has spent all she has, and sold all to her skin for him. Sir I have dwelt too long upon this unpleasing subject which I biceech you pardon."

Of Dick Hals we know much more, as he lived on terms of intimacy with his Claydon cousins, especially with Edmund Verney, who was about his own age. His father, Captain William Hals, made his will in 1637. Having returned but two years before from a West Indian voyage of great danger and suffering he was "bound forth" once more on his perilous way. He took with him a good part of his personal estate "as an adventure, in hope to improve the same, having divers debts due to him in the Ilands of the West Indies." He bequeathed his "plowland of Ballymore" and his lease of "the two plowlands of Juthimbathy," both in the county of Cork, "and the stock of some reasonable value thereon," to his "deare and well-beloved wife Bridget, and that young and tender child whom it hath pleased God but lately to bestow upon me." When we next hear of them, the sea-captain has died "in his shipp." The "well-beloved" Bridget has married again, and the boy is in England for education, where Doll Leeke, his guardian, lavishes upon him what little cash she receives as Lady Gawdy's gentlewoman, and all a maiden aunt's wealth of devotion. He ingeniously defeats her efforts to make him work in any profession, but in his nineteenth year she writes triumphantly to Sir Ralph, "My nefew has put on his gowne. I thought it had bin only discours and not a reall intension." He replies, "'Tis true your Nephew hath at last put on his gowne, but I beleeve 'twill come off againe much easier, or I am much mistaken in the Humour of the man."

Sir Ralph's forebodings were justified. Doll writes to him six months later: "My sister Hobart sends me word you will lay out ten pounds for Dick if he can get a plas, I give you humble thanks for it, I shall not fail to pay it . . . the pore boy has been willing to save his Mother's credett, tho' he has left himselfe in the lurch, and to the Charity of his frinds hear, He lost his time extremely while he was with his mother, and spent his twenty pound a year. The Master that I sent him to, gave a very good Carractur of him, and sence you are plesed to take notis of him, I pray obledg me so much, if you know of any lawer or aturney that wants such a servant, that you will asist him in the procuring of it. Reallie he was a very good conditioned youth, and can write 2 or 3 good hands."

"I find by my sister you have layed out some monies for Dick, I shall not fail to see it payed, as sone as I receve it. I am sorry we should give you such a trouble, but it is the fate of nedy peopel to opres ther frinds . . . it trobles me very much that Dick can get no preferment, I cannot endure to think he should goe back to his mother (in Ireland), whear he has lost so much time allredy, I had rather he wear a souldier, which is the worst of all professions. I have filled the paper therefore should think of a conclusion, but I fancy myself with you all this time and that is so great a plesur that I forget it is but a fancy."

In the spring of 1663 Aunt Doll comes once more to the rescue. "You see the condision of pore Dick Hals," she writes to Sir Ralph, "if I healp him not his life may be lost upon that accunt, which wold give me a very great troble." The shiftless boy who was idling about the Law Courts in 1656 had taken a long step in his downward career by the time this letter was written to Mun Verney:

"Sir, Since it was my unhappinesse to returne into England soe much contrary to your advise, I was unfortunately betrayed to the Master Keeper of Newgate and sold for 100*l.* by a tretcherous frind in February last, where I have ever since remained in Irons. I cannot express with what joy I should kisse your Hand should you vouchsafe to visit mee, which if you should please to thinke mee worthy soe greate a happinesse, you might not bee seene to come to the prison, but to the Fountayne Taverne by St. Sepulchre's Church, and send one of the drawers to the Keepers, and they will bring mee to you. Sir herein you would make mee infinite happy. I knowe not howe it may goe with mee, but my Life is in much danger but till I see you I shall be silent. . . . You may send for mee by the name of Captain Granger, for by that name I am known in prison. I lye on the Master's Side in Newgate."

In 1666, Richard Hals has found an outlet for his energies more worthy of his father's son; he thanks Mun for innumerable kindnesses, and tells him that he is "once more in a fayre way, eyther to intreate or force fortune to bee my frinde, I meane I am gott on board the Revenge. I have waighted both on the Duke and Prince. The Duke hath promised me that the next councell of warr shalbe for my good. I hope hee wil be his words' master. Our Flage men doe really beleve that the Dutch will ingage in the beginninge of June. Pray God send itt prove true. . . . We shall have but 80 sayle this summer to fight the Dutch, the rest are designed for the western station to keepe the French Privaters in awe. . . . We shall sett sayle for the Downes within six dayes."

He gives Edmund an account of their engagement with the Dutch, which had lasted from a Friday to a Monday night. "It was oure fortune att first to be out of the fight, our ship beinge one of Prince Rupert's squadron and bound to the Westward; on Sunday afternoone we came in and did the best we could to se the ende of itt. The Dutch had notice of our fleetes dividing, by two dogger boats they keept on the outside of the Goodwin Sands, our fleete then riding in the Downes, there could be noe hiding our intentions from them. The Duke was not above 46 sayle when wee began, the Dutch were 90 besides 16 fresh shipps that on Sunday came out of Flushinge. When we joyned with the Duke he had lost some shipps, the Prince Royall, the Swiftsure, the Essex, the Bull, the Ouverture [?], the Eagle, the Loyall George; besides many others that were soe farre disabled in their masts and rigginge, that they were forced to leave the fight soe that when the Prince joyned with the Duke, wee could not make above fiftie sayle, most of them not fitt to ingage . . . yett did wee continue to doe our duties to the uttermost of our abilities." "The Dutch for ought I could see were as willinge to leave fightinge as ourselves which was enough. The gasett will informe you what commands we have lost, whereof I must needs lament one, Sir Xopher Mynns, hee dies so much like a man, that he lyes more the subject of envy then pitty. Lord Admirall Harman lyves too as much honoured as the other died."

Dick Hals sends Edmund his journal written on board the "Loyall Colchester," from 19 July to 14 August 1666. "I have adventured to send your worship a breife account of my last viage and ingagement, in the most seamanlike tearmes my small travell in that art would furnish me with" —it is chiefly a log of wind and weather.

He has reached London, and acknowledges Edmund's letter of 21 November, "in which you generously condole the losses of our navy by sea, I hope we shall regaine our lost flags and honours next springe. . . . I am tryeing to gett an

imploy. Pray God send me good lucke. I have lardge prom-
isses but noe sure ground as yett. I want frends to stirr a little
for me."

"I find the maine stopp of both my biussnesses," Dick Hals
writes to Sir Ralph, "to be want of money to the clarkes att
the Navy Office, and to my Lord Generall's Secretary. I have
tryed all meanes and wayes to gett in my owne wages which
amounts to neare 16*l*., but I find I cannot doe itt till after
Christmasse." He asks the loan of 3*l*. till his pay comes in,
which Sir Ralph sends him. "Remember I was borne," he says,
"a trouble to my friends." Without pay or employment poor
Dick could not long keep out of mischief on shore, and there
is an urgent note from Lady Hobart to Sir Ralph, "As you
love me let me have one of your whitist wigs and you shall
have a new one for it. It 'tis to help away a frind. You shall
know all hereafter. Fail not to send it, and let it be that that
is lest curled."

Richard Hals is choosing some armour for his cousin in
London; he has tested it "with as much powder as will cover
the bullet in the palme of your hand"; Mun wants to test it
again, which the armourer objects to, as "it is not the custome
of workmen to try their armor after it is faced and filled. . . .
As for tasles noe horseman in England weares them and as
for a quilted gorgett," but here a mouse has dined, and the
postscript alone remains. "I have seene all the best armors in
the gards, but can see none such as yours are, my Lord Gerard's
excepted." Lord Gerard commanded the eighty gentlemen of
the King's Life Guards; Charles had knighted the Commissioners sent by the City to greet him on arrival, with Lord
Gerard's sword. Edmund's armour sent down by Plaistow,
the carrier, was valued at 14*l*. 2*s*. 8*d*., the box and cord at
2*s*. 6*d*.

"The armour fits well enough, only the man did cut away
to much just under the Arme pit both of back and breast;
but for the head-piece, it is something heavy, yet I think it
well enough if it did not come downe so low upon my forhead,
as to cover all my eyes and offend my Nose, when I put my
head backwards to look upwards."

Dick congratulates Edmund on the birth of his eldest son, "God make him a better man than his father; that's blessing enough."

In 1669 "divers Highwaymen are taken, and had not Dick Hals leaped out of a window 2 storeys high leaving his horse and his cloathes behind he had been taken. Warrants are out for him and many more, the King will pardon none but such as come in and discover and convict their fellows."

In 1670 "Cousin Dick says he is married to a sailor's wife at Wapping." In 1671 he writes to Sir Ralph and Edmund from Exeter gaol: "I, the most unfortunate amoungest men, am now forced to act a strange part in this westerne stage of our English world, imprisoned for noe offence. . . . Whether I live or die, is not much matter, itt not beinge the part of a man to testifie too much fearefulnesse of that which of necessitie will come one time or other, besides I doe not beleve itt ever lay in my power to prevent the stroke of my destenie. I have written to my cossen, your brave sonn, for a whindinge sheete, that in itt I may with my boddy winde in the eternall remembrance of his aboundinge spiritt."

"Your pardon I beg," he writes to Edmund, "as beinge the person to whom I am most obliedged of mankind, nor may you justly deny itt, iff you consider you give itt not now to the liveinge but to the dyeinge admirer of your person. Thet over-rulling hand of fate nic't me in the bud, when I least thought of harme, and in a place where I never did any, soe that lyeinge in gayle onely for want of bayle for the peace, I am like to be made knowne for what in truth I have bene. . . . I am att present in St. Thomas' ward Exon, and, Sir, would bee much att peace could I see three lines under your hand. My Aunt Hobart will send itt to mee. My thoughts are unsettled, and sometimes unwillinge to leave this world, but when I think of my misserable life past, I againe recover, and possest with thoughtes becominge a soldier I passe by all concerns."

Dick Hals might abuse himself but he allowed no one else to do so. He writes indignantly "to Mrs. Hannah Baker, in Chancery Lane at Sir Nathaniel Hobart's," "Because I am att present sunck by the hand of the most powerful God, you amoungest the rest make me your scorne."

Next comes a melancholy letter to Edmund from Newgate in April 1672: "I have made a hard shift to hould out three or fower yearres in a bad kinde of life, I meane, the highway, for which I am att last condemned to die, justly as to the law, though by the unjustnesse of a falce frende, who fainte-harted, swore against fower of us, to save his owne life. But, Sir, his Majestie, out of his infinite mercy, hath bene pleased to save our forfeited lives by his royall repreeve. My Aunt Hobart was the maine instrument, under God, who proved herselfe a mother and an aunt both in this affayre. That verry day I was taken in my bed by 4 in the morninge. They then robbed mee of every pennysworth of my illgotten goodes, and enclosed mee in a dungion, where I was keept without candle, fire, pen, inke or paper or frende, till they brought me before the Judges. Neyther could they then have done me any hurt, had not Judge Morton, by his insinuatinge facultie, over perswaded one William Ward to confesse, and to appeach Andrew Palmer, John Britton, James Slaughter and myselfe, which he impudently did, and, by his evidence alone, was we convicted. I have not wherewithall to subsist but what I have from the charitie of my frendes, for truly, Sir, they left me not worth one farthinge, when I was taken."

A few days later Hals appeals to Sir Ralph. "The Kinge goes out of towne to see the French Fleete, as wee heard this verry day, soe that we shalbe left in danger of Judge Morton's ffury, which is implackable, especially to me, for goeinge by his name, as hee is informed. Now if I could possibly make the Recorder my frende, he is able to ballance Judge Morton, and overway him on the Bench, which is not to bee done but by his clarke, Mr. Rumsey. It appeares that my Aunt Hobart did promise him a gratuitie, for the non-performance of which, hee did, in plaine termes, threaten my life in the gayle by in-sencinge his unckle, the Recorder against mee, and itt's verry probable may doe me some greate injury, if not prevented in tyme by sattisfation. The other three that were condemned with mee gave him 5*l.* each man, and soe would I but that I cannot as yett gett in money which I have in hands abroad. They tell us heare in Newgate that we may be endited uppon other Enditements next Sessiones, which, if soe, our lives will againe lye on the Recorder's good report to the Kinge. I beseech you, honnoured Sir, aske advice on this poynte and let Mr. Fall resoulve me, and out of your aboundant charitie be pleased to assiste the most unfortunate of your honner's captivated kinsmen."

He writes again: "The Kinge crost us out of the generall pardon and to what intent I know not; some say to goe to Tangere, but I beleve to be hanged, which I am sure stands with most reason. They intend to endight us againe as I heare, which if they do I am resolved to pleade guilty to all, and if there comes a thousand pardons still keepe me to the Kinge's mercy, except you send me other advice." Two months later he thanks Edmund for his great kindness, and wishes him "a merry buck season." "Were I in any other gaole then Newgate, I would venter a tryall of skill to see you, but this place is made past all hope." . . . "Tomorrow beinge Wednesday, I and the rest of my fraternitie are to pleade a pardon of transportation, some say for the Tangeir Gallies, and others, more moderate, tell us for Virginia."

It would have been worse than death for a naval officer, who had served with distinction in action, to be sent to the galleys; but Hals was not without old shipmates who remembered his better days. "Capt. Thomas Elliott my former Capt. att sea, attended the Duke of Yorke in this Citty, in order to his Knighthood for his service done in this and the former warr; and hearinge by a friende of mine, that I have neade of his assistance, gave me a vissitt the second day of his arrivall; hath promised to begg on his knees for my releasement; will to my advantage declare my service under his command in the last Dutch warr, will engage for my future Deportment (which is much) and carry me with him to sea in this present expedition to the streights. Soe God seemes att last to be passified."

Probably Captain Elliott's intercession was unavailing, as Dick refers next spring to his recent "happy escape out of prison," and laments his ingratitude "to soe deare a frende as

Mr. Palmer," which he can "never sufficiently repent of." For Doll's sake he is being nobly entertained at Croweshall, "and indeed above the merrits of any kinsman though more happy and fortunate than myself." . . . "And on my yet inviolate faith I protest, I would hast to the place I am ordered to"; he sends his "harty acknowledgments to Sir Chas. Gawdy & that incomparable lady his Mother, that if I die in this expedition my Goast may not be troubled to cross the seas to do it. . . . I am not sent away naked, but with Sword, Clothes, and Money, and to Eternize the obligation all wth so free & generus a soule, that I some times beleve y^t I can bee nothinge lesse then a sonn to the one, or a brother to the other."

"My Cossen Frances receaved a note from me," he writes to Sir Ralph in February 1674, "wherein was a full discovery of all persones I did or doe knowe that use the pad, but my keeper haveinge bene att London finds thinges, I judge, worse than he thought . . . my discovery was made the 21st of the Last mounth, to Sir Edward Smyth att Woodford, and to Mr. Justice Maineard, who committed me, with Matt Roberts, Toby Burke alias Faulkner, Thomas Dwite alias White, and Harris, which Harris and Burke or Faulkner are taken and in the Gatehouse. Sir Edward Smyth may easely sattisfie himselfe by seeinge Harris, for he tooke him by the bridle first. The King's proclamation acquits the first discoverer, and soe will the judge, iff Captain Richardson doe not prevayle to the contrary. I humbly beseech you to use your interest with Judge Twisden to this effect. Serjant Bramston, Sir Mundivile Bramston and Sir John Bramston are powerfull men with my Lord Twisden."

Dick's confessions were not yet full enough. The wretched man gave abjectly all the information asked for. "When I came into this gaole," he writes from Chelmsford, "I was resolved to die unknowne to my frendes, but Providence orderinge itt otherwayes, to my greate advantage, for althowe I am to be banished, itt is but what I should have courted iff left to my owne dispose, being assured that England, Ireland or Scotland are not places for me to rayse my fortune in, so, that to be sent, as I am promised, by that noble gentlemaen

Esquire Cheeke, into Flanders, Holland, France or Spaine, is the compleate sume of my desires or ambition." But his fate is yet uncertain; he despairs again. "The tyme drawers neare. I am yett a lost man, sure, sure, sure." . . . "That I am a deade man is most certeyne. I knowe itt from too good a hand to doubt itt. I had itt from Esquire Cheeke, who loves me more than I deserve, and promised yet once more to try the Judge."

The path of the informer is thorny. Dick feels that he has sold himself to the devil, without getting his wages. "All the miseries which attend humanity have fallen on my head. . . . This onely must afflycte me, that I was soe weake, on promise of life, to discover others, and yett by the severitie of my new masters, the Judges, to be tyed up for my good service. Besides this, all the gentlemen and Justices of the Peace in this county of Essex have bene made staulkinge horses. The noble Sarjant and his ffamily to come severall tymes to take my examination, and to retorne itt to London, and then Judge Whindam him-selfe to promise life on the tearmes aforesaid, yett all these poyntes in controversy to be throwne aside and nothinge but death thought on—this is Justice when the Devill shalbe Judge! Could they not as well have pressed me or hanged in my state of inocency, I meane, while I was a pure theife, with-out blott or blemish, as to make me stincke in the nostrills of my ould assosiates, and then out of love to hange me for my new service to my new masters."

He makes one more despairing appeal to Sir Ralph from Chelmsford gaol. "I am ashamed to discover my weake-nesse unto you, but I must. The sight of the executioner, who is still keept in the house in expectation of my execution on Monday next, is the greatest torment to me in the world, worse than death itselfe."

But Dick was to have another chance. "I have, I thanke God and good frendes, got the weather gage of ill fortune. . . . That most worthy and generous gentleman, Capt. Collins, into whose hands I putt myselfe after my escape out of gayle, will give an account for his fidellitie eyther here or hereafter." Sir Ralph has sent him a welcome gift of twenty shillings by his laundress.

H

But in the spring of 1675 he is back in Chelmsford gaol, and in mortal fear of the associates he had betrayed who have come from France to witness against him. "Iff thinges had not bene soe privatly carried," he writes to Sir Ralph, "I should not now have troubled all my noble kinsmen and frendes. How they will deale by me this Assisses, I know not nor can I learne of anyboddy what is done for me . . onely a she frende, wife to Carew writ me downe word (ould love will not be forgotten) that her husband, and Stanley and Palmer and the rest have layed their heades togeather to cutt me off, the way they intende to goe to worke she could not informe me, but soe soone as she knowes she will. Least I doe not live to write more unto you pray Sir . . . present my respects and service to my generous cossen Verney . . . and with my soule I wish I had taken his counsell when time was. . . . Iff I am not hanged, I shall goe, like Mounseir Le Gue, without a shirt. My Aunt hath promised me an ould one a longe tyme, but her many troubles makes her forgett me." There is a postmark on the letter, "Essex Post goes and coms every day."

Dick Hals' next letter is to Lady Hobart. "What will become of me I know not in this miserable place. Were I a ship board to be transported to any place (Tangiers excepted) I would be well content. The truth is I have deserved the worst that can bee, but God will not allowe each man his desserts, least more perrish than hee is willinge to loose. Sir John Bramston wrote me word before the Assiyes that he had written to a very good frende of mine att London, I knew he meant one of his generous brothers, to insert me in the Newgate pardon. Iff soe I must be removed by Habeas Corpus to London to pleade itt. . . . Sir John Howell, the Recorder, was very briske with me, I beleve he remembred ould stories. Iff my noble Cossen Edmond knew my condition, I doe verryly beleve he would doe more for me then all my new frendes."

A note received by Sir Ralph in Chancery Lane is docketed from "Dick Halse, a Highwayman—since hanged." "I am in greate want, this cold winter will kill me outright. The bearer sits on horsebacke while I write."

The charity of Dick's relations was not exhausted, and he

writes to Sir Ralph "next dore to the Black Balcony in Lin-
colln's-Inn Feilds in Holburne Row." "I wish my gratfull
soule were not confined within the narrow limmitts of a foole's
brest. . . . I dare say you beleve I pray for you, and wish you all
prosperitie, and that I have just cause to admire and adore
that providence, whose carefull eye amoungest soe many
greate men, my frends, pitched upon yourselfe to preserve me."
But neither God nor "greate men" could long help poor Dick
against himself; a piteous line reaches Sir Ralph in June 1676,
written apparently from London. "I am now arrived at the
worst place in England, where sinne and vice abound to an
infinite. I trust my newborne grace will defende me and ittselfe
from participating this sinck of humers and disorders."

Three years later Sir Ralph writes to John: Lady Hobart
is at Claydon—"well, but somewhat weake of her leggs—she
brought downe her daughter, her two Maydes & little Will—
And least they should bee too few she invited Dick Hals too, &
never acquainted me with it. He came downe in a cart with her
Cooke mayd, but he is at your Brother's house."

After this he gets an appointment: "Dick Hals is a Baly
but dos not dou no duty," Lady Hobart writes, "he has tou
men but he is to over se all the balys, for they have cheted
hyly; he receives all the mony of the cort, and has rased it
much senc he cam in, he is very hones, and I hop will kep so,
my stomack is not so good as it was at cladon, I mis your good
bear, I find the ale mor havey."

Dick turns up again in unwonted surroundings. His cousin,
Doll Smith, Anne Hobart's grandchild, is to be married at
Radcliffe to Mr. Wythers, and these warmhearted relations,
who have stood by Dick in his darkest days, have bidden him
to the wedding.

Edmund Verney, who had been looking after his hay-
makers through the long July day, watched from his garden
gate the smart cavalcade as it passed through East Claydon
in the evening. The great Sir William Smith, with his usual
taste for splendour, drove the bridegroom's family down in
his coach, with eight men on horseback in attendance. Dick
Hals, riding with the other wedding guests, turned into the

White House, to greet his old friend as he went by. "He sent over the next day," Mun writes, "by a Messenger-expresse for a Plaister for his side, from my Chirurgeon, & withall sent word that to morrow is the wedding-day, so Pegg must dance barefoot, otherwise Thom. Smith, Mr Wythers, Mr King & Dick Hals were to have dined with me, but when people marry wives, they cannot come." There was much merry-making at the wedding; "ten shillings were given to the Ringers at Buckingham, the fiddlers of Gawcott were sent for." Hester Denton drove over from Hillesden in her coach; and Parson King made love to Pegg, the bride's lively little sister, in such wise that the aunts and cousins gossiped pleasantly of another festive gathering to be held ere long. The grim highwayman must have been a tragic figure in the peaceful old grey church, and amid the village festivities, the music and dancing, the sunshine and the roses.

These were the last gleams of light in a stormy day. Hals soon resumed his desperate courses; his one remaining link with better things being his love for his child, whom he could seldom see. To his faithful friend, Edmund Verney, he writes: "After 30 yeares service I feare I am lost, left to the wide world, but bee itt how itt will, whielst the Emperor and Turke are at variance, I will not want. All that troubles me is my little boy, but God is able to provide for him. I would if I could."

Two years more elapse of ignoble stratagems and hairbreadth escapes. The perils of the road are notorious. In 1685 the Banbury coach is attacked "going upp with a woman and a man riding by it for protection, 2 Horsemen met it & rob'd them all upon Grendon Common, & the Rogues are not taken." Public feeling was exasperated, and the gentlemen of the road when caught could expect no more mercy. Judge Holt about this time visiting an old friend in prison, whom he had just sentenced, asked after their college chums. The answer was, "Ah my Lord they are all hanged now but myself & your Lordship."

"I have noe great news," writes Dick Hals to Sir Ralph, with a dash of his old cheerful courage, "but only that I thinke to die next weeke. I can doe more then David, for I can number my dayes, haveinge, as I judge, 10 to live from the date hereof, nor doth the law take away my life, but the mallice of Goaler and overheate of a Chiefe Justice, who rubbs too hard upon my ould sores." He is grateful to Sir Ralph and Edmund for all their past kindnesses; no one would have been so ready to serve them "had my starrs bene soe kinde to have called me to itt." "My tryall comes on the 29th of this mounth, and that day sennight, if not before, wee die. . . . We expected a proclamation or gaole delivery, but that's past hope." John hears that "at the Old Baily 23 were condemned to die amongst wch is Dick Halsey"; further efforts to save him were felt to be in vain.

Will Hals, the brave and pious sea-captain, praised God with joy for the birth of his only son, and this son was to be hung at Tyburn. Doll Leeke, who had so often helped and forgiven the wayward boy, had passed beyond the reach of evil tidings; Anne Hobart had long ago spent her influence and exhausted her resources. Sir Ralph was in the midst of his troubled election at Buckingham; "I am sorry for Dick Hals," he writes, "and wish he might have been transported, I trust God will forgive him, and keep us from such sad ends."

There is no doubt of his fate this time, for John Verney has seen him "in the cart"; Edmund, who has always done justice to the "few virtues he had among many vices," has a last kind word to say of him—"Cozen Dick is among the number executed, I am sorry for it, I wish I could have saved him. But if he be gone, I pray God rest his soule in Heaven."

Now for the undergraduate.

"I designe you for the Universitie, if you are fit for it, for I hope in God you will take to some honourable profession of your own accord, if not I am resolved you shalbe of a meane one for of some Profession, High or Low, I will make you, for I abhor you should go sauntering up & down like an idle lazy Fellow, and soe God blesse you."

The boy thus admonished was Edmund Verney, second son of Edmund Verney and Mary (Abell) of East Claydon; he was sixteen, and a few months later in January 1685 his father entered him as a "fellow-commoner" at Trinity College, Oxford.

H*

There was a great deal of bustle and excitement in getting the boy's outfit together. He noted with pride his "new sylver hilted sword, his new striped Morning gown," and his "6 new laced Bands whereof one is of Point de Loraine."

He is thus entered in the Trinity College Admission Register: "Ego *Edmundus Verney* filius Edmundi Verney Armigeri de East Claydon in Com: Bucks: natus ibidem, Annorum circiter 16, Admissus sum Primi ordinis Commensalis Mense Januarii 168⅘ sub tutamine magistri Sykes."

And the following fees were paid:

Jan: 23. 168⅘

	£	s.	d.
Received then of Mr. Edmund Verney. Ten pounds being Caution money laid into Trinity College, Oxon: I say, Received by me.	10	0	0

JOHN CUDWORTH BURS^R

Received also one pound ten shillings for utensils.

Item, for the New Building   .   .   . £15
Item, for the Common room   .   .   . £ 2

Jan: 23. 168⅘

	£	s.	d.
Received then of Mr. Edmund Verney the sum of one pound and eight shillings to be payed to the College servants for his admission into Trinity College Oxõn: I say received by me.	1	8	0

THO: SYKES.

Stephen Penton, chaplain to the Earl of Aylesbury, has left us a quaint account of his parting with a son whom he took up to the University about the same time. Father, mother, and sisters accompanied the lad to Oxford, and received his tutor at an inn, where that learned person delivered a discourse to the family council, of so alarming a nature, on all that the undergraduate was and was not to do, that as soon as he left the room "the boy clung about his mother and cry'd to go home again, and she had no more wit than to be of the same mind; she thought him too weakly to undergo so much hardship as she foresaw was to be expected. My daughters (who instead of Catechism and Lady's Calling) had been used to reade nothing but speeches in romances, hearing nothing of Love and Honour in all the talk, fell into downright scolding at him, call'd him the merest scholar and if this were your Oxford breeding, they had rather he should go to Constantinople to learn manners. But I who was older and understood the language call'd them all great fools."

Edmund was spared any such scene, as his father allowed him to go to Oxford alone. The last day had been occupied with packing and making lists (such was the orderly family usage) of the clothes, bed-linen, and table-linen with which his father supplied him. On 21 January 1685, he left home, and on the 22nd his father wrote him the first of a long series of affectionate letters in which he followed every detail of his son's college career.

"For Mr. Edmund Verney at his chamber in Trinity College in Oxford, or at Mr. Thomas Sykes his Tutor's Chamber in the same College. With a Box And a Trunk.

"Child, I shalbee very joyfull to Heare of yr safe Arrivail at Oxford, according to my kind Wishes wch. attended you all the Way for yr prosperous journey.

"I Have this Day sent you (By Thomas Moore ye Oxon Carryer) All yr things mentioned in this enclosed Note, except yr old Camelote Coate, wch. I Didd not think you would need nor worth sending; yr old Hatt I Didd not send neither, for it was soe Badd that I was ashamed of it. All yr new Things I Bought you I Put into a new Box Lockt up, and well Corded up, and the Key of this Box I Have also Here-enclosed for you: but for the Key of yr Trunk I could not find it, and its no matter, for that Lock is nothing worth: and Thom: made a shift to Lock it wth. a Key of myne: and it is well Corded besides: In yr. old Breeches wch. are in yr new Box, you will find yr five Laced-Bands (the sixt you Carryed with you) and a new payre of Laced Cuffes: And yr two Guinnies in yr fobb, and a new Knife and forke in yr. great Pocket. And so God Blesse you, and send you well to Do. I am yr. Loving father Edmund Verney."

"In yr. trunk I have putt for you
   18 Sevill Oranges
   6 Malaga Lemons
   3 pounds of Brown sugar
   1 pound of white poudered sugar made up in quarters
   1 lb of Brown sugar Candy
   ¼ of a lb of white sugar candy
   1 lb of pickt Raisons, good for a Cough
   4 Nutmeggs."

A week passed without any reply from the boy, and his father wrote again.

"Child,—When I take any Journey I always write unto my father By every opportunity a perfect Diurnall of my Voyage, and what else occurs worthy of Remarq: I writt to you a Letter this Day seven-night when I sent you yr Trunk and Box But never Hadd any answer nor account from you since: wch. is such a peece of Omission in you, to say no worse, that I Believe neither Oxford nor Cambridge can Paralell. For why I should Bee thus Neglected By my sonne I cannot imagine: indeed I looke upon it as an ill Omen, that you should committ such a grosse solecisme at yr first Entrance into the University against yr Loving father Edmund Verney." Letters from Oxford to London are from three to five days on the road, and one from young Edmund had miscarried.

The answer when it came showed all a freshman's nervous anxiety to do the correct thing. The outfit which had looked so handsome at home seems inadequate and rustic now, and in his self-conscious shyness young Edmund imagines that all Oxford is laughing at him.

"Most Honoured Father,—I want a Hatt, and a payre of Fringed Gloves very much, and I Desire you to send me them if you can possibly before Sunday next, for as I Come from Church Every body Gazeth upon me and asketh who I am. This I was Told by a friend of Myne, who was asked by Two or Three who I was."

"Child, . . . I ffind you Have Payd the Taylor for making yr Gowne and Cappe: But that you cannot Bee Matriculated these 3 weekes yet, untill you are Better skilled in the Orders or Statutes of yr College or University: therefore I Pray Learne them as soone as you Can. I will send you yr Bible wth yr Hatt &c: And so I Conclude Beseeching Almighty God to Have you in his Keeping."

"Most Honoured Father,—I ffind by your letter that you could not bye me any Fringed Gloves, untill you knew what is generally worne in the university by reason of the Death of our most excellent King Charles the Second. I cannot ffully certifie as yet in this matter, But there are two or three ffellow Commoners of our House of wch. Mr. Palmer is one, that have bought their Black Cloathes, and Plain Muzeline Bands, and Cloath Shooes, and are now in very strict morning: and others are Preparing for it, so that within this weeke I suppose the greater Part, if not all, of the university will be in morning."

"Child,—Last Tuesday night about 11 or 12 a Clock, yrs. of the 16th came to my Hands. I Have now sent you a new black Beaver with a Rubber and yr Handkercher in the Crowne of it, all within a pastboard Hatcase: I Have Bought you a new Sylver seale, but it is not yet Engraved wth yr Coate, so I could not send it you this Bout, but it is a Doing, you suppose That within a weeke, the Greater part of the University if not all, wil be in mourning: But I Ghuesse you are in a mistake, for I met with Dr. Say the Provost of Oriall, and askt Him about it, and Hee answered mee that There would Bee noe such thing as to the Generallity, Here & There some particular Persons might goe into mourning, and That would Bee all; for one swallow or two or 3 makes no Summer. Since I writt This, yr sylver Seale is Come soe I Have put it within yr Handkercher tyed up in great Hast."

The boy writes later that mourning is worn only by families connected with the Court.

"Child, I Heare my Cosen Denton Nicholas is come to Towne: Home to his ffather and Mother. You say Hee Hath bespoke a new Table and Cane chayres, wch. will amount to 3ᶫ a peece between you, But I Do not understand why you should Bee at that unnecessary Charge, as long as you Have that wch. will serve yr turne, neither Do I like the Vanity. You do not tell me whether you are matriculated yet or noe, and I am impatient till I know Thats done. You say you want money, wch, I will supply you with very shortly, but not to Lay out in Vaine moveables, and so God Blesse you."

"Why, what's a moveable?" we are tempted to ask with Petruchio. "A joint stool," Kate replies; Denton Nicholas and his cousin were intent upon a little more comfort than this, though they were far from having "three elegant and well-furnished rooms" such as Gibbon occupied at Magdalen seventy years later.

Edmund had come to Oxford in stirring times; Town and Gown were alike excited about Monmouth's rebellion; the Lord Lieutenant and other gentlemen of the county were calling out the trained bands, and we hear of the Dean of Christ Church haranguing the students and using all endeavours to make them fight for the Crown. A bill of Mun's, "for ye mending of my Sword," suggests the exercises most in favour with undergraduates; small bodies of volunteers are enrolled at each college, and Wilding, an enthusiastic lad at St. Mary's Hall, pays threepence for Monmouth's speech. It was a disappointment to many ardent spirits that the fighting was so soon over; but the men consoled themselves with bonfires in the quads, a review on Port Meadow, and uproarious drinking of toasts.

That hot summer was a sickly time in Oxford, and Mun was ill with a feverish rash very prevalent there. In July he wants "money To Pay for my Battles for Last quarter, which Comes To £06–00–09 and to pay my Tutor's Quarterage, and some other odd Businesses." Mun goes home, but the vacation is not apparently to last much more than a fortnight.

Edmund was an autocrat with his sons, as his father had been before him. "I heare you hate learning & your mind hankers after travelling," he writes to Ralph when the boy wishes to have a voice in his own plans; "I will not bee taught by my Cradle how to Breede it up 'tis Insolence & Impudence in any Child to presume so much as to offer it." No doubt Ralph poured out his grievances to his brother, but their father was too good-natured a man for the boys to be long *en froid* with him.

John Verney with his wife and children were at Claydon,

and paid the lads a visit at Oxford after their return, which Ralph Palmer acknowledges in a grateful letter to his sister. Edmund desires to spend Christmas in town with his grand-father, father, and brother. "With All my Heart," Edmund senior replies, "for you shalbee most welcome to mee. Bring along with you (I do not meane in the Coach But) By the Carryer yr Best Waring Things, To make as good an appearance Here as you can. You shall Lye in my Chamber."

Young Edmund is back again at Trinity College in the beginning of January 1686. "I have payd all my debts besides my Booksellers, to whom I owed 2$^£$ 9^s 6^d. and out of the whole 18$^£$ 4^s 6^d, their is but 2$^£$ 1^s 0^d remaining, Therefore before I Can Pay my Bookseller, I must heare from you again."

"Child,—I would Have answered yr ffirst Letter sooner, But that yr Brother ffell sick last Tusday and continues very ill still of this Towne ffeavor, I am glad you are out of it, my uncle Dr. Denton is his Physitian, and Mr. St Amand is his Apothecary. He Remembers his Love to you; . . . I would Have you Pay yr Bookseller, and gett Him to Abate what you Can, And then all you owe in Oxford is Payd and Cleered. . . . I Am soe perplexed about y^r Brother, that I can write no more."

"My dearly beloved son Ralph departed this transitory Life yesterday morning about 11 a Clock. . . . my Heart is so incurably pierced with grief for the loss of my dear child that I can no more be comforted then Rachel was who wept for her children. . . . My poor son is this day to be put up into 3 coffins, 2 of wood & 1 of lead & is to be drawn to his dormitory in my father's vault in Middle Claydon, I shall not stir out of doors till he is gone. He is to be drawn in a Herse with 6 Horses & scutcheons & one Coach more with 6 Horses accompanies him, my brother & Jack Stewkeley goe down in it as chief Mourners, & 4 men in mourning ride by on horseback along with the body all the way." Edmund was too ill himself to go down to Claydon for the funeral.

"Child,—You and yr sister are now my only Relicts of my Deare Wife yr Mother . . . . My Deare Sonne Ralph yr Brother . . . . Lived Virtuously and Dyed Penitently: soe I Do Verily

Believe That he is a glorious Saint in Heaven. Now upon this sadd Occasion, I who Am yr true Loving ffather Do Take upon mee to Advise, Councell, and exhort you, to Bee wholly Ruled and Guided By me, and to Bee perfectly obedient to mee in all Things, according to yr Bounden Deuty, and Likewise to Behave yr selfe alwayes Respectfully towards mee and towards yr Mother, and to Honor us, That thy Dayes may Bee Long in the Land, wch the Lord thy God Giveth Thee: ffor should you Doe otherwise and contrary in ye Least, unto this my Advice, Injunction, and Exhortation to you, I am affrayed That you wilbee in that evill circumstance Snatcht away By Death in your youth, as yr poore Brother was last weeke: Therefore O Thou my Sonne and Name Sake, Hearken unto my Voyce, who Doe Give Thee my Blessing: and who Am Thy most affectionate ffather and Best ffriend Edmund Verney."

"I have Drawne affresh Bill Here enclosed upon Alderman Towneshend for 5*l.*, to Buy you a black Cloth sute. And I Have a new black Beavor Hatt for you, wch. I will send you next Thursday in a little deale Box, with a black Crape Hatband, Black mourning Gloves, and Stockings and shoe Buckles, and 3 Payres of black Buttons for wrist and neck: And I Have also sent you a new ffrench cordebeck Hatt to save yr Beavor, the Box is to Keepe yr Beavor in: no Body useth Hatcases now."

"Most Honoured Father,—I Received Both yrs. that of the 16th and that of 18th, and by the former I understand, that it was the pleasure of Almighty God to take unto himselfe the soule of my dearest and only Brother, But I hope the Thoughts of the happyness, which he enjoyes in Heaven, will in a great measure lessen the sorrow, which I undergo by loosing so near and so dear a Relation. Now seeing it has pleased Almighty God to make me acquainted with the sorrows and Afflictions of this world, by taking from me my only Brother, I hope it will be a means to make me fear God, and Honour you and my Mother, and by so doing I hope I shall render both you and my selfe Happy. I Have made me a new Black cloth suit, and a new black morning Gown, which with new muzeline Bands and Cloth shooes will stand me in very near ten pounds. . . .

"I present my Duty to you and my Grandfather and my

love to my Dear Sister, and so I subscribe myselfe Yr most dutyfull Sonn Edmund Verney."

Edmund being now heir to Claydon, and to his mother's property, became more than ever an object of solicitude to his father and grandfather. The children inherited a delicate constitution from their mother; and any ailment or tendency to low spirits naturally caused their father the gravest anxiety: no expense was to be spared when Edmund's health was concerned, but he was not to incur any unnecessary outlay in dress or in the furnishing of his rooms.

"Child,—There Bee many scurvy ffeavers Here in Towne, So that I Do not Hold it fitt that you should Bee Here at this ffeaverish hott Time of ye yeare by noe meanes. My Cosen Nicholas Comming to this Towne is no Rule to mee, for Hee is Both Pox and ffeaver Proofe wch you are not. Pray Lett me Desire you not to goe into the water till I give you Leave, for ffeare of catching Harme. Present my service to Sr. William Dormer, And as to yr Versifying Dialogue with Him, I Like it very well, if you make it yr selves not elce, But as to That wee shall Talke more of, I Hope, if I live to meete you. You Hadd Best Bee very wary of all yr words and Actions: It is sayd Here you are Growne very melancholy, when I was Told it, I made Them a smart answer on yr Behalfe: So that if you Bee serious, sober and Discreet, Thats Interpreted melancholy to yr disadvantage, But should you Bee indeed to Blame in any Thing, then yr Back ffriends would sett you out to some Purpose, Therefore Cave mi ffili, Dimidium verbi Sapienti Sat Est et Spero Te Talem Esse et futurum Vale."

"Child,—I heard that the players are gon down to Oxford," writes Edmund in July 1686, "but I am unwilling that you should go to see them act, for fear on your coming out of the hot play house into the cold ayer, you should catch harm, for as I did once coming out of the Theatre at a publick Act when it was very full and stiaminghot, and walkin a Broad in the cold, and gave me sutch a cold that it had Likt to a cost me my Life. Your best way in Sutch a cold is to go hom to your one Chamber directly from the play house, and drink a glass of Sack, therefour Be sure you send your Servant At your hand for a bottle of the Best Canary and Keep it in your chamber for that purpose. Be sure you drink no Kooleing tankord nor no Cooling drinks what so ever . . . harkon Thou unto the voyce & Advise of mee Thy ffather, Loving Thee Better then him selfe."

It is hard to imagine undergraduate Oxford without cricket or boating, but this allusion to the players is one of the few references to amusements that we have in the correspondence. In Wilding's account-book are the entries "Michaelmas Term, spent in coursing 1s. 8d., and in the Winter Term At ye Musick night 2s. 6d."; it was also open to the curious in 1686, to pay 2d. "For seing ye Rhinoceros," as Wilding did, and to view "the rarities in the Physick School, the skin of a jackall, a rarely coloured jacatoo or prodigious large parrot and 2 humming birds, not much bigger than our humble bee."

There was "swimming in Merton Pool & Scholars' Pool, some tumbling in the hay, leaping, wrestling, playing at quoits and fishing." Laud had put an end to the popular exercise at Oxford of learning "to ride the great horse," as he found in the riding school "where one scholar learns, 20 or 40 look on & there lose their time," so that the place was fuller of scholars than either schools or library; nor would he "suffer scholars to fall into the old humour of going up & down in boots & spurs with the ready excuse that they were going to the riding house." But neither Archbishop nor Puritan reformer could keep English lads and their horses long apart, and many a "fine padd" was kept "for health's sake" at one of the 370 Oxford ale-houses; and the more zealous tutors complained of the time spent by the scholar, who must needs go once every day to see that his horse eats his oats, and "the horse growing resty if he be not used often, he must have leave to ride to Abingdon once every week, to look out of the tavern window & see the maids sell turnips." The same authorities viewed with displeasure the bowling-green and the racket court, as they were public places resorted to by "promiscuous company," and such violent games tended, it was said, "to fire the blood by a fever."

There were dancing and vaulting schools at Oxford, but fencing was probably the form of exercise viewed with least disfavour by the learned, and Mun pursued it with ardour. His hopes of distinction as a reciter were doomed to disappointment.

"Most Honoured Father,—Our Act was put off this year by reason of the death of the Bishop [Fell], which hindered us of speaking verses in the Theatre, But the Priveleages and charges are the same now as if we had spoke our verses, Though I think we have quite lost the Honour of it.

"I have bought me a new sute of mourning and by reason of the excessive heat of the summer I was forced to Buy a new crape gown, which will stand me in £02 10ˢ 00ᵈ, but I have not yet payed for my gown. I want new shirts very much."

"Child,—I Received a Letter lately from Mr. Sykes yr Tutor, unto whom you are very much obliged. Take my word for it, Albeit Hee makes a complaint of you, for not frequenting a certain afternoone Lecture as you were wont to Doe, yet otherwise Hee Speakes very Hansomly of you, wch Rejoyces my Heart, ffor I Take Him to Bee a plaine Dealer, and an Honest Gentleman, and I Hope you will Deserve those many good commendations Hee Hath Given me of you.

"It seems you Tell Him, That you Have particular Reasons, That you cannot Discover, why you come not to those Lectures. This may possibly Bee, as to Him and others, But as to mee who am yr ffather, There can Bee None, Therefore Pray Lett me Know By the next Post, those particular Reasons, And if I Like Them, I will Doe what I can with civility to Gett you excused: For Looke you Child, any one may Pretend particular Reasons, which one cannot discover, for not Doing what one ought to Do, or for doing what one ought not to Doe: But That Shamme will not Passe among Wise Men: ffor such Pretences to Avoyd ones Deuty, are allwayes (wth Justice) Interpreted in ill sence, and I should Bee very sorry any such Reflections should ffall upon you: you are under Government, as all subjects are in severall Kinds, and therefore are Bound by Laws and Rules and Precepts Divine to obey: Besides it is a wrong to the Society not to Come to Lectures, ffor if all others should fforbeare Comming to them as you Doe, the Lectures must ffall, wch are a support to a College, and so By Degrees Arts and Sciences, and Learned Societies must Dwindle away and Dissolve to nothing: But I Hope none of my Posterity will ever Bee the primum mobile of such a mischief to Learning: And so I shall close up my Discourse about this Businesse for this time and Longing for yr Answer about it."

Meanwhile young Edmund had got into a more serious scrape at Oxford, and was in danger of being sent down; but the following letter from his tutor was accidentally delayed for more than three months, and before it reached his father at East Claydon the undergraduates were all scattered by an alarming outbreak of small-pox, and the letter had "through length of time grown obsolete."

"Sir,—Since my last there are arisen new troubles, not about the Lecture mentioned in my former Letter, for I suppose that is at an end according to your Letter to me, But about other matters. It so happened that Mr. Verney Lay out of the College on Wednesday night Last with another or two of our College, and that with some other Provocations hath occasioned Mr. Vicepresident to Cross his name with the others. I suppose he will give you an Account where he was, he is unwilling to do it here, and that makes the business So much the worse. I suppose he will scarce ask for his name againe, and I presume the Vicepresident will not give it him of his owne accord, and so what will be the issue of it I Know not. He speaks of removing of himself to some other College, but I much question whether that will be for his advantage or not. If he is unwilling to stay here perhaps Sir its better to remove him from the university but I leave it to you Sir to judg what is best to be done; I cannot help this and I hope he will not deny but that I have behaved myself to him in all things as a tutor ought to do, and been civil to him as far as I could, but as to this business I can only be sorry for this, but canot remedy it. It is directly against both the discipline of our College and ye University in General to Ly out a nights, And I finde I canot prevail with the Vicepresident to take off the Cross unless your Sonn will acknowledg his fault and promise not to be faulty any more in that Kinde.

"I humbly beg pardon for this trouble and give you my most hearty thankes for all your kindness to Hon^{ed} Sir, your most humble and obliged Servant Tho: Sykes."

Mun goes down with the rest of the undergraduates. "Deare Brother," Edmund writes to John, "My sonne & I, & Grosvenor, & Mr Butterfield and Dover, Have all Read yr Booke of the Seige of Buda, soe I Have sent it Back to you, wth my Thankes, and a Cheese, wch I hope will prove Good, if a Mouse's judgement may Bee Credited, you will find it soe. I Heare the small Pox Rages mightily in Trinity College in Oxon, as the Great one doth in London, so that Eight went out lately sick of them from that College, wch makes me afrayed to send my sonne Thither till albee well again. Sir William Dormer is kept still at Lee upon the same account." Two more fellow commoners of Trinity, "Mr. Chambers and one Mr. Knopher," have fallen sick. The small-pox had done young Mun at any rate a good turn; his indiscretions were forgotten, while the authorities were gathering together their scattered and diminished flocks, and he never got into trouble again.

CHAPTER FOURTEEN

Prologue to the Revolution
1686–1689

DURING the year 1686 indignation was strongly aroused at the religious persecutions in France. "The Pope himself, tis said, is very Compasinat to the poor protestants beyond sea, and has rit to his Nuntia Fr. Lenenya to receve all as coms and give them protection, and will send all provisions as fast as hee can to them, Ittyly cannot furnish them so hee will order provisions out of Millan, hee is much ther frend and tis beleved will excomunycate the King of franc if he stops not his fury."

Mun gives voice to the savage hatred of Louis XIV that was growing amongst the country squires. It is startling to hear so good-natured a man rejoicing brutally over the terrible details of the King's illness; no punishment is adequate "for his unparalelled cruelties to his Protestant subjects." "The French King . . . will never be done, Demanding & Claiming & Destroying, and Taking forcibly until the Devill hath him. In the Interim I heare he stincks Alive, & his Carkass will stinck worse when he is dead, & so will his memory to all eternity. I am a most grievous & wicked sinner, yet I will not change my Condition with him if I mought, to have his Kingdom."

The crowd show their Protestant sympathies in a congenial manner, and there are free fights between the City apprentices and the trained bands. "On Sunday some boys and rabble were very rude in Lime Street, at the residence of the Prince Palatine, where the priests were at their devotions; one had

his head broke, but by the help of constables and my Lord
Mayor the rabble were dispersed, and some taken and committed"; on the Sunday following the same scene is repeated.
Lord Powis, as a Roman Catholic Peer, was very unpopular.
He had just built a grand house in Lincoln's Inn Fields and
was known to be much trusted by the King. Mun writes how
"Mrs. Powis [his next-door neighbour] Lyeth now sick of the
small Pox, in her fine new Dampe House, with her fresco shash
windows & coole guilt leather & smelling Paint, & they say
shee is with child, so it may goe hard with Her." Penelope
hears the Duchess of Grafton lament to the Queen "that her
father dyed a papist, but lately turned; she exprest much
troble, twas not thought wisely don to show it at court." "The
D. of Albemarle has laid down all his com^{ns} on my Ld Fever-
sham being made Lieut. Genl."

The King is making a real effort to improve the efficiency
of the army; he reviews single regiments in Hyde Park, and
compliments Lord Lichfield on the smartness of his men; he is
accessible to any private who can give him information. "As
the King came from Councell 7 or 8 Souldiers Scotch & Irish
Presented themselves to him, who came from the Buss in
Holland, his Maj: tooke one of their Musquetts in his hands &
vewing it found it to be of a size longer then those his souldiers
use: after discoursing them, he Ordered they should be provided for. . . . Abundance of people go out of town, to see the
gallantry of the camp at Hounslow Heath, where it's said the
officers will be extremely fine."

The popularity of the camp is, however, endangered by
the outrages the soldiers commit on the civil population; discipline must have been difficult indeed to maintain, when the
officers were constantly engaged in fighting one another.
"Mr. Culpepper brother & heir to my Lt Culpepper shoots
with a blunderbuss one Mr Minshull of the Guards, brother
to him of Borton by Buckingham; Sir Richard Temple calls
him cousin and says he was not dead on Saturday." "One
Mr. Ash (whose mother was Nancy Harrington's eldest sister)
being a small officer in the camp, was killed by Capt. Cooke
(who bought Skipwith's command), who darted his sword at

Ash and killed him, for which he is at present withdrawn. Capt. William Freeman, who killed Mr. Ralph Freeman, of Surrey, at Epsom, is at Calais, and some say Lord Dartmouth hath obtained his pardon of his Majesty." "Capt. Bellinger and Capt. Pack fought in Leicester Fields, the former was wounded, but parted by Harry Wharton and Mr. Smith." "The small officers" are amply warranted by the behaviour of their seniors. "Admiral Herbert coming with Colonel Kirk from dining in the City to the Play House, cut (on what provocation I know not) Lord Devonshire's coachman; on which his Lordship said nobody should correct his servant but himself. I heard they were to fight, four against four. But his Majesty hath been pleased to prevent it." "A soldier pistoll'd a watchman in Southampton Buildings, saying, some time before, he had been affronted by a watchman there, of which he was resolved to be revenged, and therefore went to them and killed one, whether he that affronted him or another it mattered not."

Murders are too common to excite much comment, but the civil worm turns at last when "Six or 8 souldiers goe from the Camp to Robb an Orchard. The Provo's seized them, & bringing 'Em near their own Regiment, about 200 men with drawn swords Rescued 'em, & the Provo's made their Escapes into the Officers Tents, who protected 'em untill the Generalls came who appeazed 'em, yet 2 or 3 were Kill'd in the fray." The sacred rights of property being thus threatened, "His Majesty came himself to the Camp" to avenge the sack of the orchard, "& drew out the Army, where some of the Mutiniers were Punished."

"On Sunday, the rabble got together again about the Welsh Camp (as they call the fields about the Cow-keeper Griffith's house) where with brickbates, which they had from a Brickill near at hand, and which they conveyed about with 'em in wheelbarrows, they pelted the Trainbands, but they did not any great hurt nor received any, only 'tis reported that handsome Fielding with his naked sword scower'd amongst 'em and wounded some of the rabble, and one of the Militia shot a maid dead (in the breast); she only came to see fashions. . . ." " 'Tis said that Capt. Swifnix, who in Ireland would not deliver his commission to the Lord-General, is in that kingdom by 15 or 16 men cut to pieces; he was formerly a highwayman in England."

"Some days past, a barge or pleasure boat going up the river, with four young women and a blackmore, were all drowned on their way to the Camp about Twittenham, by the barge's oversetting, but all watermen were saved; they were young Greenwich ladies, two of them great beauties, a third very handsome, the fourth plain; the eldest of them about 22 years, the beauties 15, and one of them an only child. On Sunday the rabble were again disorderly in Lambs Conduit Fields, and pulled down a Music-house Booth, making merry with wine and other liquors, and the brickbats did also fly about, but there was no mischief done, only one citizen (a scrivener, I think), coming thither to see fashions," evidently a very dangerous amusement, "was shot thro' the leg, and so was carried off, and one of his legs is since cut off." There was the further excitement of "a whale who came up as high as Woolwich, and was hunted and shot at and much wounded, but she made towards Gravesend so I suppose she got to sea again, having had quite enough of the turbulent city."

At Claydon, the joy felt at Sir Ralph's return to the House of Commons in May 1685 was damped by the prorogation of the Parliament in December, and by a grievous private calamity—the loss of John Verney's young wife, in 1686. Her life came gently but swiftly to a close; the responsibilities of a wife and mother had been laid too soon on girlish shoulders, and though she carried them bravely, her strength was not equal to her courage and capacity.

Elizabeth Verney died in London, in the twenty-second year of her age. When John buried his "Dearest Joy" in the vault at Middle Claydon, he buried with her the happiest chapter of his life. There was no break in the outward activities of his career; he was not a man to trouble others with his sorrows; to them he was the efficient, successful, rather cold man of affairs he had always been.

Sir Ralph was extremely unwell at the time of Mrs. John Verney's death, and the Claydon people, who are "heartily sorry" to hear of it, are yet more anxious about their kind old landlord. Dr. Denton is pining "to let blood under his tongue," which Sir Ralphe "has noe minde to." Coleman, the steward, writes: "I am soe concerned to hear your illness to continue, that I am not able at present to wright to you about any businesse for teares; my prayers I am sure & some hundreds in the County about you, are for your long life & health, both amongst us your Servants & them your neighbours. . . . I will to the best of my power bee careful of all your businesse I am imployed in, & observe all your commands about Mrs. Verney's comeing downe to be buryed."

John is attending to every detail of the funeral, and of the mourning for the motherless babies: they are to wear crape at 17*d.* a yard, Sir Ralph's cloth-crape costs but 14*d.* The portly coachman, Philip Buckley, is to have two specially large dimity waistcoats at 10*s.* and "a Pair of mild Serge breeches at 11*s.*" Mrs. Lillie, the housekeeper, sends up "a bitt of silk for a pattern of the church cushings," which are evidently to be also garbed in black. Coleman writes again: "Here are people daily to inquire of your good health . . . most that know your Worship doe pray for your health, Mr. Butterfield last Tewsday praid for you in the Church & I hope it will please God to heare our prayers, it being I am sure from mee with an humble heart. Mr Fall & Mr Rutherford of Roxton was here at Mrs Verney's buriall, but did not stay to supp here, Mr White & his daughters & Mr Jos: Churchill & his wife & 3 children stay'd supper."

Mun, who is deeply grieved for his brother's loss, is at his wit's end to devise more remedies for Sir Ralph, as "he hath been Blooded, Vomited, Blistered, Cupt & Scarifyed, & hath 3 Physicians with him, besides Apothecary & Chirurgien"; strange to say, "hee continues still very weak." Mun himself takes "Venice Treacle every night & many other nasty Apothecarys things." He is recommended Islington, Epsom, or Tonbridge waters. Grosvenor believes that the waters of Astrop, which he might drink at home, are "as sanative as the waters about London, which are so chargeable they resemble those of Bethesda, which had noe virtew till an Angell had stirr'd them."

On 3 September 1688, Edmund wrote from East Claydon another of his chatty letters to John in London. "Deare Brother, I Received yours of the 29th last past, and understanding from my Cosen Natt Hobart and my Sonne what good sport There was at Quainton Race the first day where Chesney the Horse Courser made Thousands of Men Runne after Him with their Swords Drawne, He shott his Pistol at Sir Thomas Lees man Mr Cull, and overthrew Him and his Horse together, and swore like any Lover that Hee would Have the other Pluck at Mrs. Hortons 5,000£ still, so the next Day I went my selfe to the Race, & Carryed my Cosen Cary and my Daughter in Hopes to meete with the Like diversion, But He was not so obliging to the Company as to Give them the same Pastime, so my Cosen Dentons man Valentine Budd Ridd for the Plate & wonne it, it was a Sylver server, his Horse that wonne it was a grey. There was a Child ridd over and almost Killed, & old Claver of Weeden ffell off from his Horse Being very Drunk, I saw my Cosen Charles Stafford there, & severall Ladys and Gentlemen But not T: S, nor Sʳ R. T. nor Sʳ J. B. who is gone away no Body Knows where, nor no Body Knows when He will returne. Sʳ W. D. never came to the Race, wᶜʰ troubles his Granddam Extremely, I Have a Storry to Tell in the next Sheet, that will fill it up & so I shall conclude This who am your most loving Brother & sarvent

EDMUND VERNEY."

The "storry" was never told. The next morning, hearing nothing till 8 o'clock, his servants went into his room, and sent a terrified message to Middle Claydon, that their master was sleeping so heavily they knew not what to fear. Sir Ralph arrived in his coach before nine; a surgeon was sent for, who bled him; "the Queene of Hungary's water & severall other things were applyed to him, nothing would recall him." At ten it was all over, and Sir Ralph sat down in the desolate house, and sent an urgent appeal to John to make instant preparations for the funeral, concluding in a very shaky hand, "God in mercy fit us all for Heaven, Your unfortunate father Raphe Verney."

He encloses a list of Mun's household for whom mourning will be required. "Dover his confidential servant, Harry the Coachman, Ned Smith the Groom, Thomas Very the Carter, Tom Butcher a Footman, Jacob Golding a Footboy, & little Jacob Hughes about 9 years old taken out of Charity. Your Brother's Wife, your Brother's Daughter, Cary Stewkeley, Mrs. Curzon, Two Chambermaids that attend on his wife's person, Doll the Cooke, Anne the Dayry Mayd." The names are written on the back and front of an old playing-card, another hint of the untidy condition of the house, where the kind-hearted, careless master had scarcely breathed his last, before it seemed as if every one had a debt to claim, or a story to tell against him.

The young heir was still at college; neither the widow, though just then in her right mind, nor the little terrified daughter could render Sir Ralph any assistance, and in those first miserable hours, when the old man was left alone in the deserted study to look through a mass of bills and papers, a great wave of bitterness swept over him, and he judged his dead son very hardly.

The money lent Edmund on bond, by the first rough compu-tation, amounted to some 4,500*l*. "I finde yr Brother died very much in debt," Sir Ralph writes again to John, "but as yet I cannot say how much, therefore in my opinion it will be the best way to bury him privately in the night-time, without Escutcheons, or inviting of Neighbours to attend with their Coaches, which is very troublesome & signifies nothing." He is at no pains to conceal his mortification. To Sir William Smith he writes: "You oblige me much by appearing sensible of the loss of my Sonne & if you knew in what a miserable condition he hath left his estate & Family, you would woonder at it, and hardly believe it; for its ill beyond Expression."

The elaborate mourning required keeps all the women of the family busy. Cary Stewkeley goes about with the steward and the carpenter, measuring the bed and the furniture in the widow's chamber which is to be entirely covered with black, and makes out lists for Sir Ralph, while doing her best to soothe and comfort Mrs. Verney and Molly. But it is upon the son of the house that the heaviest burden falls. Summoned from Oxford, the boy of nineteen finds his home, so to speak, in ruins, and the father who had always been so good to him beggared at once of life and of reputation. Cary sums up what the family expect from the hope of Claydon, that he should do nothing "to the prodigys of his helth," and confide absolutely in his grandfather. Young Edmund shows good sense and feeling beyond his age. The situation is difficult enough; his mother's affairs and his own are in Chancery, and he feels himself "but as it were a steward to my Father's creditors." He is surrounded by old servants and retainers, who have large expectations from the heir, which he is quite unable to fulfil; he is trying to get the superfluous men-servants into places, but they are not at all keen to leave. His father's "2 great Horses eat up a deal of horsemeate, the Coach Mares do noe work, & the Greate Barne is so full of ratts, the wheat will soon be eat up & spoiled." He tries to get in some arrears of rent, but his mother's tenants are clamorous in their requests, and with good reason; "most of them assure me that my father promised them such & such repairs, others say their Houses were begun in my father's time & I cannot tell what answer to make them." One old man's "actions," Cary reports, "is the wonder of markits as well as this towne, being called one of the Old Lords of Claydon; bot Harry Honnour has ben an old sarvant and so has his wife Doll, and both fixed heare, and therfore I wish them well setled, for I pitty every poor creature that has no shelter from wind and weather therfore care to say no more of him." Mun dares not sell a horse because there are endless delays in making out the valuation, and he cannot even get in the undertaker's bill for his father's funeral; "he is allwayes a burying somebody or other they tell me at his house when I call." The garden alone seems to be in good order, "very pleasant to walk in & the fruite is as it should be."

The attention of the relations has been concentrated on East Claydon, but public events are now too grave to be ignored. "War is in the air," and such of the family as are living in London have the cheering conviction that the Metropolis will be the Seat of War. Riots increase; "all meat risis in town & everything is snatched up, fearing the prince of

I

orange sh^d stop provisions comeing to this toune." "The rabble very rudely went to Barge Yard, defaced the Popish Chapel, breaking the windows, drinking up the Priest's liquors both wyne & beare, carrying out what portable, to make a bonfire in the Marketplace, Ld Mayor's show was very poor this year."

Young Edmund had seen some of the dreaded Irish troops at East Claydon. "This day passed by here 500 Irish ffoot souldiers in their march to London, & just at the townes end they quarrel'd amongst themselves about going over a stile in Newfield, and one of them was knock'd down & his scull much broken & he now layes insensible at Thomas Millers, 'tis thought he will dye very shortly if he is not dead allready."

Sir Ralph, on his return home in November, is roused up at two o'clock in the morning to send men and horses for the Militia levies at Stony Stratford within twelve hours, "all the Buck^m trained bands are gon with thos forces as is to march against the Prince." On the whole there is a strong feeling that "the King will put all to a push & fight," and this in spite of the desertions to the Prince of Orange, and the Princess Anne's "prank, wch dus not a littell disples the King." Cary Gardiner reports the town talk, "that ther is grat hops of a hapy Settillment in fue months, all the protistants being in most things of a mind, & believed no blod will bee shed in warr, & that our King will rain more happily than he has dun, only thar is great doubts maid how the title of the P. of Wails [no bad name for that luckless infant] will be desided. . . . The Princ marchis slow his resons is not known." Lord Abingdon and Tom Wharton were amongst the first to join his standard. The story Lord Macaulay has told once for all need not be repeated, but after reading in the letters day by day of the contradictory rumours that keep up the tension of suspense in London, one feels that Cary sums up the situation admirably to Sir Ralph, who is awaiting events at Claydon: "You will wonder at nothing now. Sertanly no Cronacill can paralell whot has bin produced in a fue weeks time—to have A King & Prince of Wales & A Queene fly from an Invader without A blow. . . . Ther is so many gon in A Weeks time as wod A mase you; night & day the water is full of barges. . . . Sir R.

Temple is this day gon to the Princ, but thos as gos in now signifys Littell bot are rather laughed at. . . . We expect the Princ here, in the mean time the moboly will pull downe all the chapels as is nuw set up. Skilton is fled & the City has seased the Tower . . . I thank you for your fat plovers & so conclud." Dr. Denton writes "We are all in a strange confusion, abandoned by K, Qu. & Pr. all gone cum pannis, confounded be all they yᵗ worship graven Images & boast themselves of idols. . . . Its said yᵗ my Lᵈ Chanʳ is gon along with them & consequently ye Seales, & a world more gone or goinge."

John's letters in a crisis are as calm as a bill of lading, but the plain facts are too dramatic to need any dressing up; "the Lᵈ Chancellor yesterday morn goeing a long in a seaman's habit in Anchor Alley in Wapping was discover'd, his Lordship presently told the discoverer he would goe along with him but desir'd him to keep it private for fear of the people soe they went into an Ale house by & sent for a Constable, who with a Guard brought him to Town, all the people huzzaying, & with difficulty did his guard keep him from the Rabble, nay one did strike at him, he was brought in to the Lord Mayors just at dinner time who when he saw ye Lᵈ Chan: thro' feare fell a Cryeing then into a fitt, for which he was blouded & put to Bed, soe the Lord Mayor being ill he coud not sign any warrant, the L. Chanc: satt downe & Eate heartily, but turning about he saw Sʳ Robᵗ Jefferyes Late Mayor who cryed & came to kiss his hand & then the L: Chan: alsoe cryed, he said what have I done that people are soe violent agˢᵗ me, one answᵈ: Remember Cornish, he said he would have savd him, but when he coud not he savd his Estate, & had not a penny for't, at length My Lord Lucas took charge of him & convey'd him to the Tower, he design'd for Hambrow & the Vessell was fitting with all Expedition wh: created some jealousy that some greate person was to goe off in that ship. The K. left the D. of Northumberland asleep in his chamber when he went away." John had dined with the Lord Chancellor some six months before, "being feasted by him as being one of his Jury."

London went through a short but anxious crisis. John

describes the sacking of the Spanish Ambassador's house, and how "The Mobb" [an abbreviation of *Mobile vulgus* now first coming into use] carried away the very boards and rafters. "The Amb^r valued his library at 15,000*l*., the Plate, Jewells, Clothes, etc., were of vast value and Papists had carried all their best things thither presuming they would be safe. Ld. Powis has removed his things & my Lady lyeth at a neighbour's for fear they sh^d come thither." John's friend Mr. Fall "is a great sufferer, his windows are all beaten down & his house defaced." "Sir Henry Bond's fine house at Peckham" is threatened. "The Capt. of the Trainbands (one Douglas) guarding the Florentine Resident's house in the Haymarket, was shot dead, 'tis beleivd by one of his own men. . . . Aunt Adams was up all night for fear of the Mobb there being 7 Papists, lodgers in her house." The terror of the Irish night is still upon him as he writes: "Last night twixt 1 & 2 we were all alarm'd by Drums & Bells that the whole Citty and subburbs were up, upon a Report that the Irish were assaulting houses & killing people near the townes End, all men gott to theire arms & lighted Candles in all theire Windowes & at their doores, but about 4 or a little after we began to be undeceiv'd & soe went to bed again leaving one or two in a house up: my Aunt Adams heard nothing of this for I went to Covent Garden this morning to knowe how they all doe; In James Street & in the Piazza they were up upon the alarm." Lady Abdy writes that the panic spread over "most parts near London but the Irish did no harm but by their big words." The best news John can send is that the King has gone off for the last time escorted by the Prince's Guards; " 'tis said he wept as he left Whitehall, the P. of Orange is at St. James'." "His Majestie's going away is of great consequence higher than I can understand," writes the prudent Mr. Cary, but to most people it meant that the game was up; the strong hands that now grasped the reins were not likely to drop them.

Sir Ralph and Sir R. Temple represented Buckingham once more in the Convention Parliament, that sat from January 1689 to February 1690. Mun has been over to Oxford to pay up his bills, and "has given a Treate to his Acquaintance in Trinity College." His sister is anxious to join him in London for "the Crownenasion, and I want clothes so mitily that I doe not know what to do, they will scarse hang on my back." A tailor's bill for "a close fitting Taby jacket" seems to prove that Molly had her wish.

The oppressor being dethroned, men are now free to pity him, and to find fault with their deliverer. Cary writes to Sir Ralph: "I hear the K is bying the E. of Notingham's hous at Kensington & implys 700 men in fitting Hamton Court for him, & the coronation I heare is talkt of, all thes things requires great sums of money: I confes popery wod A bin much wors for that wod A destroyed thousands of bodies & souls & estates in A short time; bot I heare there is great discontents now. I have sent you the K's speech wch I liked & disliked, hee being subject to sinsures as well as his meanest subjects."

"I was apt to beeleve King James was dead, not for the report of it, but because I think hee has a load heavigh enoufgh on him to waigh downe the greatest speryted man in the world: and ware hee the bitterest enymy to mee I could not but pity him, and bee glad to heare he had dyed a naturall death, afflictions causing too often great sperits to mak them selvs a way, wch I pray God presarve all christians from; I am satisfied by him and others that grif kils none; but God knows what is fitest for all, and therefore best to soffar patiently and wait till ther chang cometh." There is still a ground swell after the storm, and Cary continues, "I cannot bot put the present differences of thos as sits at the Helm amonxt my own afflictions, I feare a cevell worr, sinc both Ch: & Laety are so divided, & poor Iorland Lys a bleding."

CHAPTER FIFTEEN

Exeunt Severally
1689–1696

As THE eventful seventeenth century draws to its close, those who have played their parts with Sir Ralph in the Claydon drama are gradually leaving the stage. While their places are being filled by a younger set of actors, a word may be said concerning the exits of some old friends.

In the elder generation, the evergreen and incorrigible Tom claims the first place. He is still liable to sudden and unaccountable changes of abode, and his "quarteridge" has of late been claimed from Welsh villages whose many-syllabled names have the desired flavour of remoteness. He was unreasonably abusive of a world in which he found so many kindly dupes, and flourished unabashed till 1707, when he was well over ninety. He then died "merely of old age, his speech and memory perfect to the last." Richard Seys of Boverton, Cardiff, writes to inform John Verney that "ye old gent: yʳ uncle has at last gone to his long home, I find his late quarterly Revenue (like so many of ye former) was in a great measure Anticipated, but Jⁿ Deere by keeping him for some time to a weekly allowance has cleared all his old scores." He died possessed of "22ˢ & 1ᵈ" and John asks Mr. Deere whether he had not "some goods, as Books, Clothes, Plate, etc. wch being disposed of wᵈ suffice for his burial, without either you or I being out of pocket for your old acquaintance & my relation, whom I never saw in my life, tho' he hath had many a pound from me." The venerable Tom's personalty consisted of "a Bible & a Treatise of piety," but he was "very decently interred" at his nephew's expense, 1*l.* being spent in distributing bread to the poor "by his own desire," and he was "attended to his grave by a numerous company of the Neighbourhood," the bell-ringers were properly fed, and the genteeler guests provided with wine, so that there is room for hope that Tom may have been satisfied at last!

Dr. Denton's life, prolonged to the age of eighty-six, was vigorous and fruitful to the end. In middle life he had been more of a Royalist than Sir Ralph ever was, but so heartily did he approve of the Revolution, that one of his last literary efforts was a work, "Jus Regiminis," dedicated to William III, vindicating the King's position and the action of the English people. In 1691 Sir Ralph hurried up from Claydon on the news of the Doctor's illness, and as they were together we have no account of his last hours—only that "Mr. Banck of Preston preacht his funeral sermon," and a crumb of gossip that Sir Richard Temple failed to appear, after his cousin's death, in all the "blacks" he was in duty bound to wear. The Doctor himself would have justified Sir Richard. His very epitaph in Hillesden Church has the joyful note which was so conspicuous in his life: "He was blessed with that happy composition of Body & mind that preserved him chearfull, easy & agreeable to the last, & endeared him to all that knew him."

In 1692 John Verney makes his family very happy by his second marriage, with "Mary, one of the daughters of the Honble Sir Francis Lawley, Baronet, of St. Powell, Shropshire, Master of H. M. Jewel-office," and of Anne Whitmore his wife. Mary was a tall, dignified woman, aged thirty-one, of a gracious presence, and the mode in which her black hair towered above her forehead made her statelier still. John presents her with "a breast jewel worth about 100*l.*": "Diamonds are cheaper than they were a dozen years ago, I design to buy her another toy of 50*l.* after marriage in what she likes best." He gives her a set of "Dressing table plate, & brushes & a looking glass; she said her Mother designed her such a thing but now she would have it in somewhat else . . . I have put side glasses to my Coach, & taken off the redd Tassels from my harness

& put on White ones & also white trappings on ye bridles & made new Liveries for my Serv^{ts}, the Arms I will alter shortly by putting her Coate with mine." It is suggested that they should be married privately at the Abbey "after Morning service on Sunday wch ends at 11 a'clock; her mother saith that as the Quire is the publickest so it is the privatest place; but as the Doores are all of open wainscote soe that people may look in at any time, & you know it is a thorowfare, I do not admire my Ly. Lawley's contrivance of privacy, but I said nothing."

John has a negro page, who waits upon his wife; he is described, when he is first brought to Middle Claydon, as "a Moor of Guinea of about six years of age." His baptism (6 October 1689) is entered in the Parish Register; the little black boy's gossips were "his Master Mr John Verney," and the party from the White House, "Edmund and Molly Verney & Cary Stewkeley"; he was named Peregrine Tyam. He appears in the background of Mrs. John Verney's picture, and on 14 September 1707 there is an entry of his burial at Claydon. My Lady Latimer has "a dwarf" in her household at this time; it was one of the fashions of the day that fair Englishwomen should be served by such uncouth pages.

There is a bright little letter from Mrs. John Verney to Sir Ralph, thanking him for a happy visit with her husband and his children to Claydon; "My father and mother send thare sarves, they have bin to give joy to Sir Marten Beckman y^t is new maried, he is 67 & his bride 60, this increases my feare of a mother in law, but nothing shall make me remane les then Yr ever Dutyfull & obedint Dau^r & sarvant, Mary Verney."

She writes to John at Wasing that "Bro. Palmer" has dined with her; "Cousin Kellin & Cousen Denton" are with her; she nurses little Ralph very kindly through a fever, and wins all hearts in the family circle. John's happiness seems complete when a son is born to them, to whom the two grandfathers and Lady Whitmore stand sponsors; then the child dies, and Mary falls a victim to small-pox when she is expecting for the second time to become a mother. Her husband sums up the story on her monument: "She had one son named John who dyed within the year, and lyeth with her in the vault within the Chancell [at Middle Claydon]. She departed this life on the 24th Aug. 1694 aged 33 years."

It will be seen by this review of the family history, that Sir Ralph was paying the penalty of protracted life; he had outlived almost all his contemporaries.[1] Two infirm widows, Cary Gardiner and Betty Adams, alone remained of the large circle of brothers and sisters except Tom, who could scarcely be said to belong to it. His old friends and correspondents, Dr. Denton and Sir Roger Burgoyne, Sir Nathaniel and Lady Hobart, Doll Leeke and Dame Vere Gawdy, had entered into rest. The Great Rebellion, the Restoration, the Revolution, in all of which he had played his part, had become matters of history. Having thrown himself with much zest into the work of the Convention Parliament, which consolidated the work that the Long Parliament of his youth had begun, he expected to be re-elected for Buckingham in February 1690, but that inveterate schemer Sir Richard Temple had secretly taken measures to secure the two seats for himself and for Alexander Denton, whose share in the transaction was as little creditable. There was an outburst of indignation in the family, but Sir Ralph saved the situation by his magnanimity. With gentle dignity he reminded his godson and his old colleague that it was needless to intrigue against a man who had no private interests to serve, and was ready to retire whenever the borough found a worthier representative. He had the satisfaction of feeling that he had left Buckingham the better for his long political connection with it. He had, as Mr. Butterfield writes, "erected a lasting monument of his munificence" in the town hall (often promised by rival candidates, and forgotten when the elections were over), "built about 1685 at the expense of Sir Ralph Verney." The borough was in good humour, for the long vexed question of the locality of the Assizes had been settled in its favour. "The Bailiffe & 2 Burgesses of Buckingham have been att London to give the Queene thanks for the Assizes, & have

[1] Like our present Editor.

kist her Majestie's hand, & are come down with great joy beyond expression."

Sir Ralph spent the spring of 1696 in town; he was racked with a cough, which the east winds increased even when he kept "close at home," and the "dryed walnuts," which he took medicinally, do not sound like a comfortable remedy. His lean figure was worn to a shadow, and he suffered from many infirmities of old age without being mastered by them; the letters he dictated were clear and precise as of old; his head was as sound and his heart as kind as ever.

In the early summer Sir Ralph made the last of his many journeys from London to Claydon. It was an inclement season, "the ordinary sort of people find it as cold as in winter," yet the relations hear with horror that Sir Ralph has had made for himself "a bathing tob." He revives a little with the satisfaction of being at home again, he gets into the Fir Tree Walk in the warmest hours of the day, and "on all faire days he goes out in the Coach to take the aire."

There is a break in the letters when John is at Claydon; by the middle of September 1696 he is back in Hatton Gardens, and on the 20th Sir Ralph sends him up a hamper, and dictates an admirable business letter. He has sent to Mr. Busby about "Son Keeling's bill in Chancery"; he acknowledges the return of "the Cloth your pigg went in," and concludes "for my owne health, I still grow weaker, pray God bless you and yours."

It was almost the last effort of the brave spirit and the failing body; "he lyes in his bed all the morning, and upon it all the afternoon," and "dus not now rise from it at night to eat his supper nor say his prayers."

Sir Richard Temple comes over to dine with his old House of Commons colleague, but, finding Sir Ralph in bed, he goes on to London. Cary Gardiner prays for him many times a day on her knees, and her friend, the saintly Lady Russell, sends him an affectionate message that she makes it her daily petition that he may recover. But the prayers of devout women were no longer to keep the tired old man from his rest. On the morning of the 24th Cary Stewkeley found on her arrival that the master of the house knew not whether she went or stayed, so to her cousin's great relief she settled herself at Claydon House and took her part in watching by the bedside, and in writing the detailed accounts sent daily to John. Edmund would have shared their vigil; John, having satisfied himself that his father was well-cared for, could not stand the long days of inaction.

"He lays pretty quiet, but says nothing but rambling discours nor knows nobody now." "All his servants are as diligent and careful as possible, two have watched with him every night." "Sometimes I think he may live 2 or 3 days then I think not so long, God knows all we have now to lose in him good man, I do so pray for his happy passage out of this world. I am in so great a consarn I can hardly tell what I say or do."

Mr. Butterfield was sent for to recommend Sir Ralph's soul to God. There was a solemn pause of some hours, and then a horse was saddled in haste to carry letters to town. "My dear Uncle, your good father," Cary writes, "dyed at 12 o'clock this night." Both ladies address their letters to Sir John Verney, Baronet, and while praying that he may bear his loss with resignation, wish him joy in the same breath of his new estate and honours.

John sends down orders immediately to Coleman about "the next duty and service that can be performed for my father, which is to have him laid where he commanded. . . . His body is to be embalmed. . . . I had thought to invite the neighbouring Gentry to the funerall which I computed to be about 40 or 50, but this afternoon meeting with some near relations and opening my Father's sealed-up will, wee find that he orders to be buried *as privately and with as little pomp as may be*, these are his very words," and John "not being able to find a medium (without giving offence) betwixt a private buriall and inviting all the neighbouring gentry," decides upon the former and desires his letter to be read out to the ladies and to Mrs. Lillie. "Pray give my service to my kindred and to my friends," he writes, "and have a care of my Deare Father's body." He desires that the Hall should be hung with black baize, "the entry from the Hall door to the Spicery door, and the best Court Porch, likewise the Brick Parlour from top to bottom," where a dozen chairs are to be covered with black and the three great tables.

John's decision was not approved of; Peg Adams expressed the general opinion of Claydon when she wrote, "I should have thought that a man so generally known to be loved in the country, it would have been very decent to have some of the gentry carry him to his grave"; and Cary Gardiner in her bed "told all the clocks from one to six" thinking over her nephew's interpretation of his father's will; "to have no pomp," she writes, "may relate to straingers. . . . I confes on serious thoughts I think tis best to bury him publickly, without thos lengths as my brother may mean pomp."

Her daughter Cary had remained on a few days at Claydon House, that she and her cousin might receive the Sacrament together, on that first Sunday when they had leisure to realise the greatness of their loss. She now wrote from East Claydon: "Let me know when my deare Uncle is beried that I may steall out to waight on his body to the grave since it is so privat." But the relations acknowledged that there was no want of affection on John's part, "no child dus more lament for a father than he does," and when "he went out of town to attend his father to his grave with all the four children," Cary Gardiner had no other regret than that she was "too infirm to pay him that last love and service, who loved him as the best of brothers ought to be loved . . . and that must shortly go to him that I beeleave a blest Saint in Heaven."

It was a cold, wet autumn day when the family gathered round the vault in Middle Claydon Church; the neighbours, rich and poor, waited not for an invitation to show respect to their old friend. "The rooms looked very handsomly, though the Heavens wept with all his relations at his funeral." "You had so much mob," writes Nancy Nicholas, "what would it have been otherwais [than private] Ye King was last Sunday at Whitehall Chapl, tis the first time since the Queen dyed, and I was told by one that was their he looked full of trouble and concern."

"I thank God that we all got home without any accident,"

writes Cary to John from East Claydon after the funeral, "but all one side of me was as wet as if I had been abroad, for it was so dark we durst not put up the glass, and the wind and the rain did beat so in, and indeed I have taken a cold and have been ill ever since."

.   .   .   .   .   .

When, in after years, a master-hand drew the picture of an old English squire, the "Coverley Papers" furnished "so living a likeness of the man, and endeared him to their readers to such a point, that his death had at last to be announced with all the circumstances of an overpowering affliction. 'I question not,' says Addison, 'but that my readers themselves will be troubled at the hearing of it.' "

After sharing the viccissitudes of Sir Ralph's long life, in the "Verney Letters," it is impossible to stand by his grave without a kindred feeling of regret. Over two hundred and fifty years have elapsed since that stormy October day when he was laid to rest, but Claydon still has kept his memory green, and we would part from him with some comfortable words, written while Sir Ralph Verney was yet a boy:

"But above all, beleeve it, the sweetest Canticle is, Nunc dimittis, when a Man hath obtained worthy Ends. . . . Death has this also, That it openeth the Gate to good Fame."

CHAPTER SIXTEEN

Postscript—to 1900

SIR RALPH was dead. This was the thought weighing down all hearts, as the company dispersed after his funeral in the fading light of a wet October evening, in the year of grace 1696. The gentry departed in their lumbering coaches through the muddy lanes, the farmers on their heavy horses across the fields, the heir and his children hurried back to their London home. With the death of the old Knight and Baronet a chapter was closed for Claydon, and for the County.

Sir Ralph was not a man of commanding ability, but he had played the part of an Englishman honestly and fearlessly in difficult times. He had lived under the four Stuart kings; he had sat with Eliot and Hampden in the Short and the Long Parliaments; had lost his father in the first battle of the Civil War; had seen the Commonwealth, the Protectorate and the Restoration, and had sat in the Convention Parliament which had placed William and Mary on the throne.

Sir Ralph's fidelity to his political and religious principles had made him the centre of the Whig and Protestant interest in the County, and when his housekeeper, Mrs. Lillie, and his faithful servant, Hodges, were clearing up after the guests' departure, they were putting away more than the broken meats of the funeral feast.

The House and the Church were both draped in black hangings; the Rector, Mr. Butterfield and the family were left to share in the grief of the parish and Mr. Coleman, Sir Ralph's faithful steward and friend remained in charge till the new master could gather up the reins.

His son John was as different as possible. At the age of eight he went to Blois where his father was in exile and was brought up in French surroundings as a second son to know nothing and care nothing for Claydon and its past. He was primarily a rich merchant from Aleppo with his three wives—the pictures of all four of them are in the Pink Parlour at Claydon House. He was efficient but unemotional and cold.

The overwhelming swarms of letters of the previous century stopped. Now there was no one to consult; there was no one to feel that everything in writing however trivial must be kept. Every conceivable question had been put to Sir Ralph and answered often with a copy of the reply. So the letters soon dwindled both in number and in interest. In due course Sir John became Lord Fermanagh, his son the first Earl Verney and his grandson the second and last Earl Verney succeeding to Claydon in 1752.

Then suddenly Claydon lives again and the name of Ralph emerges. He got through a vast fortune, before becoming bankrupt in 1784. He gambled; he lent money to all and sundry. A fellow sufferer writes "my loss has been nearly £100,000; your Lordship's I suppose much more." He financed Edmund Burke to be Member for Wendover and the Burkes between them owed him £31,000, not to mention £40,000 with no security except honour.

But Claydon can never repay the cost of building at Claydon House. There can be found an interior perhaps the most beautiful of all the Houses in the care of the National Trust. There are three rooms all 50 ft. long and 25 ft. high; two of them—the Great Diner and the Library—are each double cubes, the Centre Room—the Saloon—being wider than the other two by 10 ft. In all three rooms the wood carving, not plaster, is unique; very large doors of a different pattern in every room with wood carving over them is dominant, and the design is clearly that of a great artist. Above the three big rooms are to be found the Muniment Room, the Chinese Room, the Museum and the bedroom and sitting room of Florence Nightingale, left very much as when she lived there.

Who the artist was is unknown. There is a Mr. Lightfoot who probably did much of the work. Sir Thomas Robinson only appears after the big rooms and the Inlaid Staircase have been nearly finished. He it was who designed the vast Rotunda to the north of the house and beyond the large Ball Room the size of the three big rooms put together. So the entrance to the House was through Sir Thomas Robinson's Rotunda. After the bankruptcy all his work was pulled down leaving Claydon House as it is today with no front door. The entrance is through a hole in the wall instead of from a magnificent hall. Several rich visitors, seeing no front door, have driven away in disgust, depriving themselves of the sight of the interior glories of Claydon House.

A poet, Samuel Rogers, may well be right in claiming that Lord Verney was his own architect:

> You your own Monument have raised
> Thro distant ages to be praised.

Certainly this Ralph was a true artist and the completed wing of the new House has not a single false note in it.

But the most glorious monument of these days is enshrined in Lord Verney's Inlaid Staircase. It is still in perfect condition with every step inlaid with ivory, ebony and satin wood on mahogany and with a balustrade of wrought iron with corn that rustles as My Lady walks downstairs. This may well be considered the most beautiful bit of work in England to which the public has access.

Two misfortunes overtook the poor man in the same year 1791. His wife died and his creditors were after him like a pack of hounds. He is said to have escaped them in his wife's hearse.

In the nineteenth century the Verneys of Claydon centre round Sir Harry Verney, the second Baronet; his dates were 1801–1894. His father, another Sir Harry, the first Baronet, was a distinguished soldier and became Adjutant General at the War Office at the time of the Battle of Waterloo. Mr. George Russell, one of Mr. Gladstone's Ministers, who knew all about the family, proclaimed that the first Sir Harry, on hearing that he was unexpectedly to succeed to Claydon, died of joy.

The Rt. Hon. Sir Harry Verney used to quote a four-line rhyme about an imaginary talk between Napoleon Bonaparte and John Bull:

Said Boney to Johnny, "I'm coming to Dover,"
Said Johnny to Boney, "That's doubted by some";
Said Boney, "But what if I really come over,"
"Then really," said Johnny, "You'll be overcome."

That was proved to be true—Trafalgar at sea, Waterloo on land; we were invincible; there would be no more war and therefore no wounded soldiers. Hence neglect.

Sir Harry spoke French, German and Italian fluently. As a young man he made a perilous journey across the snow-covered Andes and learnt Spanish by the way.

On returning to Claydon he gave himself up to managing his large estate, repairing farms, building cottages and planting trees. He made friends with George Stevenson and encouraged railways on his estate when other landowners opposed them.

He was elected in 1832 as M.P. for Buckingham and retained a seat in the House of Commons for most of the next fifty-two years.

He was rather the typical "Fine old English Gentleman." When he inherited there was little money to keep the large house and estate in good order; but he did inherit a useful court yard built, as the blue bricks still show the date, in 1754. There was a brewhouse—home-made beer was an essential—a carpenter's shop with a skilled succession of Webbs to repair old carving and devise new, the dairy for rich butter and cream, a forge for repairs, a bakehouse, a laundry, an ice house and a slaughterhouse, with a woodyard behind, not to mention horses and carriages, and over these vital needs a spinner and a weaver, a bevy of grooms and gardeners and hoards of apples: all still in use within living memory today, but every corner is now adapted for a modern estate—no more beer brewing. For with wages at a low level plus extras there was no nonsense about overtime and holidays, and workmen walked to their work and children walked to school.

Some letters survive between two sisters in 1866, one

twenty-two and the other twenty, both to marry Verneys in due course. There are innumerable aristocratic and tory aunts. It is recorded that one of them when her fire went out was angry and shouted to be brought "pongs and toker." The sisters are "excessively amused" by a poem:

> Where London's City skirts the Thames
> In ball room met two rival dames.
> Quoth one "What means this youthful sham?
> You now are but a *has-been* Ma'am."

> "Well better far," was the reply,
> "To be a has-been, such as I;
> Than still to hang upon the shelf,
> A *never-was-er* like yourself."

They dress up for a ball and "we all pack into a wee little Brougham behind a rampart of petticoats, while our male escort was always trying to devise some expedient for condensing his interminable legs." After dancing eight times running "it was then one o'clock and we went away."

About now the cricketer W. G. Grace was coming into fame; in 1866 he made 224 not out for England against Surrey. Gossips say that he went down to a prep school where a small boy bowled him out; that evening at the school prayers the hymn chosen was No. 28, Sweet Saviour, in which the line occurs, "The scanty triumphs grace has won," which the school sang with éclat.

Sir Harry knew everybody, man, woman and child, living in the Claydons, Middle, East, Botolph and Steeple, most of which he owned. When at home, every afternoon would see him on his white pony enquiring after the old and sick and superintending estate building. What with the estate workmen, the Home Farm and the indoor and outdoor servants of both sexes most of the houses in the village had some connection with the big House.

Perhaps the most remarkable on the staff was William Cubbage, the water finder; he remained at work all his life and

never failed to decide with certainty whether water was there or
no. Sceptics came to scoff and stayed to be convinced that the
little two pronged stick was never wrong. After a day at his
work, Cubbage was completely exhausted and he was guarded
like a precious rare specimen, which indeed he was. Living next
door to him in Middle Claydon was the forester, old Selwood;
he never seemed to make a mistake; if he pronounced that a
tree should come down, down it came. His estimate as to the
number of feet in a standing tree was uncanny. Another
remarkable case was that of Miss Lepper; her mother saw an
advertisement for a secretary on the Claydon Estate. "Why
not try it for a fortnight." She stayed fifty years.

A more commonplace old man, William Webb, lived alone
at the North Lodge; no water, no light, no sanitation. But no
job was too dirty for him to undertake and nothing could make
him dirtier than he was already. He was known to be an
incorrigible thief and his chief passion was for butter. One
day on his way home across the Park he saw Sir Harry approaching. What to do with the pound of butter. It was a hot day
and he put the butter under his hat. By the time he met his
boss, melting butter was pouring down his cheeks.

The House itself was bitterly cold with log fires in winter in
every room and countless abigails to answer bells; these—
twenty-nine of them—were and still are at the back door with
indicators waiting to swing when its bell has been rung; in
the kitchen a revolving spit in front of the fire was cooking
"barons of beef." In the Park was a Decoy Pond, famous in the
neighbourhood, still supplying wildfowl.

Some "improvements" were done to the House in the middle
of the century and—alas—a previously unknown secret room
was broken into behind the Cedar Room fireplace where
ten men could, and did, hide in times of panic. Now there is
no secret room; only part of a passage.

The muster of the whole staff took place on Sunday evening,
when all and sundry came to Family Prayers. Quite short—a
hymn, a reading and a prayer. But the staff entry was dramatic.

Perhaps the procession is worth recording. First the housekeeper, then her Ladyship's maid with any visiting ladies'

maids, then the cook followed among the middle ranks by a highly trained kitchen maid and lower down, a scullery maid somewhere among the crowd; a little more important, a house parlour maid to carry trays upstairs with a housemaid or two in the offing, then any remaining refuse, but at all costs the last female must be the most recently arrived, Tweeny.

The male ascent began with a shy page boy in buttons with a garden boy or two trying to hide behind some grooms; after, a footman, if present a visiting "Gentleman's Gentleman" and at length the first footman to open and shut the door for . . . no, not a butler but the house steward whom guests found too proud to accept a tip (what a waste thought the boys)—perchance twenty or so.

Nobody knows what came over the immaculate example, but one Sunday, instead of sitting down to be read to after the hymn, he knelt down to pray. A newly arrived footman thought that this is what men did and promptly himself knelt down. Grandpapa never knew.

One of the mid-nineteenth century puzzles for a respectable county family was the question of grace before and after meals. How could children be taught to give thanks for "what we are going to receive" without knowing what it was; it might be boiled mutton, mostly fat, and cabbage with tapioca pudding to follow. But there was one certainty about "what we have received," because dessert could not go wrong—fruit in season, crystallised fruit, nuts, chocolate and the rest. Then an amazing thing happened: thanksgiving took place before dessert. Why? The true reason was never disclosed, but seventeenth century habits died hard and there was the possibility that some of the weaker brethren might, by the end of dessert, be under the table in no position for prayer. Grace was indeed a problem, but a vanishing one. One newspaper suggested:

> Thanks for eggs and buttered toast
> Father, Son and Holy Ghost.

Perhaps at City dinners it is wiser to dispense with an oblation at the end.

A curious letter has turned up from a very aristocratic lady to her distinguished husband dated 14 June 1859 about the use of leeches to cure tooth ache. Do leeches say grace before meals? If so, the leech in this letter might well consider the delicious meal it is "going to receive." Here is the letter:

> Dearest Love, I am so concerned at this pain in your teeth going on—if the gum is inflamed, no doubt a Leech would do good, but you cannot apply it without a proper glass for the purpose and that we have; if Mrs Humphreys will look in my Physic Closet, she will find the Leech Glass in the small sieve and plenty of Corks in the Card Box The way to do is putting the Leech in with his mouth towards the small end, and then corking the other, so that he cannot get out—apply him at once on the spot desired and he will take to it without the smallest difficulty—the glass must only be held steady and as he fills take out the cork.
>
> Your ever loving Wife.

Well known initials follow. It may be observed that the leech is male.

There were three other septuagenarians at Claydon during a good deal of the century. Sir Harry's brother Frederick, Q.C., born in 1806, tried to be a Member of Parliament; he was elected for Aylesbury in 1850 and was promptly unseated for bribery. After that, Frederick made money, lots of it, at the Parliamentary Bar, and when he died in 1890 he left a quarter of a million, which was supposed to be coming to the family and did not He had no gift with children, having none of his own. He thought children should be seen and not heard. The children agreed and only wished they need not be seen, because the poor old man had that tiresome affliction of a drop on the nose. The children drew lots as to who should kiss him good-night first.

Later still he became "funny"; now and again when the footman brought round the potatoes he would eat from the whole dish and when the pompous butler appeared with the claret, he drank out of the decanter. The children whose mother was teaching them from the Book of Daniel wondered if, like Nebuchadnezzar, Uncle Frederick was eating grass in the Park.

Another septuagenarian was Parthenope, Lady Verney, the elder sister of Florence Nightingale. She had great talent as an artist and all her sketches are worth seeing; but she thought how lucky Florence was to have such a charming elder sister. Florence somehow did not agree. So gradually she became jealous and did not fancy playing second fiddle and that out of tune; she took to her bed with two nurses to relieve the agonies of arthritis. In 1858 Sir Harry had married Parthenope and, though always the faithful husband, he gave most of his time to the younger sister.

Sir Harry did not seem to have any faults and his faith was a reality. Perhaps he was least successful in choosing a wife. He tried twice. His first wife Miss Hope (daughter of Admiral Sir George Hope, one of Nelson's Captains at Trafalgar) was a mighty Protestant and Fundamentalist, believing firmly in Hell Fire. Her eldest son at the age of 12 left Harrow (where he and his forbears and successors have been since "Grandpapa's Grandpapa") to go to sea in the Royal Navy. His last letter home before sailing reads "Yes, dear Mamma, I will try to avoid the everlasting bonfire." She wrote an immensely dull book called *Practical Thoughts on the Book of Isaiah*. After her death a copy was found with, written on the first page:

> If there should be another flood,
> Hither for refuge fly.
> Though all the world should be submerged,
> This book will still be dry.

After the Crimea, Miss Nightingale spent almost all her time, when not in London, at Claydon, often being there latterly for months at a time. She published anonymously a pamphlet showing that the majority of deaths in the Crimea were due, not to the war, but to preventable disease Then under her own name she proved with statistics that mortality in military barracks was more than double that of the ordinary public. For forty years she worked to improve conditions in hospitals and to establish a team of devoted women who gave up their lives to becoming trained nurses of the highest efficiency, as we know them today.

A great deal of this work was done at Claydon and Sir Harry Verney devoted himself to helping her. It is painful but true to record that not a single member of her own family helped at all.

A survivor can still testify to the astonishing hold that Great Aunt Florence Nightingale exercised over children All children are of course troublesome at times, and all grown ups seem constantly to be saying No no don't, but Aunt Florence seemed to say Yes yes do She understood and stood by the child's point of view. So sobbing young would pour out their troubles, stealing, yes, taking seven chocolates for 1*d*., when only six were legal. "Well in later life you may even come upon greater crimes"; lying, "Yes, but we have all lied in our time."

And all questions, however embarrassing, were answered truthfully, "Yes, that is just what I wanted to know at your age." And then constant little notes about her bird table or birthday presents. ("I choosed it, but Aunt Florence buyed it.") Or a climax with an inscribed diary on New Year's Day 1895, "For our dear Harry with Aunt Florence's love, and may each day of this year 1895 be better and happier than yesterday and may the young Boy and the old Woman make and find this a better and a happier year than any that has gone before. So help us God. New Year's Day 1895." She was perhaps the greatest influence in many young lives. No wonder they loved her.

Miss Nightingale had the reputation of never being wrong (no man likes that) but she obtained her accurate information by getting her brother-in-Law, Sir Harry Verney, to ask questions in the House of Commons upon any subject of doubt. Before long he became known not as the Member for Buckingham but as the Member for Miss Nightingale. She worked incessantly, always in poor health, to the end of the century and one of her professional outside helpers records this:

Nobody who has not worked with her daily can have an idea of her strength of mind, her extraordinary powers joined with her brilliant intellect; she was one of the most gifted creatures God ever made.

Her dedicated life was due to her personality, her strength, her indomitable courage, her immensely high standards both of work and conduct and her loving kindness, for like Abou ben Adhem, she loved her fellow men.

One other name must be recorded. As Miss Nightingale's own relations would not recognise the value of her work, perhaps her greatest friend was the very competent Margaret, Lady Verney, 1844–1930.

There are about 4,000 letters at Claydon written by Miss Nightingale, many of them written to this friend and the letters gradually change from My dear Margaret to Dearest Blessed Margaret. This Margaret was certainly the cleverest and the most successful of the countless Lady Verneys who for 500 years have made Claydon House a home of welcome and peace.

She wrote *The Verney Memoirs*, 1600–1696, *The Verney Letters*, 1696–1799, and all the six biographies of the Claydon Verneys in the *Dictionary of National Biography*—she herself being included in a supplementary volume.

There is a last name that can just qualify for the nineteenth century. William Temple was born in 1881. As a Freshman at Balliol College, Oxford, he came over to Claydon and announced that he would get a First in Mods, a First in Greats, be a Bishop and probably an Archbishop. He did and was.

There is a seventeenth century letter "to in Quier how the Verneys of Claydon doe doe." The answer today is "They doe doe quite nicely thank you."

APPENDIX

The Verneys in Parliament

THE Verneys were a very Parliamentary family. Sir Ralph Verney, as before mentioned, was member for London in 1472, and from that time there was seldom wanting a representative of the name for the county of Bucks, or for one of its five boroughs, always on what would now be seen as the "liberal" side in politics.

Edward VI	1552	Sir Edmund Verney for Buckinghamshire, and Francis Verney, Esq., for the town of Buckingham.
Philip & Mary	1556	Sir Edmund Verney and Francis Verney, Esq., for Bucks.
James I	1624	Sir Edmund Verney (on his return with Prince Charles from Spain) for Buckingham.
Charles I	1628	Sir Edmund Verney (Knight Marshal) for Aylesbury.
Charles I	1640	Sir Edmund Verney for Wycombe, and Ralph Verney, Esq., for Aylesbury (the Short Parliament).
Charles I	1640	Sir Edmund Verney for Wycombe, and Sir Ralph Verney for Aylesbury (the Long Parliament).
Charles II	1680	Sir Ralph Verney, Bart., for Buckingham.
William & Mary	1688–89	Sir Ralph Verney for Buckingham (Convention Parliament).
Anne	1710	Sir John Verney, Bart., for Buckinghamshire.

Anne	1713	Sir John Verney, Lord Fermanagh, for Amersham.
George I	1714	Viscount Fermanagh for Amersham. In his place deceased, Ralph Verney, Viscount Fermanagh.
George I	1722	Ralph Verney, Viscount Fermanagh, for Amersham.
George II	1735	Ralph Verney, Viscount Fermanagh, for Wendover.
George II	1747	Ralph Verney, 1st Earl Verney, for Wendover.
George II	1754	Ralph Verney, 2nd Earl Verney, for Wendover.
George III	1768	Ralph Verney, 2nd Earl Verney, for Buckinghamshire.
George III	1790	Ralph Verney, 2nd Earl Verney, for Buckinghamshire. (The last male of the old family of Verney.)
William IV & Victoria	1832	Harry Verney, 2nd Baronet for Buckingham.
Victoria	1885	Edmund Verney, 3rd Baronet, for North Bucks.
Edward VII	1906	Frederick W. Verney, for North Bucks.
George V	1910	Harry C. W. Verney, 4th Baronet for North Bucks.

Index

Abell, Mary *see* Verney, Mary (2)
Abercromby, Susan 117
Alcock, Mrs. 82
Algiers 177
America, Puritan emigration to 17
Apprentices 129–31
"Aulnage" 12, 38
Aylesbury 11, 17

Barbados 19–20, 97
Barn Elms 127
Barrymore, Lord 28–30
Battles
   Edgehill 33
   Newbury 37
   Worcester 77
Blacknall, Mary *see* Verney, Mary,
   Lady Verney
Blarkes, Captain 169
Blois 62
Bludworth, Sir Thomas 166
Bray
   Elizabeth 5
   Sir Reginald 5
Brickmaking 88–9
Bridges, Major-General 123
Browne, Lady 70–2
Buckingham, Bucks 245
Burgoyne, Sir Roger 37–9, 45, 50,
   56, 64, 74, 79, 114, 130, 138,
   160, 245
Burke, Edmund 251
Busby, Sir John 172

Carlisle 24
Charles I 63–6

Charles II 185–98
   at Newmarket 187
   poverty in reign 191
Child marriages 186–7
Claydon 9–10
   deer park 136
   garden 135
   house 241–52, 253, 255
   orchard 88
   park 88, 114
   poor 85
   re-habiting 80–4
   sequestration 50–3
Cockram 65
Coffee 77
Colchester 58–9
Convention Parliament 151, 240,
   245
Council of Officers 146
"Cow club" 86
Cowley 27
Cromwell, Oliver
   death 140–2
   on Drogheda 61–2
Cromwell, Richard 112, 143
Cubbage, William 254–5
Curzon, Nurse 171

Dawson, Richard 199–200
Decimation Bill 124
Denton
   Alexander 245
   John 114
   Margaret 110
   Nicholas 221
   Penelope 114

263

Denton—*contd.*
  Sir Thomas   9
  Dr. William   25, 52, 63, 110–11,
    118, 200, 243
Devonshire, Earl of   49
Ditchley   114
Dobson, William   111
Drogheda   61
Dryden, John   170
Duels   189–90
Dungarven   30
Dutch War   158, 179–83
Du Val, Claude   198

Earle, Dr.   164
East Claydon   169–84
  plague   161
Eikon Basilike   65–6
Elliott, Capt. Thomas   211
Elmes, Sir Thomas   87
Essex, Lord   32
Evelyn, John   141

Fleet Marston   1
  sale   8
Fleet prison   93–5
Fleetwood
  Charles   112
  James   127
Florence   77

Gape, William   135
Gawdy, Vere   155
Gibbon   222
Giffard, Sir George   4–5
Grace, W. G.   254
Grafton Park   136
Great Fire of London   165–8

Hackney coaches   11–12
Hale, Sir Mathew   191
Halfe Cowes Common   174
Hals, Richard   202, 217
Hammond, Col. Thomas   116
Haselrigg, Arthur   135

Henrietta, Duchess of Orleans   177
Henry VII   3
Herbord, Sir Charles   108
Highwaymen   198–217
Highway robbery   188–90
Hillesden   9, 38, 110–11
  destruction   41–3
Hinton, Dr.   105
Hobart
  Lady Anne   116, 152, 165, 245
  Sir Nathaniel   152, 245
Holland   37–8
Holmes   137
Hope, Sir George   258
Hounslow Heath Camp   231–3
Hyde, Anne   179

Isham, Mrs.   44–5, 115
Isham, Sir Justinian   117, 138, 163

James I   10–11
Jones, Col. Michael   60

King's Langley   4

Lasly, Lord   26
Lawley
  Sir Francis   243
  Lady Mary   243
Lee, Sir Francis Henry   194
Leeke
  Dorothy   13, 116, 118, 124, 245
  Sir John   27–8, 37
  Thomas   118
Lenthall   144
Lepper, Miss   255
Levellers   67
Lilburne, John   91–2
Lithgow, William   8
London riots   238
  Irish assault   240–1
  Spanish Ambassador's house
    sacked   240

Long Parliament 112
Louis XIV 177, 230
Luke, Sir Samuel 42–3

Marshalsea prison 204
Mary of Modena 179
Middle Claydon 1, 121
Monk, General 145–7, 177
Monmouth's rebellion 222
Monson, Lord 45, 136
Morley, Dr. George 79
Municipal charters 196
Mursley 121
Muxwell wood 84

"New Disease" 134
Newton, Sir Henry 46, 60, 66,
69–71
Nightingale, Florence 251, 258–9

Oxford
court at 162, 164
Trinity College 217
fees 1685 218

Penley Hall 3
sale 8
Pembroke, Lord 22, 185
Plague 159–65
Powis, Lord 231
Puckering
Jane 70
Sir Thomas 70

Quainton 4
sale 8

Roberts, Gabriel 130–1
Robinson, Sir Thomas 252
Rochester, Lord 194–5
Rogers, Samuel 252

Rouen 41
Rump Parliament 144
Rye House Plot 196–7

Saint Martin Pomary 1–2
Sandford, Thomas 121
Scotch war 16, 22–8
"Second Bishops' War" 27
Sequestration committee 120
Sheppard, Luce 73–4, 75, 82–3
Sidney, Col. 197
Sladburne 106
Smith, Col. 40–2
Smoking 160
Soest 133
Steeple Claydon 42, 174
Stevenson, George 253
Stewkeley
Cary 146–8, 236–7
Ursula 187–8
Strafford 27
Sussex, Lady 34, 39
Switzerland 76–7

Temple
Jack 203
Sir Richard 114, 245
Susan 110
William 260
Thinn, Sir Thomas 105
Treaty of Berwick 26
Turville, Frederick 202–4
Tyam, Peregrine 244

Ulster rebellion 27–8
Uvedale, Robert 142

Vaughan, John 109
Venice 78
"trekle" 78
Verney
Sir Edmund (1) 5–6
Sir Edmund (2) 6–7

Verney—*contd.*
Sir Edmund (3) 9–35
    death 33–5
    in civil war 30–5
    in Scotch war 22–8
    standard keeper 32
    will 23
Sir Edmund (4) 57–62
Edmund (5) 70, 74, 115, 135,
    150, 152, 157–63, 169–84,
    235–6
Edmund (6) 173, 183, 237
Elizabeth 233
Francis (1) 5–6
Francis (2) 6–9
Frederick 257
Harry, 1st Bt. 252
Harry, 2nd Bt. 252
Henry 81, 90, 112, 139, 199
Isabella 1
Sir John (1) 2–3
John (2) 70, 127–34, 186, 190,
    198, 222, 233, 239, 251
    apprenticeship 130–3
    in Berkshire 175
    schooling 128–9
    to Aleppo 133–4
Margaret, Lady Verney xi, 260
Mary, Lady Verney 13–14, 68–9
Mary (2) 153–7, 171–3
Mary (3) 173, 183–4
Parthenope, Lady Verney 257–8
Sir Ralph (1) 1–2
Sir Ralph (2) 3
Sir Ralph (3) 3–4
Sir Ralph (4) 4–5
Sir Ralph (5) 13–15
    arrest 115–19
    arrest of 5 members 36
    back in parliament 150, 233
    death 247
    decimation 122–5
    flight abroad and exile 40,
        45–56, 62–80
    funeral 248

illness 234
in civil war 33–5
in Rome 77
Lord Rochester's guardian
    194
marriage 14
sequestration 120–2
Ralph (6) 171–2, 182, 222, 223
Ralph (7) 244
Sir Ralph (8) 251–2
Robert 1
Susan 37
Thomas 17–21, 89–109
    at sea 100
    death 242
    "emigration" 18
    in army 99
    in Barbados 19–20
    in civil war 36–41
    in the Fleet 93–5
    in Paris 56, 67
Volunteers 192

Warwick
    Lady 116
    Lord 58, 138–9
Webb, William 255
Wheler, Sir George 201–2
Whigs and Tories 196
Whittingham, Sir Robert 2
William of Orange 192, 238
Wilmot
    Anne 194
    Henry 194
Wine tax 186
Wing 4
Worsley, Col. 118
Wroxall 160

Yate, Dr. Thomas 162
York
    death of Duchess of 178–9
    Duke of 178